KEYBOARDING

AND APPLICATIONS

For use with microcomputers
electronic typewriters
and typewriters

SECOND EDITION

Chiri • Kostner • Seraydarian • Stoddard

Judith A. Chiri, Smoky Hill High School, Aurora, Colorado
Jaclyn Kostner, Telecommunications Consultant
Patricia Seraydarian, Oakland Community College, Farmington Hills, Michigan
Ted D. Stoddard, Brigham Young University, Provo, Utah

GLENCOE

Macmillan/McGraw-Hill

Lake Forest, Illinois   Columbus, Ohio   Mission Hills, California   Peoria, Illinois

AUTHORS

Judith A. Chiri is Department Chair, Business Education, at Smoky Hill High School in Aurora, Colorado. She has taught typewriting, electronic keyboarding, and other business courses at middle school through college levels. In addition to writing for business journals, Ms. Chiri is a frequent speaker at workshops and seminars for business teachers. She is active in many business education teacher organizations and has served as editor of keyboarding articles for *Business Education Forum*.

Jaclyn Kostner is a telecommunications and technology expert, currently working with private industry worldwide. Dr. Kostner is a former teacher of business and technology at the secondary through college levels. Subjects include information processing, business software and applications, and keyboarding. She currently heads her own consulting and training business, specializing in helping people use technology more effectively to improve their company's competitiveness in global markets. She is author of numerous books and articles about technology and global communication.

Patricia E. Seraydarian is Professor at Large at Oakland Community College, Farmington Hills, Michigan. She is former Department Chair of Office Information Systems at Oakland Community College and has taught at both secondary and post-secondary levels. A recognized expert in information processing, Dr. Seraydarian lectures on the topic around the country. She is also the author of a variety of materials for secretarial training as well as for the professional secretary.

Ted D. Stoddard is Professor of Information Management at Brigham Young University in Provo, Utah. He lectures and writes extensively in the areas of keyboarding, typewriting, and information processing. Dr. Stoddard is a specialist in business/computer education, business communication, and computer information systems. He is past president of Western Business Education Association and is active in numerous professional teacher organizations.

CREDITS

Cover and Part Opener Designs: Thomas Vroman & Associates Gains, PA

Illustrations: David Archambault: Pages xii–xx, 4, 5, 6, 7, 8, 9, 12, 16, 18, 20, 24, 27, 34, 44, 57. Peggy Brier: Pages 2, 23. All other art by Graphics Etcetera.

Photo Credits: Page ix top-Courtesy IBM; bottom-Dario Perla/After Image. Page x-left, Peter Chapman; right-Ellis Herwig/The Picture Cube. Page xi-left, Panel Concepts; right top-Protype; bottom-Compuscan. Page xvii, Courtesy IBM.

This program was prepared with the assistance of Publishing Advisory Services.

Keyboarding and Applications, Second Edition

Send all inquiries to:
GLENCOE DIVISION
Macmillan/McGraw-Hill
936 Eastwind Drive
Westerville, OH 43081

ISBN 0-02-800602-X (Student's Edition)

Printed in the United States of America.

1 2 3 4 5 6 7 8 9   RRD-W   00 99 98 97 96 95 94 93 92

CONTENTS

Preface

Keyboarding is a key to the future. With the explosion of electronic technology, keyboarding skills are rapidly becoming life skills—skills needed to survive and succeed in personal and professional life.

Keyboarding skills are also marketable skills. Developing such skills involves a mastery of the knowledge and skills associated with keyboarding, formatting, and document processing. In today's office, keyboarding skills are used to process information ranging from simple electronic messages to professional looking reports prepared with desktop publishing software.

Regardless of what a student's ultimate career objective may be, the keyboarding skills learned today will help open the doors to success tomorrow.

OBJECTIVES

This edition of *Keyboarding and Applications* offers a comprehensive instructional program—one that trains fast, accurate, and competent keyboard users of typewriters and computers. Critical objectives of this edition are:

- To develop proficiency in keyboarding.
- To develop decision-making skills, language arts skills, and positive work attitudes.
- To familiarize students with critical information-age procedures, terminologies, and technologies.

COMPONENTS

A complete package of instructional materials is available to help students master these objectives. The package includes the student text; teacher's annotated edition; teacher's resource files with posters, overhead transparencies, resource masters, and other activities; a student workbook, a test package, ancillary simulations, drill materials, cassettes, and disks. A teacher's reference guide is also available.

FEATURES

This edition promotes proficiency in keyboarding, formatting, and processing knowledge and skills through a variety of special features.

Skill-Building Program. Intensive technique development through technique timings, speed-building drills, and accuracy practices are the basis of the skill-building program, enabling learners to develop speed and accuracy.

Simplified Instructions. Directions for completing each activity and explanations of formats and procedures are presented in simple, easy-to-read language that is enhanced by the liberal use of color. Simple-to-complex presentations and realistic cycles of learning help students become proficient.

Communication Skills. The unique Language Arts activities help students to master critical capitalization, punctuation, grammar, and related language skills. Proper spelling of frequently misspelled words is also emphasized. Keyboard Composition activities give students practice in composing in a carefully sequenced confidence-building way.

Decision-Making Skills. Activities are structured to give students increasing responsibility for the details of their work. The sequence is show, tell, and remind to help students remember. New applications are accompanied by complete instructions. In later applications, detailed instructions are replaced by reminders called "cues" and "checkpoints." Finally, students are expected to remember the format—or to look it up in Need to Knows. A simple-to-complex philosophy is inherent in these activities.

The Electronic World. All lessons and vocabulary accommodate the equipment, terminology, and procedures of today's electronic world. Specific instructions, where needed, are provided for electronic typewriters, microcomputers, and electric typewriters.

Testing Program. The Measuring Mastery lessons in the text can be used for informal or formal evaluation of student progress. Longer tests in the separate test booklet contain alternate timed writings, applications, and objective questions—all designed to check student progress and comprehension of basic concepts and formats.

J. Chiri, J. Kostner, P. Seraydarian, T. Stoddard

Index

Special Index

Electronics at Work

A little child injured in an accident needs a blood transfusion. First, the child's blood must be analyzed and matched with the correct blood type. That work is done by computer.

A job applicant in a distant city needs to send her resume to a prospective employer immediately. She decides on same-day delivery via the telephone line—using a FAX (facsimile) machine.

An auto mechanic thinks the electronic component of a car brought in for repair is faulty. He confirms his guess by testing the part on special electronic equipment.

An elderly couple does a week's shopping at the supermarket. The cashier rings up their purchases with the aid of an OCR (optical character recognition) scanner that reads the product bar code into the cash register.

Computers and electronic equipment have become a commonplace part of everyone's life. From the most extraordinary events, like blood transfusions, to the most everyday ones, like shopping for groceries, electronic equipment plays a major role in how we work, play, and live. In order to make choices about how we live and work, we need to become as familiar as possible with electronic equipment—what it is, what it does, and how it works.

Just about every job involves some writing—anything from composing a brief letter or two to keyboarding book-length manuscripts. Computers handle it all.

As an office manager in a small arts and crafts gallery, you might use an electronic typewriter to compose the few letters and bills of sale you need to write. Most electronic typewriters have a memory, so you can proofread the letter before getting a printed copy to send. The memory will also hold different form documents that you can call up, change as needed, and then print out. To send an announcement of an upcoming gallery show to a list of your best customers, you create a form announcement and then store it in the typewriter's memory. You can then merge the letter with a stored list of customers' names and addresses in order to print out, say, fifty personalized announcements for the show.

If you worked in a law firm, on the other hand, you could be responsible for the keyboarding and printing

of a great many important legal documents, such as leases, contracts, and wills. You might use a microcomputer with a very large memory. The legal documents, stored as "boilerplate," can be called up on the screen and filled in for the specific situation. A spell checker in the microcomputer helps you make sure the spelling is correct before you print the document. Your microcomputer might be linked into a computer network so that you could share files and other information with others in your office.

In the job you choose, you might need to create graphs, charts, and other illustrations for inclusion in printed documents. With a desktop publishing pro-

only areas in which computers are used. Computers excel at all tasks involving numerical calculations.

If you worked in the payroll department of a company that manufactures sporting equipment, you'd use a microcomputer to automatically prepare payroll checks for all employers. The computer program figures out and itemizes the necessary deductions and then prints out the checks.

Suppose you owned a small catering business. You could use a computer spreadsheet program to keep track of what you paid for food, supplies, equipment, advertising, and salaries and what you earned from the jobs you catered. By changing figures on the spreadsheet, you could see how paying more rent for a larger kitchen would affect your profit. The spreadsheet would tell you, for example, whether the greater earnings from the bigger parties you'd be able to cater would more than offset the higher rent for the kitchen.

Even if your job does not call for much writing, illustrating, or calculating by computer, you will find yourself using computers for a host of other applications. Electronic mail will enable you to receive long-distance messages on your computer screen—from a branch office that is hundreds of miles away, for example. A FAX machine in your office will make it possible for you to send actual copies of printed matter over telephone lines. If you have a lot of data to send—say, a lengthy report—you can use a modem to connect one computer to another over telephone lines.

gram, run on microcomputers, you would do the work easily and efficiently.

Suppose you worked in the public relations department of a nonprofit organization. A desktop system would enable you to select an attractive size and style of type for the monthly newsletter or contributors or the informational flyers distributed to members.

As a sales assistant in a company that sells CDs and tapes, you would use a hand-held "mouse" and your desktop equipment to create pie charts, graphs, and other illustrations to include in keyboarded sales reports. The entire report is printed out with a laser printer to produce sharp, good-quality copies. Word processing and graphics are by no means the

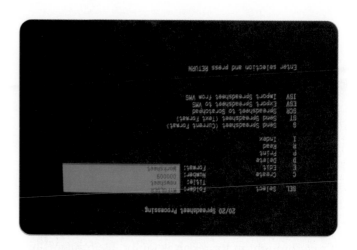

As a utilities company worker, you might use a hand-held computer to record a customer's use of electricity and gas. As a police officer, you would use a computer to check on the license plate number of a car you suspected was stolen.

You could use an electronic appointment calendar, in your job at a real estate office, to keep track of meetings, appointments, and other critical dates. Special computer programs will inventory houses for sale, keeping you up to date on which ones have been sold—and for how much.

Large, mainframe computers that have substantial power and run very sophisticated programs are used in many industries to run scientific tests, analyze the results of research, and carry out complex calculations and projections. As an employee in a drug company or an engineering firm, you might use a scanner to input large amounts of statistical data into such a system.

If you work in an industry where security is important, you might use an electronic voice recognition system to gain entry to secured information. When you speak your name, the computer compares a digitized print of your voice with one it has on file to make sure you are who you say you are!

In just about any field you choose, computers will be there, serving a range of needs with a wide variety of applications. You may come in contact with computers only a few minutes a week—or you might spend much of your day working on one. The choice is yours, and the more you know about electronics in the workplace, the better informed your choice will be.

About Your Equipment

Electronic Typewriter

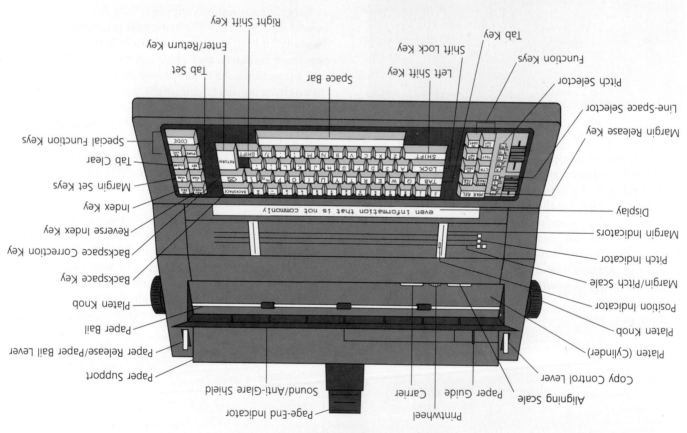

Line-Space Selector controls the space between lines of text.

Left Shift Key is used to capitalize letters keyed with the right hand.

Index Key moves the paper without returning the carrier to the beginning of a line.

Function Keys are those keys other than the alpha/numeric keys that allow the user to perform special functions such as auto centering.

Enter/Return Key enters information into memory and/or returns the carrier to the left margin and moves the paper up to a new line.

Display shows text keyed for checking accuracy.

Copy Control Lever moves the platen forward or backward to adjust for paper thickness.

Carrier is the movable unit containing the printwheel and ribbon carrier.

Backspace Key moves the carrier to the left (backward) one space at a time without deleting characters.

Backspace Correction Key backspaces and removes an incorrect character.

Aligning Scale helps locate the text line when reinserting paper.

Margin Indicators are adjustable tabs on the margin scale that can be positioned to show where current margins are set.

Margin/Pitch Scale indicates horizontal spaces, the position of the carrier, and the pitches available. It may also show the position of the margin sets.

Margin Release Key allows the carrier to move beyond the margin stops.

Margin Set Keys set the margins to control the beginning and ending of lines.

Page-End Indicator shows the lines/inches left on a standard 8½ × 11-inch sheet of paper.

Paper Bail holds the paper against the platen.

Paper Guide guides the paper into the machine so it is consistently in the same position.

Paper Release/Paper Bail Lever frees the paper for removing or straightening.

Paper Support supports the paper for reviewing.

Pitch Indicator shows the pitch that has been selected.

Pitch Selector allows the user to choose a pitch from those available.

Platen (Cylinder) is the large roller around which the paper turns.

Platen Knobs are used to turn the platen by hand.

Position Indicator shows the position of the carrier on a line.

Printwheel is a circular disk containing all the keyboard characters.

Reverse Index Key moves the paper down without returning the carrier to the beginning of a line.

Right Shift Key is used to capitalize letters keyed with the left hand.

Shift Lock is used to key all capital letters.

Sound/Anti-Glare Shield reduces noise and adjusts for glare.

Space Bar spaces the carrier forward one space at a time.

Special Function Keys are those keys that do not produce a letter, number, or special symbol.

Tab Clear clears, or removes, tab stops.

Tab Key moves the carrier directly to a tab stop.

Tab Set sets, or puts in, tab stops.

Microcomputer

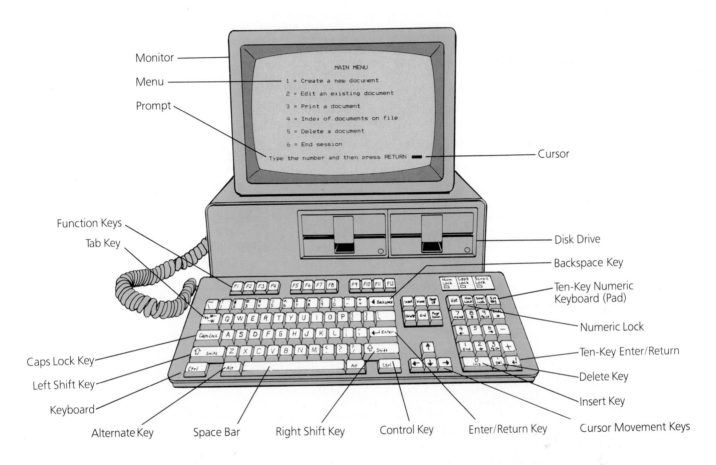

Alt (Alternate Key) is used with other function keys to access software options.

Backspace Key moves the cursor to the left (backward) one space at a time. On some equipment, the backspace key may delete characters.

Caps Lock Key is used to key all capital letters.

Control Key is usually used with other keys to perform specific functions such as temporary indent.

Cursor is a lighted indicator on the display screen that shows a user's exact position within a document.

Cursor Movement Keys allow the cursor to be moved up, down, left, or right within text.

Delete Key is used to delete text.

Disk (Diskette/Floppy Disk) is the most common storage medium used with microcomputers. Disks are usually made of thin plastic, magnetically coated. Disks are protected by a jacket with openings to allow the disk drive to read or write information.

Disk Drive is the component of a microcomputer system that reads and writes data on a disk.

Enter/Return Key is used to enter information into a microcomputer or to return the cursor to the beginning of a new line.

Function Keys are those keys other than the alpha/numeric keys that allow the user to perform special functions such as auto centering.

Insert Key allows the user to insert text without deleting previously keyed text.

Keyboard is a device similar to a typewriter keyboard containing alphabetic, numeric, and special function keys.

Left Shift Key is used to capitalize letters keyed with the right hand.

Menu is a list of options available in a software program.

Monitor is an electronic screen that displays data. The monitor may also be called a CRT (Cathode Ray Tube) or a VDT (Video Display Terminal). Monitors can be color or monochrome (one color).

Numeric Lock is used to activate the numeric keypad.

Prompt is a line displayed on the monitor to request specific input from the user.

Right Shift Key is used to capitalize letters keyed with the left hand.

Space Bar spaces the cursor forward one space at a time.

Tab Key moves the cursor directly to a tab stop.

Ten-Key Enter/Return is used to enter numeric data from the ten-key numeric pad.

Ten-Key Numeric Keyboard (Pad) is a set of keys that resembles a calculator and is used to enter numeric data.

Paper Release Lever frees the paper for straightening or removing.

Pitch Indicator shows the pitch that has been selected.

Platen (Cylinder) is the large roller around which the paper turns.

Platen Knobs are used to turn the platen by hand.

Position Indicator indicates position of the type element on a line.

Right Shift Key is used to capitalize letters keyed with the left hand.

Shift Lock is used to key all capital letters.

Space Bar spaces the carrier forward one space at a time.

Tab Clear/Set clears and sets tab stops.

Tab Key moves the carrier directly to a tab stop.

Type Element is the ball-shaped device containing all the keyboard characters.

Variable Line Spacer is used to permanently change the text line.

Index Key moves the paper up without returning the carrier to the beginning of a line.

Left Shift Key is used to capitalize letters keyed with the right hand.

Line Finder allows for keying above or below a line and then returning to the same line.

Line-Space Lever controls the amount of space between lines of text.

Margin/Pitch Scale indicates horizontal spaces, the position of the carrier, and the position of margin sets.

Margin Release Key allows the carrier to move beyond the margin stops.

Margin Sets control the beginning and ending of lines.

On/Off Control turns the electric power on and off.

Paper Bail holds the paper against the platen.

Paper Centering Scale centers the paper on the platen.

Paper Guide guides the paper into the machine so it is consistently in the same position.

Aligning Scale helps locate the text line when reinserting paper.

Backspace Key moves the carrier to the left (backward) one space at a time.

Card Holder holds cards and envelopes against the platen.

Carrier is the movable unit containing the element and ribbon carrier.

Carrier Return Key returns the carrier to the left margin and moves the paper up to a new line.

Copy Control Lever moves the platen forward or backward to adjust for paper thickness.

Correcting Key backspaces to the error and moves the lift-off tape into position to make a correction.

Dual-Pitch Lever (special models only) resets spacing for 10 pitch or 12 pitch.

Express Backspace Key moves the carrier rapidly to the left without spacing the paper up.

Half-Backspace Lever moves the carrier to the left a half space at a time.

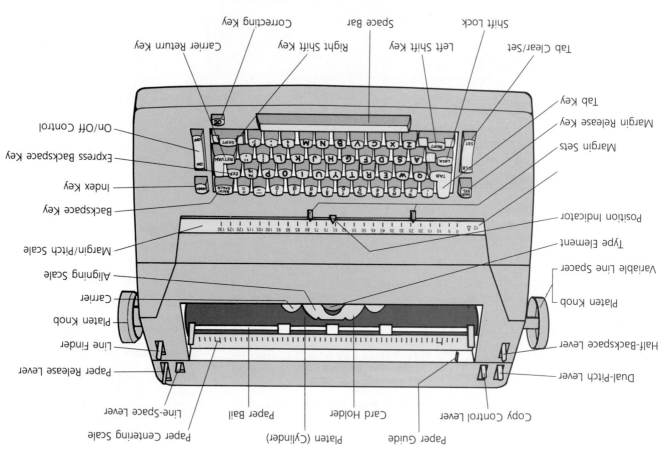

Element Typewriter

Learn About Software

Disks

A **disk** is a magnetic storage device. Disks are sealed in a protective jacket. Through holes in the jacket, the disk drive "reads" information from or "writes" information to the disk. Never insert or remove a disk while the red "in use" light of the disk drive is on.

Disks must be handled with care to avoid damaging information stored on them. To avoid damage, follow these guidelines:

Hold the disk by the corner. Do not touch the exposed recording surface of the disk.

Do not bend or fold the disk.

Do not expose the disk to extreme heat or cold. Never store the disk in direct sunlight.

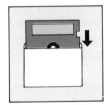

Store disks in their protective sleeves in an upright position away from liquids, dust, smoke, and ashes.

Do not store disks near x-ray devices and magnetic fields such as telephones, dictation equipment, magnets, monitors, and other electronic equipment.

If it is necessary to write on a disk label, use only a felt tip pen. Do not use ballpoints, pencils, or paper clips.

Menus

The **menu** lists the options that are available on a software program. When the microcomputer is operating and a program disk has been inserted properly, a menu will appear on the display screen. A **prompt** will also appear. The prompt tells you how to choose a menu option.

Learn About Pitch (Type) and Paper Size

Pitch (Type) Size

Size of type, or **pitch,** is the number of horizontal spaces/characters to an inch. Most printwheels and

Standard vertical line spacing is 6 lines to 1 vertical inch. Therefore, a sheet of paper 11 inches long (27.94 cm) has 66 lines (11 inches × 6 lines = 66).

Determine the Pitch of Your Equipment

[E T] Electronic Typewriters/Typewriters

Multi-pitch typewriters can print in either 10 pitch, 12 pitch, or 15 pitch. When using a multi-pitch typewriter, always check to see if the printwheel or element is 10, 12, or 15 pitch. Set the pitch selector to correspond to the pitch marked on the printwheel or element. Be sure yours is set correctly.

Multi-pitch typewriters also have 10-, 12-, and 15-pitch margin scales. Be sure to use the proper scale to set the margins for the pitch you are using.

 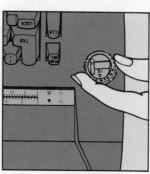

If you are not using a multi-pitch typewriter, align the left edge of the paper with zero on the margin/pitch scale. If the right edge of the paper ends at 85, you have a 10-pitch typewriter (8½ inches × 10 spaces = 85). If the right edge ends at 102, you have a 12-pitch typewriter (8½ inches × 12 spaces = 102).

If your margin scale does not start at zero, key a line of characters and measure off 1 inch. Count the number of characters in the 1-inch space to determine whether you have a 10- or a 12-pitch typewriter.

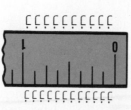

12-pitch has 12 characters in 1 inch

10-pitch has 10 characters in 1 inch

---

elements are either 10 pitch (10 characters to a horizontal inch) or 12 pitch (12 characters to a horizontal inch). Some equipment also has 15 pitch (15 characters to a horizontal inch) and proportional spacing (a kind of pitch where the spacing for each character varies). More advanced software programs and printers may allow you to print in still other sizes. Notice the difference in the major pitch sizes shown in the type samples that follow.

This is a sample of 10-pitch type.

This is a sample of 12-pitch type.

This is a sample of 15-pitch type.

Paper Size

Standard-size paper is 8½ inches wide by 11 inches long (21.59 cm × 27.94 cm). With 10 pitch, there are 85 horizontal spaces across the page (8½ inches × 10 spaces = 85). With 12 pitch, there are 102 spaces across the page (8½ inches × 12 = 102). With 15 pitch, there are 127 spaces across the page.

The center point of the paper for 10 pitch is half the number of spaces in the line, or 42½. Drop the half, and use 42 as the center point. For 12 pitch, the center point is 51. For 15 pitch, the center point is 63.

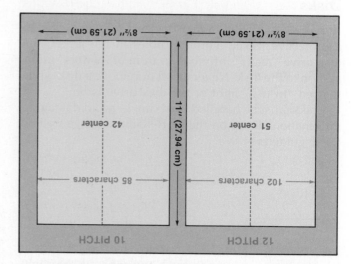

[M] Microcomputers

With software, the center is found by dividing the number of spaces/columns displayed on the screen by 2. If 80 spaces (columns) are displayed, the center point is 40.

Ⓜ Microcomputers

Hard copy is text printed on paper. To obtain a hard copy of text prepared on a microcomputer, you must connect the microcomputer to a printer. The two most common kinds of printers are letter-quality printers and dot-matrix printers. A third type of printer, a laser printer, is also available. The laser printer is a sophisticated printer that produces letter-quality documents using technology that is similar to the technology used in photocopiers. Laser printers also have the capability of printing high-quality graphics.

Letter-Quality Printers

Letter-quality printers produce typewriter-quality text. Most letter-quality printers are equipped with either a 10-pitch or a 12-pitch printwheel. Other pitch sizes are also available. The pitch may be set through the software, usually by an option on the print menu. The pitch is also marked on the face of the printwheel. Set your margins to correspond to the correct pitch of your equipment.

Dot-Matrix Printers

Dot-matrix printers form individual characters with a series of closely spaced dots. The pitch and style of the characters depend on the software and the kind of printer in use. Many software packages offer a variety of pitch sizes. However, some dot-matrix printers are very close in size to 10-pitch typewriter type. When using a dot-matrix printer, choose the 10-pitch selection from the menu, and use the appropriate margin settings for 10 pitch.

Adjust Your Paper

Ⓔ Ⓣ Electronic Typewriters/Typewriters

The paper guide helps you to insert paper into the typewriter so that each sheet is consistently inserted in the same position. The paper guide also helps to keep the paper straight. Adjust the paper guide before you insert a sheet of paper into the typewriter. Slide the paper guide to the left or right so it aligns with zero on the paper centering scale or margin/pitch scale.

Ⓜ Microcomputers

Two kinds of paper may be used in computer printers: continuous feed and individual sheets of standard-size paper. With continuous-feed paper, the vertical perforation on the left side of the paper should align with zero on the margin/pitch scale. If your paper cannot be adjusted, adjust your left margin to allow for the narrow strip of paper to the left of the perforation.

If your printer uses individual sheets, set the paper guide or align the paper with zero on the margin/pitch scale.

Figure Your Margins

Once you have determined the correct pitch and adjusted the paper, you need to determine where to set

Set Your Margins

The following procedures are for most standard kinds of margin sets. If the procedure for setting margins on your typewriter or computer is not given here, refer to the equipment's operating manual, or ask your teacher for help.

12-PITCH 102
margin settings 12 — 90 1"

10-PITCH 85
margin settings 10 — 75 1"

the margins. Margins allow you to control the amount of space on either side of the printed line. For most documents, left and right margins have equal in width. For example, reports usually have 1-inch side margins.

To determine margin settings, multiply the number of characters per inch (usually 10 or 12) by the number of inches you want in the side margin. The result is the left margin setting. For example, the left margin setting for a 1-inch margin using a 12-pitch machine is 12 (12 characters × 1 inch = 12). With 10 pitch, the left margin setting is 10 (10 characters × 1 inch = 10).

To get the right margin setting (when margins are equal), subtract the left margin setting from the total spaces across the page. On a 12-pitch machine, the right margin setting for a 1-inch margin is 90 (102 − 12 = 90). On a 10-pitch machine, the right margin is 75 (85 − 10 = 75).

Note: Some software uses line length rather than side margin settings. To determine the line length of a document when margins are given, subtract the left margin from the right margin. For example, if your side margins are 12 and 90, subtract 12 (the left margin) from 90 (the right margin) to get a line length of 78 characters.

M Microcomputers

Most software has default (preset) margins. These margins are automatically set when you load the software into the computer. Changing the default margins is usually done in one of the following ways:

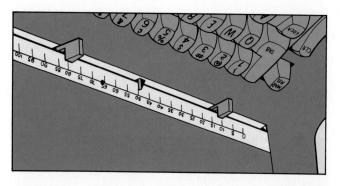

Note: You may have to move the carrier to the right before you can slide the margin set past the position indicator.

T Element Typewriters

1. Push in the left margin-set lever.
2. Slide it to the left or right to the desired setting on the margin/pitch scale.
3. Release the lever.
4. Repeat this procedure to set the right margin.

E Electronic Typewriters

1. Locate the left and right margin-set keys on your keyboard.
2. Move the printwheel or element to the desired setting for the left margin. (You may need to use the margin release to move the carrier/cursor past a previously set margin).
3. Press the appropriate margin-set key.
4. Follow this procedure to set the right margin.

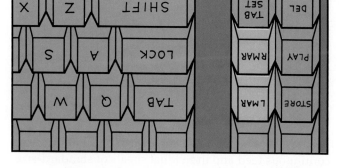

Special Command

1. Enter the special command used by your software to change default settings.
2. A prompt appears on the screen and asks you for the desired margin set number.
3. Respond to the prompt by keying in the desired margin settings.

Ruler Line

1. Move the cursor along the ruler line displayed on the screen. A margin symbol will move as you space left or right.
2. When the symbol is at the desired setting, press enter/return.

Print Menu

Some software programs require you to set margins when you are ready to print a document.

1. Access the print menu. The print menu lists options for changing margins.
2. Select the option you want to change.
3. Enter the new margin settings.

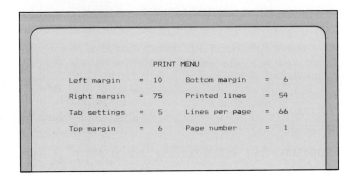

```
                    PRINT MENU

    Left margin    =  10    Bottom margin    =   6

    Right margin   =  75    Printed lines    =  54

    Tab settings   =   5    Lines per page   =  66

    Top margin     =   6    Page number      =   1
```

Set Your Tab Stops

The tab key is used to move the carrier/cursor directly to a specific position on a line.

E T Electronic Typewriters/Typewriters

Before you set tab stops, clear any previously set tab stops along the line.

To clear all tabs at once, check your typewriter to see if it has a total tab clear key. If it does, press the total tab clear key to clear all tab stops.

If you have an element typewriter, move the carrier to the far right. Hold down the tab clear while you return the carrier.

To clear tab stops one at a time, move the carrier to the left margin. Tab to the first stop and press the tab

clear. Continue this procedure until all tab stops are cleared.

To set a tab stop, move your carrier to the desired position and press the tab set.

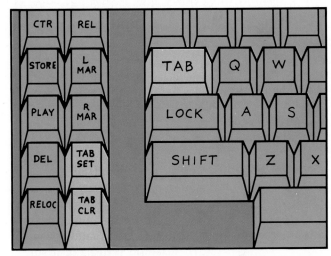

Electronic Typewriter

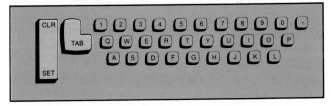

Type Element

M Microcomputers

Use the method required by your software to set new tab stops. The two most common methods of setting tab stops are:

Special Command

1. Give the tab set command for your software.
2. When the prompt asks for a column number, key in the column number for the first tab setting.
3. Repeat this procedure to set the remaining tab stops.

Ruler Line

1. Access the ruler line.
2. Move the cursor to the first desired tab position.
3. Press the appropriate key for setting tabs (usually the tab key or the letter T).
4. Repeat this procedure to set the remaining tab stops.

Set Your Line Spacing

When you select single spacing (SS), text appears on every line. When you select double spacing (DS), one blank line is left between printed lines. When you select triple spacing (TS), two blank lines are left between printed lines, and so on, as shown in the following illustration.

1 single	double	triple	quadruple
2 single	blank	blank	blank
3 single	double	blank	blank
4 single	blank	triple	blank
5 single	double	blank	quadruple

E T Electronic Typewriters/Typewriters

On some typewriters, the line-space selector/lever can be set on 1 for single spacing or 2 for double spacing. Some machines also have settings for triple spacing and for half-line spacing (1½ or 2½). The settings may be indicated by a light on the line-space selector or by notches or numbers beside the line-space lever.

M Microcomputers

Most software programs use a default line-space value of 1 for single spacing. Line spacing may be an option of either the format or the print menu. To change the default setting, you may need to use a command or enter the desired setting.

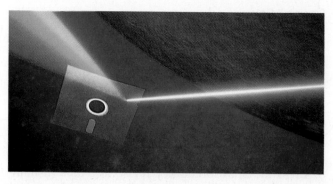

Care For Your Equipment

E T Electronic Typewriters/Typewriters

1. Clean the printwheel/element with a dry, stiff brush. If necessary, remove the printwheel or element to clean it properly.
2. Use a softer brush or lint-free cloth to clean the keyboard and the carrier.
3. Use a mild detergent to clean the plastic parts and painted surfaces of the typewriter.
4. Clean the platen with a soft cloth that has been moistened with alcohol.
5. Use only the proper replacement ribbon or correction tape for your typewriter. Check the owner's manual for installation instructions.
6. Keep the machine covered when it is not being used to keep it dust free.

M Microcomputers

1. Wipe the screen with a soft cloth to keep it dust free. If necessary, moisten a cloth with glass cleaner and then wipe the monitor.
2. Clean the cabinet with a damp, lint-free cloth.
3. Use only the proper replacement ribbon for your printer. Check the owner's manual for installation instructions.
4. Keep the machine covered when it is not being used to keep it dust free.

Careers

Retail Marketing

Did you ever think, while shopping in a store, "If I were in charge here, I'd do things differently"? If so, consider a career in retail marketing.

You might start as an assistant buyer for a large department store. You'd visit showrooms and decide which merchandise was right for your customers. Then, you would use your computer to place orders, and to track the merchandise through delivery, distribution to branch stores, and sales to customers.

Electronic mail would be your communications life line; you'd get "E mail" messages all day long from stores, vendors, and distribution centers.

Or you might go into store management, starting as a group manager. You'd be responsible for stocking, displaying, and selling the merchandise selected by the buyers.

PART 1 Developing Keyboarding Skills

JOB 4 ————————

Announcement
File name: L74C4

Center vertically and horizontally.

EDUCATIONAL SYSTEMS, INC. presents a

RECEPTION

in Recognition of

ESI Scholarship Recipients

7 p.m.

February 14, 19——

Hamilton House

Grossbeck Room

449 Pine Bluff Drive

Southfield, Michigan

(Regrets only 349-3155)

Please come!

JOB 5 ————————

Letter
File name: L74C5

Date: Line 15

Send to:

Mr. Donald Swanson
Manager
Dorseth, Inc.
3745 High Point Road
Westport, CT 06880

From:

Dolores Troesch
Sales Manager

Have you put off buying payroll database software because
you thought only large companies could afford to use
database software? If you prepare over 50 payroll
checks each month, our FAS-PAY payroll database software
can save you money.
FAS-PAY was created for the needs of businesspeople
just like yourself. The software processes payrolls for
25 to 100 employees in minutes at an average cost of
about 10 cents per employee. Not only will your payroll preparation process be faster and more accurate,
but you will have well-organized records of each pay period.
Let's get together and see how the FAS-PAY software can
work for you. Please call me today at 609-438-2851 to
make an appointment.

Sincerely

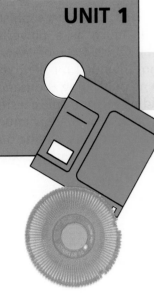

UNIT 1

Alphabetic Keys

Keyboards are everywhere—most notably on typewriters, word processors, and computers. Keyboards can be used for your personal, business, or professional needs. In this course, you will develop keyboarding and formatting skills.

UNIT OBJECTIVES

In this unit, Lessons 1–16, you will:

1. Key all alphabetic keys by touch.
2. Locate selected machine parts and use them correctly.
3. Use proper techniques in striking the keys and using various machine parts.
4. Figure your speed on timed writings.
5. Identify misstrokes.

ELECTRONIC CONCEPTS

automatic return (p. 36)	monitor (p. 4)	scroll (p. 6)
command (p. 7)	option (p. 8)	software (p. 3)
cursor (p. 5)	print (p. 8)	store (p. 7)
default settings (p. 8)	program disk (p. 4)	student disk (p. 4)
file name (p. 4)	prompt (p. 4)	word wrap (p. 36)
menu (p. 8)		

LESSON 1

Margins: Default or 1" (12 pitch, 12-90; 10 pitch, 10-75)
Spacing: SS or default

1A
READ AND DO

Goal: To learn to arrange your work area   3 minutes

Follow these steps to arrange your work area:

1. Clear your desk.
2. Make sure the keyboard is even with the front edge of your desk.
3. Place your textbook to the right of the keyboard at a comfortable reading angle.
4. Place paper, pencils, and so on, on the other side of your desk.

print shop. ¶ Desktop publishing saves money and time. Using in-house desktop publishing can drop the cost of a typeset page from $50 to $10. The editing chores can be reduced by as much as 60 percent (Friedman 1987, 69), partially because the paste-up process is eliminated. An added plus of desktop publishing is that it does not require highly skilled labor. Most keyboarders can easily learn to use desktop publishing. ¶ A disadvantage of desktop publishing is its original cost. The most inexpensive system costs about as much as a top-of-the line microcomputer. The most sophisticated system can cost as much as a powerful mainframe computer (The Office 1987, 67). Also, the desktop system is not intended for high volumes of materials, such as publishing thousands of textbooks. ¶ The deciding factor in purchasing a desktop publishing system lies in how much money and time are already spent on having materials printed that could be done with desktop publishing (Friedman 1987, 69).

JOB 2

Table

File name: L74C2

DS

Leave 10 spaces between columns.

Center horizontally and vertically.

Projected Job Openings in 1995

Computer Programmers	586,000
Computer Operators	353,000
Accountants and Auditors	1,189,000
Secretaries	3,064,000
Accounting Clerks	2,091,000
Receptionists	542,000
General Office Clerks	2,629,200
Administrative Assistants	2,417,500
Computer Technicians	1,759,600

JOB 3

Letter

File name: L74C3

Date: Line 15

Send to:

Mr. David McKenna
203 Asbury Drive
Wilmore, KY 40390

From:

Estelle MacLennan
4435 Hacienda Drive
Dallas, TX 75233

Your talk last week to our local users' group on accessing computer databases really opened my eyes to what databases could do for me. Since hearing your speech, I have used several different databases and have enjoyed experimenting with them.

As an expert on databases, could you recommend one for use in my home business? I run a small mail-order catalog business and sell local handicrafts throughout the country. I would like a database that can index my customers' names and the frequency of their orders, flag states that require taxes, and keep an inventory of my most-requested products.

Any additional insights that you can give me will be appreciated. Thank you for your help.

Sincerely

1B

Goal: To learn proper position at the keyboard   5 minutes

Refer to the illustrations as you read and follow the instructions.

Curve your fingers

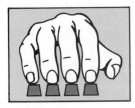

Correct alignment

Correct position at the keyboard is important as you learn and build your keyboarding skills.

1. Sit up straight with your back touching the chair.
2. Sit directly in front of the keyboard.
3. Put both feet flat on the floor with one foot slightly in front of the other.
4. Curve your fingers and place them on the keys.
5. Hold your forearms so they slant with the keyboard.
6. Keep your wrists low, but do not rest your hands on the keyboard.

Correct position at the keyboard

1C

NEED TO KNOW

Goal: To learn about the symbols E, M, and T   2 minutes

This textbook has directions for electronic typewriters, microcomputers, and electric typewriters. Some directions are general. They relate to all the equipment. When specific directions and activities are needed for the different kinds of equipment, the symbols E, M, and T are used.

The symbol E indicates directions and activities for

electronic typewriters. If you use an electronic typewriter, ignore directions that are labeled for the microcomputer and electric typewriter.

The symbol M indicates directions for microcomputers. NOTE: You need word processing **software** for your microcomputer.

The symbol T indicates directions for typewriters.

1D

READ AND DO

Goal: To learn how to insert paper or load a disk   5 minutes

E T *Electronic Typewriters/Typewriters*

1. Turn on the typewriter.
2. Set the paper guide at zero on the margin/pitch scale. (Figure 1)
3. Place the paper behind the platen, long edge against the paper guide. (Figure 2, next page)
4. Pull the paper bail/insertion lever toward you (or up on some machines).
5. Feed the paper into the machine. Use the automatic paper insert or turn the platen knob.

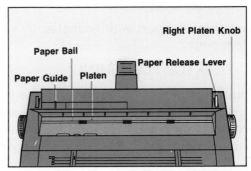

Figure 1

(Continued next page)

74–75A

WARMUP

Goal: To strengthen keyboarding skills   5 minutes

Key each line twice. DS after each pair of lines.

Speed
Accuracy
Number/Symbol

1 The panel of eleven girls may handle its amendment problems.
2 Wes quickly went to Quebec as Quincy wired the weekly quota.
3 About 342 cases of meat were shipped to 243 West Oak Avenue.

| 1 | 2 | 3 | 4 | 5 | 6 | 7 | 8 | 9 | 10 | 11 | 12 |

74–75B

GOAL WRITING

Goal: To measure timed-writing progress   10 minutes

DS or default.

Take two 3-minute goal writings.

If you finish before time is called, start again.

Record your speed and accuracy.

	1'	3'
In a recent survey, a group of top executives was	10	3
asked to name the major weakness of their newly hired	21	7
college graduates. Eighty percent of the executives said	33	11
that by far the biggest weakness is poor writing skills.	44	15
The executives said that most of the business majors	55	18
and the science majors whom they hired are not able to write	67	22
even a short memo that is clear and has the right style.	78	26
The executives noted that the graduates are well prepared in	91	30
their degree fields. However, it seems to come as a big	102	34
surprise to many of the graduates that thirty percent or	113	38
more of their time is spent writing memos, letters, reports,	126	42
proposals, and notes to document research.	134	45

1' | 1 | 2 | 3 | 4 | 5 | 6 | 7 | 8 | 9 | 10 | 11 | 12 | AWL
3' | 1 | | 2 | | 3 | | 4 | 5.7

74–75C

PRODUCTION
MEASUREMENT

Goal: To measure production skills   85 minutes

JOB 1

Report   File name: L74C1

Prepare the unbound report with endnotes.
Prepare a title page.

DESKTOP PUBLISHING

Desktop publishing is an outgrowth of the increased sophistication of personal computers and word processing software. ¶ Desktop publishing uses a personal computer and an advanced word processing program, but the concept is broader than word processing. In desktop publishing, the user is able to select type sizes, perform layout tasks on the screen, create graphics, draw illustrations, and then see the full page on the computer screen as it will appear in printed form. The hardware and software are combined with a laser printer that can print graphics and produce documents that look as if they have been printed in a

(Continued next page)

6. Check to see if your paper is straight. If not, pull the paper release lever forward, straighten the paper, and return the paper release lever to its proper position. (Figure 3)
7. Place the paper bail/insertion lever back into position. Adjust the paper bail rollers to divide your paper into approximately equal sections.
8. Unless directed otherwise, leave about 1 inch at the top of the paper. With auto paper insert, your paper is automatically positioned with a 1-inch top margin.
9. Return the carrier to the left margin.

Figure 2

Ⓜ *Microcomputers*

1. Open the door to the disk drive.
2. Insert the **program disk** into Drive 1 and close the door. (Figure 4)
3. Insert the **student disk** into Drive 2 and close the door. (If you have a single disk drive, follow any screen **prompts** to determine when to remove the program disk and load the student disk.)
4. Turn on the **monitor** and the microcomputer.
5. Follow the screen prompts.
6. If required to give a **file name,** use: **Lesson1**.

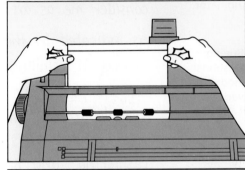

Figure 3

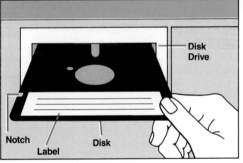

Figure 4

Insert the disk into the disk drive with the label facing up.

1E

NEW-KEY ORIENTATION

Study the keyboard chart. Note which finger strikes each home key.

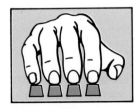

Correct alignment

Goal: To learn the home-key position   5 minutes

1. Place your left index finger on Ⓕ and your right index finger on Ⓙ. This positions your hands on the home keys: left hand on Ⓐ Ⓢ Ⓓ Ⓕ; right hand on Ⓙ Ⓚ Ⓛ Ⓙ. Keep your fingers curved and aligned on the keys.
2. Using the correct fingers, lightly touch each key as you say the letters to yourself: asdfjkl;.

(Continued next page)

71–73I

APPLICATION: EMPLOYMENT DOCUMENTS

Goal: To format and key an application letter and a resume

JOB 1

File name: L73I1

Key this application letter.

Use your name and address as originator.

Send to:

Mr. Marvin Bueing
Director of Personnel
Baker and Rhodes, Inc.
56 Fourth Avenue
Portland, OR 97202

Supply a salutation.

Supply a complimentary closing.

CUE: When enclosing a resume with your letter, include an enclosure notation on your letter.

While reading today's edition of the <u>Salem Tribune</u>, I was delighted to see your advertisement for a sales associate. Please consider me as an applicant for this position.

As indicated in the enclosed resume, my sales training includes courses in retailing, advertising, and public relations. During the past year, I worked full time as a sales clerk in the gift department at Reynolds Department Store. My responsibilities included assisting customers in making gift selections, cashiering, and preparing advertising copy.

You will find me cheerful, highly skilled, and eager to learn. May I have the opportunity to discuss my qualifications with you. My telephone number is (503) 555-0190.

Checkpoint: Did you include an enclosure notation?

JOB 2

File name: L73I2

Key this resume. Use your name, address, and telephone number in the heading.

CAREER OBJECTIVE To obtain a full-time sales manager position with opportunity for advancement. / EDUCATION Wilkens High School, 783 Wilkens Road, Salem, OR 97312. September 1989 to June 1992. Course work included retailing, advertising, and public relations. Received DECA Salesperson of the Month Award for March, 1992. Graduated with 2.75 grade point average in all course work. / EXPERIENCE Sales clerk in the gift department at Reynolds Department Store, 105 Main Street, Salem, OR 97303. June 1992 to present. Duties include assisting customers in making gift selections, cashiering, and preparing advertising copy. / Cashier at Jack's Donut Shop,

521 Elm Street, Salem, OR 97312. September 1991 to January 1992. Duties included cashiering and frying donuts. / Cashier and sandwich maker at Hamer's Sandwich Shop, 473 Pine Street, Salem, OR 97314. June 1991 to September 1991. Duties included cashiering, making sandwiches, and cleaning tables. / ACTIVITIES Member of the Salem Council for the Arts / Member of the Blue Mountain Tennis Club / Member of Metropolitan Community Church Youth Club / REFERENCES Provided upon request

JOB 3

File name: L73I3

Proofread your application letter and resume. Mark corrections with proofreader's marks. Prepare a corrected copy of each document.

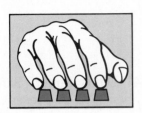

Incorrect alignment

3. Remove your hands from the keyboard.
4. Replace your fingers on the home keys. Check for correct finger and wrist position: fingers curved and wrists low, but hands not resting on the keyboard.
5. Strike each home key with the correct finger while saying each letter to yourself. Use a quick, sharp stroke: `asdfjkl;`
6. Strike each home key again as you say each letter: `asdfjkl;`

1F
READ AND DO
Goal: To learn the proper technique for the return/enter key   4 minutes

When you reach the end of a line, use the return/enter (R/E) key to move the carrier/**cursor** to the beginning of a new line.

*Using the **sem** (semicolon) finger, press the return/enter key lightly, and release it quickly.*

1. Locate the return/enter key.
2. Place your fingers in home-key position.
3. Key the letters: `asdfjkl;`
4. Keep your other fingers on the home keys while you extend the **sem** finger to the return/enter key.
5. Press the return/enter key.
6. Return your **sem** finger to its home-key position immediately after pressing the return/enter key.
7. Key: `asdfjkl;`. Then press return/enter.

1G
READ AND DO
Goal: To learn to operate the space bar   5 minutes

The space bar is used to space between words and after marks of punctuation (such as the semicolon).

1. Locate the space bar.
2. Place your fingers in home-key position and key: `asdf`.
3. Hold your right thumb over the space bar and keep your fingers in home-key position. Tap the space bar with your right thumb using a quick, down-and-in motion.
4. Key: `jkl;` and then *quickly* tap the space bar.
5. Do not pause before or after spacing.
6. Key: `asdf`. Then space quickly and key: `jkl;`.
7. Press return/enter to begin a new line.

1H
NEED TO KNOW
Goal: To learn about Technique Timings   3 minutes

Keyboarding skill can be developed using good techniques. The Technique Timings in this textbook will help you master good keyboarding skill.

During a Technique Timing, focus on a single goal. That is, try to use one technique properly. For example, during a 1-minute Technique Timing for eyes on copy, your goal is to key for one minute without taking your eyes off the textbook copy. Key at a comfortable pace. Concentrate only on the technique. Don't be concerned about how fast you key or how many misstrokes you make.

At the end of a Technique Timing, evaluate how successful you were in meeting the technique goal of the timing.

71–73F

APPLICATION: RESUME

Goal: To format and key a resume

File name: L110F

Key this resume. Proofread and correct errors.

JOHN BLACKHAWK / 2528 Palm Circle Drive / San Antonio, TX 78228 / (512) 555-4581 / CAREER OBJECTIVE To obtain a part-time position as a computer-aided drafting technician. / EDUCATION Davis Technical College, 634 East Corrina Lane, San Antonio, TX 78206. September 1992 to present. Will receive an Associate of Science degree in Computer Science upon graduation. Degree includes courses in mathematics, drafting, engineering, and microcomputers. Grade point average is 3.0 in all academic work. / Sam Houston High School, 312 Novena Street, San Antonio, TX 78226. September 1989 to June 1992. Course work emphasized computer science, art, and mathematics. Maintained a 3.95 grade point average in all courses. Graduated with honors. / EXPERIENCE / Sales clerk at The Computer Connection, 3641 Davis Street, San Antonio, TX 78204. September 1992 to present. Duties include stocking shelves, cashiering, and assisting customers. / Carpenter's helper at the All-City Construction Company, 126 Third Avenue, San Antonio, TX 78217. June 1992 to September 1992. Duties included measuring and sawing lumber, running errands, and cleaning. / Print framer at Tate's Gallery, 141 Quechemaca Street, San Antonio, TX 78228. June 1991 to June 1992. Duties included making frames, cashiering, answering telephone inquiries, and assisting customers in making decisions. / ACTIVITIES Vice president of Davis Technical College Computer Club / Volunteer guide at the San Antonio Native American Museum / Member of San Antonio Symphony Society / Member of San Antonio Trinity Chapel Choir / REFERENCES Provided upon request

71–73G

NEED TO KNOW

Goal: To learn about application letters

You send an application letter to a prospective employer when you apply for a job. The purpose of the letter is to obtain an interview.

Use the personal business letter format to key an application letter. A copy of your resume is always enclosed with your application letter. Be sure to include an enclosure notation in your letter. Refer to 33C to review the format for a personal business letter.

71–73H

SELF-CHECK

Goal: To review resumes and application letters

Key the statement number and your answer: True or False.

Check your answers in Appendix B.

1. Resumes should be double spaced.
2. The purpose of an application letter is to obtain an interview.
3. The purpose of a resume is to provide a prospective employer with information about previous work experience.
4. A resume should never be sent with a letter of application.

1I

TECHNIQUE TIMING

Take two 1-minute timings.

Strike each letter, then tap the space bar the number of times shown.

Do not pause when spacing.

Press return/enter when you see R/E.

Goal: To improve keyboarding techniques 4 minutes

Tap the space bar with your right thumb, using a quick, down-and-in motion. Keep your left thumb tucked out of the way.

a 3sp a 2sp s 3sp s 1sp R/E d 1sp d 2sp

f 5sp f 2sp R/E j 1sp j 3sp k 1sp k 3sp

l 4sp R/E l 1sp ; 2sp ; 2sp R/E a 3sp

s 4sp d 3sp f 2sp R/E j 1sp k 2sp l 1sp ; R/E

a 2sp ; 2sp s 3sp l 1sp d 2sp k 1sp f R/E

> **Checkpoint:** Were you successful in meeting the technique goal of the timing?

1J

KEYBOARD PRACTICE

Key each line twice.

Goal: To practice proper keystroking 5 minutes

Strike the keys with a quick, sharp stroke (A). As you strike a key, snap the finger toward the palm of your hand (B).

Ⓕ *and* Ⓙ 1 ff jj ff jj ff jj fj fj fj fj fj fjf fjf

Ⓓ *and* Ⓚ 2 dd kk dd kk dd kk dk dk dk dk dk dkd dkd

Ⓢ *and* Ⓛ 3 ss ll ss ll ss ll sl sl sl sl sl sls sls

Ⓐ *and* Ⓘ 4 aa ;; aa ;; aa ;; a; a; a; a; a; a;a a;a

1K

TECHNIQUE TIMING

Take a 1-minute timing on each line.

Think and say each letter to yourself as you strike it.

Space once between words.

Goal: To improve keyboarding techniques 6 minutes

Return/enter quickly when you come to the end of a line. Do not space before pressing return/enter.

1 as ask as ask all lass all lass as ask a R/E

2 ad ad lad lad ad lad all a lad all a lad R/E

3 all all fall fall all all fall fall fall R/E

4 a lass; a lass; a lass asks; a lass asks R/E

5 ask a lad; a lass asks; a lad; ask a lad R/E

Ⓜ As you continue to key lines of text, the text may begin to **scroll** (disappear) off the screen.

> **Checkpoint:** Were you successful in meeting the technique goal of the timing?

71–73E
PROJECT PREVIEW

Goal: To format and key a resume

File name: L110E

SM: Default or 1"

Tab: Center

Key as much of the resume as you can in 6 minutes.

Ignore misstrokes.

If you finish before time is called, start again.

line 13↓ AMANDA LEA WAINWRIGHT
1422 Rangeview Road
Sacramento, CA 91104
(916) 555-6113 _{TS}

CAREER OBJECTIVE _{DS}

To secure a data entry position with opportunities for growth. _{TS}

EDUCATION _{DS}

Central Junior High School, 1023 Clement Way, Sacramento, CA 91103. September 1992 to present. Will graduate in June, 1995. Course work emphasizes data entry and accounting. Trained on a microcomputer using word processing, database, and spreadsheet software. Keyboarding speed is 45 wpm with 95 percent accuracy. Grade point average is 3.5 in all course work. _{TS}

EXPERIENCE _{DS}

Office assistant at Accounting Services, Inc., 33 Federal Street, Sacramento, CA 91110. June 1993 to present. Duties include answering the telephone, data entry, using spreadsheet software, making photocopies, delivering express mail to the post office, and running errands. _{DS}

Sales assistant at DeSoto's Card Shop, 723 Old Milford Road, Sacramento, CA 91107. September 1992 to June 1993. Duties included stocking cards, dusting display racks, assembling advertising displays, taking inventory, cashiering, and assisting shop customers. _{TS}

ACTIVITIES _{DS}

President, Central Junior High School Business Club
Member of Central Junior High School Microcomputer Club
Member of Sacramento City Junior Swim Team
Member of Nobel Little Theater Actors _{TS}

REFERENCES _{DS}

Provided upon request

1L
READ AND DO

Refer to the illustrations as you read and follow the instructions for your equipment.

Goal: To end the lesson   3 minutes

E T *Electronic Typewriters/Typewriters*

1. To remove the paper from the typewriter, follow these steps:
   a. Pull the paper/paper bail release toward you. (On some machines, this will cause the paper to eject. If so, go to Step 2.)
   b. Take the paper out of the machine and return the paper/paper bail release to its original position.
2. Turn off the typewriter.
3. Cover the machine if told to do so.
4. Clean up your work area.

M *Microcomputers*

Ending procedures vary. Follow the specific instructions for your equipment or these general steps:

1. Read and respond to any prompts that appear on the screen.
2. If necessary, **store** your document using the store key or **command**, and exit the program.
3. Be sure the red light of the disk drive is off before you open the door of the disk drive.
4. Carefully remove the disk.
5. Place the disk into its envelope.
6. Turn off the power to the monitor and to the microcomputer.

Use the paper/paper bail release lever to remove the paper from your typewriter.

Always store disks in their protective envelopes to prevent damage to stored documents.

7. Store the disk following your instructor's guidelines.
8. Clean up your work area.

LESSON 2 Reinforcement

Margins: Default or 1" (12 pitch, 12-90; 10 pitch, 10-75)
Spacing: SS or default

2A
READ AND DO (REVIEW)

Goal: To get ready to key   3 minutes

Clear your desk of anything you won't need during your keyboarding class. Arrange your work area as described in 1A.

(Continued next page)

71–73C

Goal: To measure timed-writing progress

DS or default.

Take two 5-minute goal writings.

If you finish before time is called, start again.

Record your speed and accuracy.

	1'	5'
Experts believe that how people dress has a major	10	2
impact on how they are perceived and how successful that	22	4
they will become. Some executives hire wardrobe consultants	34	7
to help them select the most effective colors and styles.	45	9
Consultants say that to dress for success, both men and	57	11
women should choose a conservative business suit. They say	69	14
that a dark blue or a black suit conveys an image of power	81	16
and competence. A dark gray suit is also a good choice,	92	18
but a pale gray suit makes its wearer look weak. They say	104	21
a brown suit is best avoided because it makes its wearer	115	23
look dull and cloddish. Consultants prefer simply tailored	127	25
shirts and blouses in white or ivory.	135	27

1' | 1 | 2 | 3 | 4 | 5 | 6 | 7 | 8 | 9 | 10 | 11 | 12 | AWL
5' | 1 | | 2 | | 3   5.7

71–73D

Goal: To learn to format and key a resume

A **resume** is sent to a prospective employer and lists your qualifications in an easy-to-read format. A resume contains information about your career objective, educational background and skills, previous work experience, relevant activities, and references.

1. Margins: Default or 1"
2. Heading: Center the SS lines containing your name (keyed in all caps), address, and telephone number.
3. Section headings: Key each heading, beginning at the left margin, in all caps. TS before and DS after each heading.
4. Body: Key all the lines beginning at the left margin. SS the items within a section, DS between the items.

AMANDA LEA WAINWRIGHT
1422 Rangeview Road
Sacramento, CA 91104
(916) 555-6113

CAREER OBJECTIVE
To secure a data entry position with opportunities for growth.

EDUCATION
Central Junior High School, 1023 Clement Way, Sacramento, CA 91103. September 1992 to present. Will graduate in June, 1995. Course work emphasizes data entry and accounting. Trained on a microcomputer using word processing, database, and spreadsheet software. Keyboarding speed is 45 wpm with 95 percent accuracy. Grade point average is 3.5 in all course work.

EXPERIENCE
Office assistant at Accounting Services, Inc., 33 Federal Street, Sacramento, CA 91110. June 1993 to present. Duties include answering the telephone, data entry, using spreadsheet software, making photocopies, delivering express mail to the post office, and running errands.

Sales assistant at DeSoto's Card Shop, 723 Old Milford Road, Sacramento, CA 91107. September 1992 to June 1993. Duties included stocking cards, dusting display racks, assembling advertising displays, taking inventory, cashiering, and assisting shop customers.

ACTIVITIES
President, Central Junior High School Business Club
Member of Central Junior High School Microcomputer Club
Member of Sacramento City Junior Swim Team
Member of Nobel Little Theater Actors

REFERENCES
Provided upon request

Resume keyed in an easy-to-read format

E T *Electronic Typewriters/ Typewriters*

1. Turn on the typewriter.
2. Adjust the paper guide so the left edge of your paper aligns with zero.
3. Insert a sheet of paper and straighten it if necessary.

M *Microcomputers*

1. Insert the disks in proper sequence as described in 1D.
2. Turn on the monitor.
3. Turn on the microcomputer.
4. If required to give a file name, use: **Lesson2**.

> **Checkpoint:** Is your keyboard even with the front edge of your desk or table?

2B
NEED TO KNOW

Line-space key

Line-space lever

Goal: To learn about line spacing   6 minutes

All keyboarding equipment lets you set the line spacing. When you select single spacing (SS), text appears on every line. When you select double spacing (DS), one blank line is left between keyed lines. Some equipment also allows for half-line and triple spacing. For more information about line spacing, refer to the *About Your Equipment* section of this textbook.

E T *Electronic Typewriters/Typewriters*

The line-space key/lever controls the number of lines your paper spaces up when you press return. Set your line-space key/lever on 1 for single spacing (SS), as shown in the color band at the beginning of this lesson. When your machine is set for SS, you can leave a blank line between keyed lines by pressing the return key twice. If the instructions say DS (double space), set the line-space key/lever on 2.

M *Microcomputers*

Most software programs have **default** (or preset) line spacing. Usually the default setting is single spacing (SS). When your software is set for single spacing, you can leave a blank line between keyed lines by pressing the return/enter key twice. When the instructions say DS (double space), select the appropriate **option** from the **print menu,** or give a command to change the line spacing.

2C
READ AND DO

12 pitch has 12 characters to 1 inch

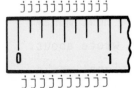

10 pitch has 10 characters to 1 inch

Goal: To learn about setting margins   6 minutes

Margins allow you to control the length of a line of text. They also allow you to position that line of text horizontally on the page.

Many typewriters and printers can print in either 12 pitch or 10 pitch.

Determine the pitch of your equipment.

Next, decide how wide to make the side margins and determine the margin settings. For example, 2-inch side margins require settings of: 24-78 (12 pitch); 20-65 (10 pitch).

Determine margin settings for 1-inch and 1½-inch margins for 12 pitch and 10 pitch.

Throughout Unit 1, side margin settings are shown in the color band at the beginning of each lesson.

(Continued next page)

Employment

You should begin developing your job-seeking skills early. You can do this by learning to format and key a resume and an application letter. These are the documents you will need to apply for a job.

UNIT OBJECTIVES

In this unit, Lessons 71–73, you will:

1. Increase your keyboarding speed and accuracy.
2. Format and key a resume.
3. Format and key an application letter.

LESSONS 71–73

Margins: Default or 1″
Spacing: SS or default   Tab: ¶

71–73A
WARMUP

Key each line twice. DS after each pair.

"th" combinations

Goal: To strengthen keyboarding skills

1 Thomas Thoma thanked the theater watchers for their thrones.
2 The thin, thankful thief escaped through the three thickets.
3 Throughout the third theme, Theola thus thrummed the zither.

| 1 | 2 | 3 | 4 | 5 | 6 | 7 | 8 | 9 | 10 | 11 | 12 |

71–73B
SPEED PRACTICE

Take a 1-minute timing on each sentence.

Goal: To build keyboarding speed

1′

1 The individual customers can give us a list of the problems.   12
2 April is the month when their customers want the most money.   24
3 They are proud of the financial system that you wrote about.   36
4 She spent most of the month touring the four national parks.   48
5 That relationship might endure open talks on various topics.   60

| 1 | 2 | 3 | 4 | 5 | 6 | 7 | 8 | 9 | 10 | 11 | 12 |

12 pitch (SM 1")	
left margin	12
right margin	90

10 pitch (SM 1")	
left margin	10
right margin	75

Equipment with Default (Preset) Margins

Many electronic typewriters and software programs have default margins. These default margins are usually 1 inch. Use default margins unless otherwise directed.

Equipment without Default (Preset) Margins

Align the left edge of your paper at zero on the margin scale. Then look at the margin settings in the lesson-opener band and set your margins.

2D
READ AND DO (REVIEW)

Goal: To review home-key position   3 minutes

LEFT HAND   a s d f   j k l ;   RIGHT HAND

1. Curve your fingers, and place them on the home keys: `asdfjkl;`.
2. Keep your wrists low, but do not rest your hands on the keyboard.
3. Keep your arms even with the slant of the keyboard.
4. Hold your right thumb over the space bar.
5. Tap the space bar several times with a quick, down-and-in motion: *space, space, space.*
6. Press the return/enter key with the **sem** finger, keeping other fingers on home keys.

2E
TECHNIQUE TIMING

Place your fingers on the home keys. Then take two 1-minute timings on each line.

Space once between letter groups.

Goal: To improve keyboarding techniques   10 minutes

Strike each key with a quick, sharp stroke. Release the key quickly.

1 `ff jj dd kk ss ll aa ;; fj dk sl a; ;lkj` R/E
2 `aa ;; ss ll dd kk ff jj a; sl dk fj fdsa` R/E

Keep your wrists low, but do not rest your hands on the keyboard.

3 `asd fjk l; aa ;; a; ss ll sl dd kk dk fj` R/E
4 `sad lads; as dad asks; sad lass asks dad` R/E

2F
TECHNIQUE TIMING

Review the correct technique for the return/enter key. Then, take two 1-minute timings.

Goal: To improve keyboarding techniques   4 minutes

Place your fingers in home-key position. Keeping your other fingers on the home keys, reach the **sem** finger to the return/enter key. Press the key lightly and release it quickly. Remember: Do not space before pressing return/enter at the end of a line.

(Continued next page)

70A
GOAL WRITING

Warm up on 69A for 5 minutes.

DS

Then take two 3-minute goal writings.

If you finish before time is called, start again.

Record your speed and accuracy.

Goal: To measure timed-writing progress   15 minutes

	1'	3'
The purpose of the reader plays an important role in	11	4
determining the kind of reading that a person does. Two	22	7
different people may read the same book in different ways	34	11
if their purposes are not the same. Speed of reading and	45	15
comprehension of the material being read vary depending	57	19
upon the purpose of the reader.	63	21
When you read for information, you should first scan	74	25
the material to preview the ideas. This process provides	85	28
an overview to aid in understanding the material when it is	97	32
read thoroughly. You should also decide what should be	109	36
covered thoroughly, what can be read quickly, and what	120	40
should be put aside and read at a later date.	129	43

```
1'| 1 | 2 | 3 | 4 | 5 | 6 | 7 | 8 | 9 | 10 | 11 | 12 |     AWL
3'|       1       |       2       |       3       |       4       |   5.7
```

70B
PRODUCTION MEASUREMENT

Goal: To measure formatting skills   35 minutes

File name: L70B   Key this report in unbound format. The title is *The Importance of Friends.* Prepare a title page. Use your name as the author.

Men and women have been described as social beings. That description helps us understand our need to have and to be a friend. From early childhood on, friends help us in the lifelong process of self-development (Rubin 1985, 34).

How do we form these vital friendships? It has been said that the evolution of a friendship is an interesting process to observe, even though it is seldom completed (Smith 1984, 145). We often begin reaching out to form friendships, but only continue to build the relationship in a few instances. Even fewer of our friendships fit the category of "best friend."

Best friends: a special kind of relationship, and a unique one, embodying the best of all the important relationships in our lives—kin, mate, and friend—along with the problems of all three, and some that belong to friendship alone. (Rubin 1985, 175)

What are the components of a genuine friendship? Friendship, like all other valued facets of our lives, requires an investment of time and energy. It requires genuine concern on the part of both people to develop (Buscaglia 1984, 177). Friendship requires a willingness to "reach out," a commitment to being open, and the courage to take risks.

WORKS CITED

Buscaglia, Leo. 1984. *Loving Each Other.* Thorofare, NJ: SLACK Inc.

Rubin, Lillian B. 1985. *Just Friends.* New York: Harper & Row.

Smith, Fred. 1984. *You and Your Network.* Waco, TX: Word Books.

Return/enter when you see R/E, not at the end of a line.

```
a as ad ads all fall
as sad; ask lads ads

a lad lads lass fall
as a lad; a sad dad;

a fall; a lad falls;
all lads; ask a lass
```

Do not space before pressing return/enter. Quickly return the **sem** finger to home-key position after pressing return/enter.

```
a as ad ads all fall R/E as sad; ask lads ads R/E R/E
a lad lads lass fall R/E as a lad; a sad dad; R/E R/E
a fall; a lad falls; R/E all lads; ask a lass R/E R/E
```

Checkpoint: Do your lines look similar to those shown in the left margin?

2G
KEYBOARD PRACTICE

Key each line twice.

Double space (DS) after each pair of lines by pressing return/enter twice.

Goal: To practice proper keystroking   8 minutes

CUE: Keep your eyes on the textbook copy as you key.

```
1 aj ak al a; sj sk sl s; dj dk dl d; a;sl  Repeat each line
2 fj fk fl f; ja js jd jf ka ks kd kf a;sl
3 la ls ld lf ;a ;s ;d ;f a; sl dk fj a;sl
4 as as ask ask asks asks ad ad ads ads as
5 sad sad dad dad fad fad lad lad all fall
6 all fall dad dads ask asks lad lads lass
7 sad dad asks a lass fads fall all ask as
```

Checkpoint: Did you remember to double space between groups?

2H
TECHNIQUE TIMING

Take a 2-minute timing on each pair of lines.

If you finish before time is called, start again.

DS after each timing.

Goal: To improve keyboarding techniques   8 minutes

Quickly return to home-key position after pressing return/enter.
```
1 a;sldkfj a;sldkfj a;sldkfj a;sldkfj lad;
2 a fall; a flask; all fall; all dads; ask
```

Sit up straight with your feet flat on the floor.
```
3 all fall fads; a fall flask; as all lads
4 all ads; a fall ad; a sad lass; as a dad
```

Strike the space bar with a quick, down-and-in motion.
```
5 aa ;; ss ll dd kk ff jj a;sldkfj jak jak
6 fall lass dad fad dads lads ask asks sad
```

69C

Choose the word or phrase that correctly completes each statement.

Key the number and the completed statement.

Check your answers in Appendix B.

Goal: To review unbound reports and author-date references   10 minutes

Answers:	alphabetical	author name	double	13
	9	1-inch	triple	
	year	6	margin	

1. The title of a report or works cited page is placed on line ____.
2. A ____ space is used after the title.
3. The body of a report is ____ spaced.
4. On the second page of a report, the body begins on line ____.
5. An unbound report uses ____ side margins.
6. Leave ____ lines in the bottom margin of an unbound report.
7. The first line of a works cited entry is keyed at the ____.
8. Works cited entries are placed in ____ order.
9. The ____ is keyed first in an author-date reference.
10. A parenthetical reference must always include the ____.

69D

APPLICATION:
REPORTS

Goal: To format an unbound report with works cited   30 minutes

File name: L69D   Key this report in unbound format. The title is *All About Modems*. Prepare a title page, using your name as author. Prepare a works cited page.

Sooner or later, every computer user has the desire to talk to another computer user. If you have a microcomputer, you probably won't be an exception. You may want to access a new service, communicate with other people, or telecommute to work. The device that allows you to do all these things is the modem.

What is a modem? A modem is a device that "translates computer input into audio tones" (Kurshen et al. 1986, 228). Another writer describes the modem as follows:

The word modem is a contraction of "modulator/demodulator," which is exactly what the modem does. The modem converts computer data into the form that phone lines can carry. In effect, computers and telephones speak two different languages. The modem acts as the translator. (Powell 1984, 111)

The prospective modem buyer needs to be familiar with transmission speeds. The usual speed for the home user is 300 bits per second (bps); a speed of 300 bps is equal to about 30 characters per second. That speed is slower than many daisy-wheel printers (Seymour 1987, 12).

Once your modem is connected, you are ready to enter the exciting world of telecommunications. Keep in mind, though, that the receiving computer must also have a modem so that tones can be translated back into computer signals.

WORKS CITED

Gabel, David A. 1986. Modems. Personal Computing, January, 109-119.
Kurshen, Barbara L., Alan C. November, and Janet D. Stone. 1986. Computer Literacy Through Applications. Boston: Houghton Mifflin Company.
Powell, David B. 1984. Buyer's Guide to Modems. Popular Computing, July, 111-120.
Seymour, Jim. 1986. Modern Prices Plummet as Speeds Skyrocket. Today's Office 22 (June): 12.

2I

READ AND DO
(REVIEW)

Goal: To end the lesson 2 minutes

E T *Electronic Typewriters/*
Typewriters

1. Remove the paper from the typewriter.
2. Turn off the machine.
3. Cover the machine if directed to do so.
4. Clean up your work area.

M *Microcomputers*

1. Read and respond to any prompts.
2. Store your document and exit the program.
3. Carefully remove the disk from the disk drive.
4. Place the disk into its protective envelope.
5. Turn off the monitor and the microcomputer.

LESSON 3

Margins: Default or 1″ (12 pitch, 12-90; 10 pitch, 10-75)
Spacing: SS or default

3A

READ AND DO
(REVIEW)

Clear your desk of
everything you don't
need, and arrange
your work area as
described in 1A.

Goal: To get ready to key 3 minutes

E T *Electronic Typewriters/*
Typewriters

1. Turn on the typewriter.
2. Adjust the paper guide.
3. Insert and straighten a sheet of paper.
4. Set line spacing for single spacing (SS).
5. Set the margins as directed in the color band at the beginning of the lesson.

M *Microcomputers*

1. Insert the disks in proper sequence as described in 1D.
2. Turn on the monitor.
3. Turn on the microcomputer.
4. If required to give a file name, use: **Lesson3**.

3B

WARMUP

Key each line twice.

DS after each pair of
lines.

Goal: To strengthen keyboarding skills 5 minutes

```
1 a;sldkfj a;sldkfj a;sldkfj a;sldkfj a;sl
2 fjfj dkdk slsl a;a; a;sldkfj a;sldkfj a;
3 all lad ask fad lass ad dad all fall ads
4 as a lad; ask a dad; all fall; a sad lad
```

3C

TECHNIQUE
TIMING

Take two 1-minute
timings on each line.

DS after each timing.

Goal: To improve keyboarding techniques 8 minutes

Space between words without pausing. Use a quick, down-and-in motion.

```
1 all lads ask dad; a sad lass; ask a lass
```

Quickly return to home-key position after pressing return/enter.

```
2 a fall; a flask; all fall; all dads; ask
```

Keep your eyes on the textbook copy.

```
3 sad dad fad lad fall all as a asks salad
```

68F

APPLICATION: REPORTS

File name: L68F

Goal: To key the title page for an unbound report   6 minutes

Prepare a title page for your report, *Documenting Sources*. Use your name and course on the title page.

> **Checkpoint:** Did you key the current date a DS below the course name?

68G

READ AND DO

Read and follow the instructions to the right as you put your report together.

Goal: To proofread and assemble the pages of a report   16 minutes

Proofread and assemble the pages of the report you prepared in Lessons 65–67, file names L65F, L67F, and L68F.

1. Proofread. Read your entire report word for word, both for accuracy and for understanding. If you are using a microcomputer, proofread on the screen before you print the report. Then, proofread the printed report. Check that all formats are correct.
2. Correct all errors.
3. Print the report.
4. Assemble the pages. Place the title page first, followed by the pages of the report, in numerical order, and the works cited page.
5. Unless directed otherwise, use a paper clip to hold the pages together.

LESSON 69

Reinforcement

Margins: Default or 1″
Spacing: SS or default   Tab: ¶

69A

WARMUP

Key each line twice.

DS after each pair of lines.

Frequently misspelled words

Goal: To strengthen keyboarding skills   5 minutes

1 questionnaire attendance explanation definite truly apparent
2 The explanation on the questionnaire apparently confused me.
3 I truly appreciate definite attendance figures on the forms.

| 1 | 2 | 3 | 4 | 5 | 6 | 7 | 8 | 9 | 10 | 11 | 12 |

69B

ACCURACY PRACTICE

DS after each group of lines.

Goal: To build keyboarding accuracy   5 minutes

Take a 2-minute accuracy timing on the lines in 69A. Repeat the timing. Try to improve your accuracy.

> **Checkpoint:** Did you improve your accuracy?

1. Locate the new key on the keyboard chart and on your keyboard.
2. Practice the first line. Watch your finger reach to the new key and re-turn to home-key position.
3. Take two 1-minute technique timings on the second line. Goal: Eyes on copy.
4. Take a 2-minute technique timing on the third line. Goal: Eyes on copy.

Goal: To learn the location of Ⓔ Ⓗ and Ⓣ   16 minutes

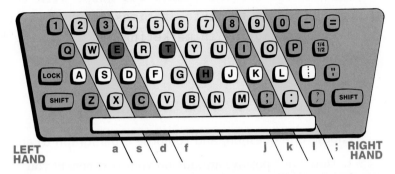

LEFT HAND   a \ s \ d \ f   j \ k \ l \ ;   RIGHT HAND

 Practice the reach to Ⓔ with the **d** finger. The **f** finger may lift slightly, but your other fingers should remain in home-key position.

1 ded ded de de de de de de de de de de de
2 see lee fees led fed lead dead feed seas
3 feel keel leaf jell seals seek ease fed;

 Practice the reach to Ⓗ with the **j** finger. Keep your other fingers in home-key position.

4 jhj jhj jh jh jh jh jh jh jh jh jh jh jh
5 half had has he she heals head hall lash
6 hash heal; shell shed sashes ashes ahead

Practice the reach to Ⓣ with the **f** finger. Keep your other fingers in home-key position. Do not let your hand move up as you strike Ⓣ.

 7 ftf ftf ft ft ft ft ft ft ft ft ft ft ft
8 tea set fat sat jet lets tell feet tests
9 feat eat least seat; sets ate late taste

Key each line twice.

DS after each pair of lines.

Goal: To practice proper keystroking   6 minutes

1 at least tell; all the sales; a sad jest
2 she has a lease; sell the jet; see these
3 take the tea sets; shed these hats; take
4 the test; feed these fat lads; ask these

SPEED PRACTICE

Take two 2-minute timings. Try to increase your speed on the second timing.

Goal: To build keyboarding speed 5 minutes

	2'
1 Bob works for the hotels and helps with the tourist manuals.	6
2 He works on the auto at times other than the early mornings.	12
3 She is majoring in marketing and is paying her own expenses.	18

| 1 | 2 | 3 | 4 | 5 | 6 | 7 | 8 | 9 | 10 | 11 | 12 |

68C
KEYBOARD COMPOSITION

DS or default.

Key as much as you can in 5 minutes.

Goal: To compose at the keyboard 7 minutes

Choose one question, and compose a paragraph to answer the question.

1. How can a positive attitude on your part benefit you and your employer?
2. What skills or knowledge would be useful to get the job you want?
3. Should an employer consider potential employees' personalities when making a selection?

68D
PRODUCTION TIMING

Take two 2-minute timings. Try to key more on the second timing.

DS between entries.

Goal: To build speed in keying a works cited list 6 minutes

WORKS CITED

Hertzberg, Lanny. 1987. A Guide to MS-DOS Desktop Publishing. <u>Electronic Learning</u>, May/June, 41-42.

Jarvis, Pamela. 1987. Desktop Publishing: Is It for Every Office? <u>The Office</u>, June, 65-68.

68E
NEED TO KNOW

Refer to the illustration as you read about the format for a title page.

Goal: To learn how to prepare a title page 5 minutes

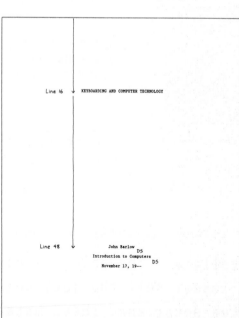

Line 16 ↓ KEYBOARDING AND COMPUTER TECHNOLOGY

Line 48 ↓   John Barlow
                      DS
          Introduction to Computers
                      DS
            November 17, 19--

Title page

The title page for a report contains the title of the report, the author's name, the name of the course, and the date. This information is keyed on a separate page that is placed at the beginning of the report.

1. Center and key the title in all caps on line 16.
2. Space down 32 lines to line 48.
3. Center and key your name; DS.
4. Center and key the name of the course; DS.
5. Center and key the current date.

3F
TECHNIQUE TIMING

Take two 2-minute timings on each pair of lines.

DS after each timing.

Goal: To improve keyboarding techniques 10 minutes

Keep your wrists low, but do not rest your hands on the keyboard.

1 the last jet; he has a fast jet; she has
2 the lake had; take all; at last; a death

Return to home-key position after making reaches to the new keys.

3 at least tell; all the fakes; a sad jest
4 she had a lease; sell the jet; see these

3G
READ AND DO (REVIEW)

Goal: To end the lesson 2 minutes

E T *Electronic Typewriters/Typewriters*

1. Remove the paper from the typewriter.
2. Turn off the machine.
3. Cover the machine if directed to do so.
4. Clean up your work area.

M *Microcomputers*

1. Read and respond to any prompts.
2. Store your document and exit the program.
3. Carefully remove the disk from the disk drive.
4. Place the disk into its protective envelope.
5. Turn off the monitor and the microcomputer.

LESSON 4

Margins: Default or 1″ (12 pitch, 12-90; 10 pitch, 10-75)
Spacing: SS or default

4A
READ AND DO (REVIEW)

Clear your desk, and arrange your work area.

Goal: To get ready to key 2 minutes

E T *Electronic Typewriters/Typewriters*

1. Turn on the typewriter.
2. Adjust the paper guide.
3. Insert and straighten a sheet of paper.
4. Set the line spacing for SS.
5. Set the margins.

M *Microcomputers*

1. Insert the disks in proper sequence.
2. Turn on the monitor.
3. Turn on the microcomputer.
4. If required to give a file name, use: **Lesson4**.

4B
WARMUP

Key each line twice.

DS after each pair of lines.

Goal: To strengthen keyboarding skills 5 minutes

1 a;sldkfj a;sldkfj a;sldkfj a;sldkfj a;sl
2 the last jet; a fast jet; seek the deal;
3 at least ask a dad; the fast jet had the
4 these lads feel that the sale has a lead

67E
PROJECT PREVIEW

File name: L67E

SS

SM: 1"

Key as many entries as you can in 6 minutes. If you finish before time is called, start again.

Goal: To list a key of works cited 8 minutes

Line 13 ↓ WORKS CITED TS

Cane, Mike. 1983. The Computer Phone Book. New York:
New American Library. DS

Fersko-Weiss, Henry. 1987. On-Line Contacts. Personal
Computing, January, 83-91. DS

Lambert, Steve. 1985. Online. Bellevue, WA: Microsoft
Press. DS

Steigler, C. B. 1984. Telecommunications. The Secretary
44 (November-December): 22-23. DS

Zemke, Ron. 1987. Are You Battling Computerphobia?
Working Woman, September, 53.

67F
APPLICATION: REPORTS

File name: L67F   Prepare a works cited page for the report in 65F. Underline titles shown in italics.

CUE: Use the same margins you used on page 1 of the report.

Goal: To prepare a works cited list for a report 14 minutes

WORKS CITED

Gibaldi, Joseph, and Walter S. Achtert. 1988. *MLA Handbook for Writers of Research Papers.* New York: Modern Language Association.

Sabin, William A. 1992. *The Gregg Reference Manual.* Columbus, OH: Glencoe Division of Macmillan/McGraw-Hill Publishing Company.

Turabian, Kate L. 1987. *A Manual for Writers of Term Papers.* Chicago: University of Chicago Press.

University of Chicago Press. 1982. *The Chicago Manual of Style.* Chicago: University of Chicago Press.

LESSON 68

Margins: Default or 1"
Spacing: SS or default   Tab: ¶

68A
WARMUP

Key each line twice. DS after each pair.

"ble" combinations

Goal: To strengthen keyboarding skills 5 minutes

1 babble able table reasonable marble fable remarkable capable
2 The terrible and horrible comedian was not laughable at all.
3 Thomas was able and capable of marking the invisible bubble.

| 1 | 2 | 3 | 4 | 5 | 6 | 7 | 8 | 9 | 10 | 11 | 12 |

4C
TECHNIQUE TIMING

Take a 1-minute timing on each line.

DS after each timing.

Goal: To improve keyboarding techniques 8 minutes

Keep your fingers curved and your wrists low.

1 head lasses; sell the shell; take a jet;
2 sell that dead leaf; she fed these seals
3 take the last sash; feel these felt hats

Keep your wrists and hands almost motionless as you strike each key.

4 jade fake leak deal self jest seek least
5 these death seals feels leads teeth feet
6 task salad dash steel lakes eat kale fee

4D
NEW-KEY ORIENTATION

1. Locate the new key on the keyboard chart and on your keyboard.
2. Practice the first line. Watch your finger reach to the new key and return to home-key position.
3. Take two 1-minute technique timings on the second line. Goal: Eyes on copy.
4. Take a 2-minute technique timing on the third line. Goal: Eyes on copy.

Goal: To learn the location of Ⓘ Ⓖ and Ⓝ 16 minutes

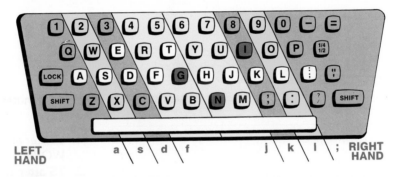

Ⓘ Practice the reach to Ⓘ with your **k** finger. The **j** finger may lift slightly. Your other fingers should remain in home-key position.

1 kik kik ki ki ki ki ki ki ki ki ki ki ki
2 its kit sit fit hit lit his lid hid kids
3 it kid lists fist kiss hill field filed;

Ⓖ Practice the reach to Ⓖ with your **f** finger. Keep your other fingers in home-key position.

4 fgf fgf fg fg fg fg fg fg fg fg fg fg fg
5 fgf jag hags legs keg lag sage aged glad
6 eggs leg gas gag gets gagged gal gaggle;

Ⓝ Practice the reach down to Ⓝ with your **j** finger. Keep your other fingers in home-key position.

7 jnj jnj jn jn jn jn jn jn jn jn jn jn jn
8 nat nets ned dens hen fan sand land hand
9 fan; tan than thank sends land hand lean

67C

LANGUAGE ARTS

Key the sentences below. Select the correct word usage. Supply quotation marks and underscoring as needed.

Review:

51B, 55C, 57E, 58C, 59C, 61C, 63C, 66D

Check your work with the key in Appendix A.

Goal: To review confusing words and punctuation   7 minutes

1. (Are/Our/Hour) committee met for an (are/hour/our), she said.
2. Pat said, I want (to/too/two) see (you're/your) materials for the national accounts.
3. (Their/There/They're) sure that (its/it's) the right bus.
4. The (to/too/two) critics praised her novel, The Hills of Home.
5. The critics liked (its/it's) first chapter, A Country Boy.
6. The Delta Chronicle reviewed (you're/your) play, One Hour to Live, in the morning edition.
7. Literary Parade will praise (its/it's) plot, (to/too/two).
8. My article, Artificial Intelligence Today, was published in Reader's Review.
9. We need to review problems, said the chairwoman, before we review solutions.
10. (Their/There/They're) sure that the woman is wise.

67D

NEED TO KNOW

Refer to the illustration as you read about the format for a works cited page.

Goal: To learn to key a works cited page   6 minutes

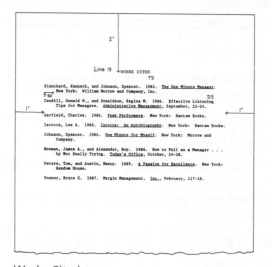

Works Cited page

The **works cited page** is an alphabetic listing of all the sources referred to or used by the writer in preparing a report or a term paper. Sources listed on the works cited page may include books, magazines, government publications, and newspaper articles. The works cited page is placed at the end of the report.

1. Center and key in all caps the heading WORKS CITED on line 13.
2. TS after the heading.
3. Use the same side margins (1-inch) as you used when keying the body of the report.
4. Arrange the entries in alphabetical order by author, or if the author is not known, by title.
5. Key each entry in this order: author's name (last name first), year of publication, title of the source, and publication data.
6. Start the first line of each entry at the left margin. Indent carryover lines five spaces from the left margin.
7. SS the lines of each entry. DS between entries.

Software Alert: If changes in line spacing are difficult or impossible to make with your software, key the heading on line 12, QS, and DS the entries.

4E
KEYBOARD PRACTICE

Key each line twice.

DS after each pair of lines.

Goal: To practice proper keystroking   7 minutes

```
1 let the king land the ninth jet in haste
2 he said that the king felt fine at night
3 she lied as she said she had faith in it
4 he asked that she feed the fast fat seal
```

4F
TECHNIQUE TIMING

Take two 2-minute timings on each pair of lines.

DS after each timing.

Goal: To improve keyboarding techniques   10 minutes

Space between words without pausing. Use a quick, down-and-in motion.

```
1 tin sing kind hint shine kindle gain tag
2 dank dangle glisten fling knitting inlet
```

Return to home-key position after making reaches to the new keys.

```
3 list fist kiss hills field killed filled
4 fig dig jig get leg keg lag jag hag glad
```

4G
READ AND DO (REVIEW)

Follow these procedures at the end of each keyboarding class.

Goal: To end the lesson   2 minutes

E T *Electronic Typewriters/ Typewriters*

1. Remove the paper.
2. Turn off the machine.
3. Cover the machine if directed to do so.
4. Clean up your work area.

M *Microcomputers*

1. Read and respond to any prompts.
2. Store your document and exit the program.
3. Remove the disk from the disk drive.
4. Place the disk into its envelope.
5. Turn off the monitor and the microcomputer.

LESSON 5 Reinforcement

Margins: Default or 1″ (12 pitch, 12-90; 10 pitch, 10-75)
Spacing: SS or default

5A
WARMUP

Key each line twice.

DS after each pair of lines.

Goal: To strengthen keyboarding skills   5 minutes

```
1 a;sldkfja;sldkfja;sldkfja;sldkfja;sldkfj
2 the then these this that thin than think
3 night sight lights fights height delight
4 hang gang sang fang dangle jangle tangle
```

Checkpoint: Did you remember to arrange your work area as described in Lesson 4A?

66F

**APPLICATION:
REPORTS**

Goal: To key an unbound report   18 minutes

> **CUE:** Single space long quotations and indent them ten spaces from the left margin.

Continue the report in 65F, file name L65F. Try to complete page 2 of the report today.

> **Checkpoint:** Did you key the page number on line 7?

LESSON
67

Margins: Default or 1"
Spacing: SS or default   Tab: ¶

67A

WARMUP

Goal: To strengthen keyboarding skills   5 minutes

Key each line twice. DS after each pair of lines.

Speed
Accuracy
Number/Symbol

1 The four lakes on the south island may be dry when he comes.
2 The guys from Yukon were huffy about hurrying for Yule logs.
3 Yes, 1 carat, 3.086 grains, and 200 milligrams are the same.

| 1 | 2 | 3 | 4 | 5 | 6 | 7 | 8 | 9 | 10 | 11 | 12 |

67B

GOAL WRITING

DS or default.

Take two 3-minute goal writings.

If you finish before time is called, start again.

Record your speed and accuracy.

Goal: To measure timed-writing progress   10 minutes

	1'	3'

Modeling is difficult and demanding work. Models sometimes work for long periods of time under hot, bright lights. Because advertisers plan ads far in advance, models may be required to pose in bathing suits during the winter and in heavy coats during the summer.

A model who is photographed earns an hourly fee to pay for his or her time. For a fashion show, a model may work for a set fee rather than for an hourly rate. A model for an artist often charges a lower fee because artists usually work with smaller budgets and their work may require more time. Modeling fees for television commercials are usually determined by a union contract.

1'	3'
10	3
22	7
33	11
44	15
53	18
65	22
76	25
88	29
100	33
112	37
124	41
130	43

1'	1	2	3	4	5	6	7	8	9	10	11	12	
3'	1		2		3		4						

AWL
5.7

5B
TECHNIQUE TIMING

Take two 2-minute timings on each pair of lines.

Key each line once. If you finish before time is called, start again.

DS after each timing.

Goal: To improve keyboarding techniques   10 minutes

Strike each key with a quick, sharp stroke. Snap the finger toward the palm after each stroke as shown in the illustration.

1 he thinks that; she feels the; list that
2 kindle; assign; knitting; knight; kitten

Tap the space bar using a quick, down-and-in motion.

3 sing king ding fling sling single jingle
4 at the jail; see a light; fish all night

5C
KEYBOARD PRACTICE

Key each line twice.

DS after each pair of lines.

Goal: To practice proper keystroking   14 minutes

1 the light; the jail; the fish; the shine
2 has a fine kite; sing a little; the sign
3 a tall tale; a keen knight; a fine sight
4 she thinks that she has signed the lists
5 he felt he needed the things at the sale
6 he thinks the kindness is a keen delight
7 he gnashed his teeth at the killing gale
8 the lads asked the king at the east gate
9 the sale at the kingfish is in his hands
10 she asks in jest; she needs his kindness

5D
SELF-CHECK

Read each statement.

On a sheet of paper, handwrite the statement number and indicate whether the statement is true or false.

Check your answers in Appendix B.

Goal: To review good keyboarding techniques   6 minutes

1. You should look at your fingers, not at your textbook, when working at the keyboard.
2. When sitting at the keyboard, sit up straight with your back touching the back of the chair.
3. You should not space before returning/entering at the end of a line.
4. For best results, press the space bar firmly and release it slowly.
5. Both feet should be placed flat on the floor, one slightly ahead of the other.
6. Rest the palms of your hands on the keyboard when you key.
7. You should always look up after pressing return/enter to be sure you are at the beginning of a new line.
8. By pressing the return/enter two times, you leave one blank line between keyed lines.

66C
PRODUCTION TIMING

Key as much of this section of a report as you can in 3 minutes.

Indent the quotation 10 spaces from the left margin.

If you finish before time is called, start again.

Goal: To build speed in keying long quotations 5 minutes

     Time management has been a popular topic for a long time. And yet, it continues to draw an audience whenever it is presented. Time management is a critical skill for managers.

          Perhaps the single most important asset administrative managers can possess is skill in managing time. If managers can effectively control their time, they will be able to devote balanced attention to interpersonal relations and production. (Smith et al. 1987, 378)

66D
LANGUAGE ARTS

Read the rule in the box at the right.

Then key each numbered sentence, supplying quotation marks where needed.

Check your work with the key in Appendix A.

Goal: To review use of quotation marks 9 minutes

> Use quotation marks to set off a direct quotation (a person's exact words).
>
> **Examples:**
>
> "When do you think," she asked, "that your work will be done?"
> "Their letter must be ready for the morning mail," Andre said.

1. Julio asked, May I have the reports now?
2. The secretary answered, The reports are on your desk.
3. If you listen carefully, Lou said, you can hear his accent.
4. I'll see you at the staff meeting, he yelled.
5. By the way, Lisa complained, the copy machine is broken again.
6. John sighed and said, I guess we'll have to buy a new one.
7. David needs more training on the equipment, Maria explained.
8. We won the battle, he said, but lost the war.
9. Margaret said, Mr. Jones, word processing increases productivity.
10. Paul said, I have just begun to fight for the new legislative bill.

66E
SELF-CHECK

Key the statement number and your answer: True or False.

Check your answers in Appendix B.

Goal: To review the format for quotations 8 minutes

1. A long quotation set off within text contains four or more printed lines.
2. Long quotations are indented 10 spaces from each margin.
3. Long quotations are enclosed in quotation marks.
4. Long quotations are followed by a parenthetical reference.
5. A double space is used before and after a long quotation.
6. Quotation marks indicate that a person's exact words are being used.
7. If the first line of a long quotation begins a paragraph, that line is indented an extra 5 spaces.
8. Long quotations are always double spaced.
9. If the author's name is mentioned in the quotation, the name is not included in the parenthetical reference.

5E
KEYBOARD PRACTICE

Key each line twice.

DS after each pair of lines.

Goal: To practice proper keystroking   10 minutes

```
1 fail said jail laid hail tail nail aided
2 sealing dealing keeling kneeling healing
3 nil neat night nines needle nigh needing
4 get gain gale gill gift glen geese glean
5 if it is in idle its ideal ignite island
6 lead the list; tells a tale; hit the net
7 set these dates; get in line; take sides
```

5F
TECHNIQUE TIMING

Take two 2-minute timings.

Return when you see R/E

DS after each timing.

Goal: To improve keyboarding techniques   5 minutes

Do not look up as you return/enter. Begin keying the next line without pausing.

```
dish fishing telling R/E delight assign shine R/E kiss
jangle knitting R/E killing shilling jig R/E fail flesh
tennis it R/E think link sink kink R/E thing sing king
sign R/E height kitten needle
```

LESSON 6

Margins: Default or 1" (12 pitch, 12-90; 10 pitch, 10-75)
Spacing: SS or default

6A
WARMUP

Key each line twice.

DS after each pair of lines.

Goal: To strengthen keyboarding skills   5 minutes

```
1 fin din sin gin kin sit lit kit hit fit;
2 jell jets jade jest jilt hand half halt;
3 skiff slash slate sleek slide sneak snag
4 slight height flight delighted sightless
```

6B
TECHNIQUE TIMING

Take two 1-minute timings.

DS after each timing.

Goal: To improve keyboarding techniques   6 minutes

Sit in correct position: back against the chair and feet flat on the floor, one slightly in front of the other.

```
1 find kind nine line fine tine fins tins;
2 is the; in the; if the; let the; see the
3 the thing is; find a site; take a flight
```

(Continued next page)

The system of documentation that is most economical in terms of space and time is the parenthetical reference keyed in the author-date format (Chicago 1982, 400).

The author-date format requires that a parenthetical reference include the author's last name and the year of publication (unless given in the text), followed by a comma and the page reference: (Wilson 1982, 73). Information cited in the text is omitted from the parenthetical reference. (Gibaldi and Achtert 1984, 161)

The reference is keyed within parentheses as near as possible to the material to be documented. Whenever possible, the reference should be placed just before a mark of punctuation (Chicago 1982, 404). However, if the quotation is set off from the rest of the text, the parenthetical reference should be keyed two spaces after the ending punctuation mark.

Endnotes provide the same information in nearly the same style as footnotes (Holmes 1987, 158). Endnotes are indicated in text by a superior figure and are numbered consecutively throughout the text. Endnotes are keyed on a separate page that is placed at the end of a report. Unlike footnotes that are identified by a superior figure, endnote numbers are placed evenly on the lines with their entries.

Footnotes are indicated in the text by superior figures. Footnotes are numbered consecutively throughout the report.

As the name implies, footnotes are placed at the bottom of the page on which the reference appears. Because footnotes require careful planning and generally reduce the level of productivity, there is a strong tendency today to use endnotes or author-date references. (Holmes 1987, 157)

When preparing a report, determine which of these documentation styles you will use, and use that style throughout the report. Consistency is the watchword when preparing reports. Using a consistent format for documenting sources is the writer's responsibility.

LESSON 66

Margins: Default or 1"
Spacing: SS or default   Tab: ¶

66A

WARMUP

Key each line twice.

DS after each pair of lines.

Frequently misspelled words

Goal: To strengthen keyboarding skills   5 minutes

1 criticism grammar embarrassing superseded congratulate ninth
2 The criticism by the teacher superseded her congratulations.
3 The grammar of ninth graders can be embarrassing to parents.

| 1 | 2 | 3 | 4 | 5 | 6 | 7 | 8 | 9 | 10 | 11 | 12 |

66B

ACCURACY PRACTICE

DS after each group of lines.

Goal: To build keyboarding accuracy   5 minutes

Take a 2-minute accuracy timing on the lines in 66A. Repeat the timing. Try to improve your accuracy.

Checkpoint: Did you improve your accuracy?

Take two 1-minute timings.

Reach to the keys with your fingers, not your hands.

4 the night; a sight; the light; the fight

5 sail the skiff; find the fish; he sings;

6 see the sites; take the light; sit idle;

6C
NEW-KEY ORIENTATION

1. Locate the new key on the keyboard chart and on your keyboard.
2. Practice the first line. Watch your finger reach to the new key and re-turn to home-key position.
3. Take two 1-minute technique timings on the second line. Goal: Eyes on copy.
4. Take a 2-minute technique timing on the third line. Goal: Eyes on copy.

Goal: To learn the location of Ⓞ Ⓡ and left (SHIFT)   16 minutes

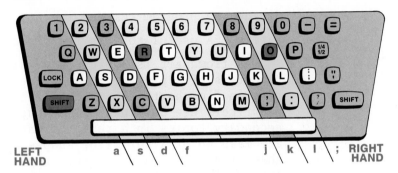

Ⓞ Practice the reach to Ⓞ with the **l** finger. The **k** finger may lift slightly. Your other fingers should remain in home-key position.

1 lol lol lo lo lo lo lo lo lo lo lo lo lo

2 lots logs old hole gone done tooth jolts

3 fool fold told sold songs good hood soon

Ⓡ Practice the reach to Ⓡ with the **f** finger. Keep your other fin-gers in home-key position.

4 frf frf fr fr fr fr fr fr fr fr fr fr fr

5 firs far jars tart dart dirt first third

6 red rag ran far free rail hard lark rake

Use a one-two count to operate the left shift key. **One**—depress the left shift key with the **a** finger. **Two**—strike the desired key with the correct finger of the right hand. Quickly release the shift key and return the **a** finger to its home-key position.

 Practice the reach to the left shift key with the **a** finger. Keep your other fingers in home-key position.

7 Lal Lal La La La La La La La La La La La

8 He His Ned Nan Janet Nate Jake Jets Kate

9 He is; Hal sat; Nan gets; Is it; Jake is

5. Key the parenthetical reference two spaces after the ending punctuation.
6. DS after the long quotation.
7. Return to the original left margin.

Software Alert: If changes in line spacing are difficult or impossible to make with your software, DS the quotation.

65E
PROJECT PREVIEW

Goal: To key a long quotation   8 minutes

File name: L65E

DS

SM: 1"

Key as much of the text as you can in 6 minutes.

If you finish before time is called, start again.

Ignore misstrokes.

Writing a software program is a complicated task even for an experienced programmer. Before writing, the programmer must divide the program components into a logical sequence of steps. A useful tool is the flowchart. DS

A flowchart is a picture or diagram outlining SS the steps of a program in sequence. Programmers rely on flowcharts to organize their thoughts just as writers use outlines to map out primary and secondary topics in a research paper. Flowcharts are made up of a series of shapes and arrows. Each shape represents a different step in the program. Arrows placed between shapes show the order in which the steps will be taken. (Atkinson 1984, 58) DS

Most programmers design flowcharts using three shapes: the oval, the parallelogram (or diamond), and the rectangle. The oval shows where the program begins and ends. The parallelogram indicates input or output. The rectangle shows internal computer processing.

Checkpoint: Did you make format changes before keying the long quotation?

65F
APPLICATION: REPORTS

Goal: To key an unbound report   16 minutes

File name: L65F   Key page 1 of this report. Do not key the author's name on page 1. You will prepare a title page in Lesson 68.

DOCUMENTING SOURCES

The writer of a term paper or formal report often includes facts, quoted material, or opinions obtained from outside sources. These sources may include books, magazines, encyclopedias, software, radio programs, and videos.

Giving proper credit to these sources is known as documentation. When writing a report, you must document everything that you borrow—not only direct quotes and paraphrases but also information and ideas (Gibaldi and Achtert 1984, 136).

The three most common styles of documentation to choose from are parenthetical references, endnotes, and footnotes. Which one you use may be determined by the subject matter of your report. For example, a business report may require parenthetical references, whereas a scientific report may require the use of either endnotes or footnotes.

(Continued next page)

6D
KEYBOARD PRACTICE

Key each line twice.

DS after each pair of lines.

Goal: To practice proper keystroking   13 minutes

CUE: Avoid pauses when using the left shift key.

1 Jo said Jan has seen the old red rooster
2 Ora had a great session on the third hit
3 He had Lee and Karl and Jake for his jet
4 Ida rode a Jetstar for the entire season
5 I said that Joanna and Neal are the ones
6 Learn the right things and get the sales
7 Jail is the right thing for John and Lee
8 Join this one; Hank is the one; Here are
9 Let her tell those stories to Janet soon
10 His Her Lee Ida Karl Jake John Ned Lorna

6E
TECHNIQUE TIMING

Take two 2-minute timings on each group of lines.

Key each line once. If you finish before time is called, start again.

DS after each timing.

Goal: To improve keyboarding techniques   10 minutes

Do not pause between words. Try to keep the carrier/cursor moving.

1 note nose none done lone tone gone groan
2 tore sore fore soar dare road roan thorn
3 fright freight grief relate render grate

Keep wrists low, but do not rest hands on the keyboard.

4 the ladies; the girls; this is; there is
5 their goods; their food; their one thing
6 Here are the letters; I sold those goods

LESSON 7

Margins: Default or 1" (12 pitch, 12-90; 10 pitch, 10-75)
Spacing: SS or default

7A
WARMUP

Key each line twice.

DS after each pair of lines.

Goal: To strengthen keyboarding skills   5 minutes

1 night tight light fight sight right then
2 tone gone none lone done this that north
3 for her; for those; for this; for their;
4 that is not; there is not; there are no;

Margins: Default or 1"
Spacing: SS or default   Tab: ¶

65A

WARMUP

Key each line twice.
DS after each pair.

"in" combinations

Goal: To strengthen keyboarding skills   5 minutes

```
1 find rind rink insights begin beginning sing mind tin finals
2 Fling the tin ring into a bin, and bind the vines in a line.
3 The line of pine design is a fine sign to bring to the sink.
```
| 1 | 2 | 3 | 4 | 5 | 6 | 7 | 8 | 9 | 10 | 11 | 12 |

65B

SPEED PRACTICE

Take two 1-minute timings on each sentence. Try to increase your speed on the second timing.

Goal: To build keyboarding speed   9 minutes

		1'
1 Utah is growing, as they saw when they wrote up their study.		12
2 They thought they would be eligible for the new health plan.		24
3 He may hope that they may be able to use him in their study.		36
4 Neither one of us can talk with her client for up to a year.		48

| 1 | 2 | 3 | 4 | 5 | 6 | 7 | 8 | 9 | 10 | 11 | 12 |

65C

NEED TO KNOW

Goal: To learn about the temporary indent   6 minutes

When more than one line of text is to be indented within a document, set a temporary left margin.

Equipment with Temporary Indent

To set a temporary left margin without changing margin settings, space to where you want the indented text to begin. Use the appropriate keys or command to begin the **temporary indent**. When you have keyed the

last line of indented text, end the temporary indent function.

Equipment without Temporary Indent

Space to where the indented text begins. Reset the left margin. Key the text to be indented. When you have keyed the last line of indented text, return the left margin to its original settings.

65D

NEED TO KNOW

Goal: To learn to key quotations   6 minutes

Long quotation in an unbound report

Quotations of three or fewer lines are enclosed within quotation marks and are keyed within normal paragraph copy. For quotations of four or more lines:

1. DS before beginning the long quotation.
2. Do not enclose the quotation in quotation marks.
3. Indent the left margin ten spaces. If the quotation is also the beginning of a paragraph, indent the first line an additional five spaces.
4. SS the quotation.

(Continued next page)

7B

**TECHNIQUE
TIMING**

Take a 1-minute timing on each line.

DS after each timing.

Goal: To improve keyboarding techniques   5 minutes

Keep **s, d**, and **f** fingers on home keys as you press the shift key.

1 He is here; I need that one; Lee has it;
2 I think I need an O; an H; an L; and a K
3 He asked Jane to send the letter to Karl
4 Here are the things that she sent to Jed

7C

**NEW-KEY
ORIENTATION**

1. Locate the new key on the keyboard chart and on your keyboard.
2. Practice the first line. Watch your finger reach to the new key and return to home-key position.
3. Take two 1-minute technique timings on the second line. Goal: Eyes on copy.
4. Take a 2-minute technique timing on the third line. Goal: Eyes on copy.

Goal: To learn the location of and   16 minutes

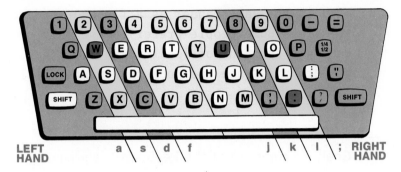

LEFT HAND   a s d f   j k l ; RIGHT HAND

 Practice the reach to Ⓤ with the **j** finger. Keep your other fingers in home-key position. Do not lift your hand as you strike Ⓤ.

1 juj juj ju ju ju ju ju ju ju ju ju ju ju
2 juts jug guns run dug hug rugs just ruin
3 unfit usual until unit under unjust dust

Ⓦ Practice the reach to Ⓦ with the **s** finger. The **d** finger may lift slightly, but your other fingers should remain in home-key position.

4 sws sws sw sw sw sw sw sw sw sw sw sw sw
5 sow saw sew wits wig wins was with shown
6 who whose what where when how while will

Practice the reach to ⊡ with the **l** finger. The **sem** finger may lift slightly, but your other fingers should remain in home-key position.

 7 1.1 1.1 1. 1. 1. 1. 1. 1. 1. 1. 1. 1. 1.
8 L. K. ft. in. Ill. Ok. La. No. Jr. Oreg.
9 L. J. and J. K. sent her to N. H. Loans.

64B

GOAL WRITING

DS or default.

Take two 3-minute goal writings.

If you finish before time is called, start again.

Record your speed and accuracy.

Goal: To measure timed-writing progress   10 minutes

	1'	3'
One out of every ten people suffers from pollen	10	3
allergies. Pollens are abundant from early spring until the	22	7
first hard frost in the fall. During this time, allergy	33	11
sufferers sniffle and sneeze as if they had bad colds.	44	15
To relieve the symptoms of their allergies, some people	56	19
have injections of the pollens that they are allergic to.	67	22
Injections help their bodies to create an immune system,	79	26
much in the same manner as a flu shot creates an immunity to	91	30
the flu. Some people prefer to use folk remedies, such as	103	34
eating a spoonful of local honey every day. Other people	114	38
suffer in silence and hope that winter will come soon.	125	42

```
1'|  1  |  2  |  3  |  4  |  5  |  6  |  7  |  8  |  9  | 10  | 11  | 12  |      AWL
3'|        1          |        2        |       3       |      4        |       5.7
```

64C

KEYBOARD COMPOSITION

DS or default.

Key as much as you can in 7 minutes.

Do not correct errors.

Goal: To compose at the keyboard   9 minutes

Choose one question. Compose a paragraph to answer the question.

1. If you could do so, how would you improve your school?
2. What is the best way to study for an exam?
3. Why is education important to you?
4. Why is it important for a cashier to be accurate?
5. If you work in public relations, what attitude should you have when dealing with the public?

64D

SELF-CHECK

DS

Key the statement number and your answer: True or False.

Check your answers in Appendix B.

Goal: To review report and reference formats   8 minutes

1. Parenthetical references are always keyed at the ends of paragraphs.
2. The page number for a continuing page is placed on line 2.
3. The page number is keyed 5 spaces before the right margin.
4. Continuing pages are single spaced.
5. Parenthetical references are keyed within parentheses.
6. An author-date reference used within the body of a report always includes the author's name, the title, and the date of the publication.
7. The side margins for continuing pages of a report should be wider than the side margins on the first page.

64E

APPLICATION: REPORTS

Goal: To key page 2 of an unbound report   18 minutes

CUE: Key the page number on line 7.

Continue the report in 63F, file name L63F.

7D
READ AND DO

Space once after a period used with initials or abbreviations.

Space twice after a period used at the end of a sentence.

Goal: To learn the spacing after the period   5 minutes

Key these sentences using correct spacing after the periods.

1 Kathie left at noon.² K.¹L.¹left at one.
2 Ned went to Ohio U.² J.¹L.¹is at Ohio U.
3 Let us work with N. H. Oaks at the sale.
4 I was with Kate. Nan wants H. J. to go.
5 I sang. Jorge jogged. Helena did also.
6 J. U. Last is here. Let Lorrie see her.

7E
KEYBOARD PRACTICE

Key each line twice.

DS after each pair of lines.

Goal: To practice proper keystroking   6 minutes

CUE: When shifting for capitals, use a one-two count.

1 Let her go. I will. Ned Jones will go.
2 I had a ft. of wire and an in. of twine.
3 Lou is here now. Jed will see her soon.
4 O. J. wrote Jo often when she was there.

7F
TECHNIQUE TIMING

Take a 1-minute timing on each line.

DS after each timing.

Goal: To improve keyboarding techniques   8 minutes

Keep the wrist from turning outward as you strike ⊙ with the I finger.

1 K. U. Hunt was our unusual Latin Leader.
2 K. U. K. Kar Kare will let J. L. use it.
3 N. U. Hill and H. U. Heath were willing.

Return to home-key position after making the reach to the new keys.

4 sun fun run gun dug rug hug lug tug just
5 working white would writing wrong within
6 I was the one. He is at war. Let Jake.

7G
TECHNIQUE TIMING

Take two 2-minute timings.

Key each line once. If time allows, start again.

DS after each timing.

Goal: To improve keyboarding techniques   5 minutes

Quickly return to home-key position after pressing return/enter and begin keying without pausing.

1 H; How; J; Jet; K; Keg; L; Let; I; India
2 Ned Harris left. Ora Howe will go soon.
3 Oregon Iowa Utah Kansas Illinois Indiana
4 Linda K. Hanson will go to Utah in June.

---

require recall, tests that require thinking, and tests that require applying skills (Gall and Or 1985, 143).

To become a more confident test taker, you need to become familiar with the kinds of tests you may have to take. People are creatures of habit. Teachers are no exception. Out of preference and habit, an instructor is likely to give students the same kind of tests. How do you find out a teacher's testing style? The best way is to look at tests you have already taken. Are there patterns—multiple choice, true/false, or essay? Former students are another excellent source of information. Their firsthand testing experience may give you valuable insight into an instructor's testing style. You could also ask the teacher. Most instructors will tell you their favorite testing methods. They also may provide guidelines and tips on the best way to prepare for one of their tests.

Once you know the kind of test you'll be given, you can prepare with confidence for success. For example, if the test emphasizes recall, carefully study class notes. Scan the textbook—it's too late to reread all the material. When preparing for the test, ask yourself, "What kinds of questions will be asked? What has been emphasized in class?"

Many people say that the test situation itself causes the most stress and anxiety. What can you do to get rid of this stress? The confident test taker begins by scanning the entire test (Geoffrion 1986, 28). Read and follow all directions. Read each test question twice before you answer it. Pay attention to limiting words that affect the answers, such as "never" and "always." These steps help you approach the test bit by bit rather than all of it at one time.

As soon as you take these steps, you can begin to answer the questions. Most people don't complete test questions in the order they are given. Instead, they answer easy questions first (Gall and Or 1985, 151). Then, they go back to answer questions that require more thought. During the course of the test, take many, short breaks by resting your eyes away from the test copy. Breaks of 10 or 15 seconds are best. A relaxed approach is important to reducing stress and anxiety.

Finally, always check the test before handing it in. Have you answered all the questions? Are your answers readable? If the answers are in essay form, do your words explain exactly what you want to say? Experienced test takers advise against changing answers at this point; first answers are most likely to be correct.

Successful, confident testing is a learned and practiced skill. However, no test-taking secret or gimmick can replace for thorough preparation (Lengefeld 1986, 47).

LESSON
64

64A

WARMUP

Goal: To strengthen keyboarding skills   5 minutes

Key each line twice. DS after each pair of lines.

Speed
Accuracy
Number/Symbol

1 Susie and her mother did sign the title over to the members.
2 The four overtures may perturb this new, neutral metropolis.
3 Which address (1528 East Grove or 313 Princeton) is correct?

| 1 | 2 | 3 | 4 | 5 | 6 | 7 | 8 | 9 | 10 | 11 | 12 |

8A
WARMUP

Key each line twice.

DS after each pair of lines.

Goal: To strengthen keyboarding skills   5 minutes

1 all an are at do for has he his if in it
2 we should; we would; we think; we shall;
3 new no not of one our should than the is
4 Jane John Jennifer June Jewell Jill Jake

| 1 | 2 | 3 | 4 | 5 | 6 | 7 | 8 |

8B
NEED TO KNOW

Goal: To learn about word scales   3 minutes

In keyboarding, every five strokes—including spaces—count as a "word." Each drill line in these lessons contains a total of 40 letters, spaces, and punctuation marks. To figure the number of "words" in a line, divide the number of strokes in the line (40) by the number of strokes in a word (5). So each 40-stroke line in these lessons equals 8 words (40 ÷ 5 = 8).

The word scales below the Warmup drill lines divide the lines into 5-stroke (1-word) groups. By using these word scales, you can quickly see how many words you have keyed in a line.

8C
TECHNIQUE TIMING

Take a 1-minute timing on each line.

DS after each timing.

Goal: To improve keyboarding techniques   12 minutes

Do not pause between letters or words; keep the carrier/cursor moving.

1 few get need later least head note offer
2 seen shall she soon sure used wish sheet
3 jest dealer feel file free here high and

Tap the space bar with a down-and-in motion of the right thumb.

4 an at do if in is it no of to we go his;
5 all are has his new not one our the two;
6 than that were will with good note seen;

Keep your wrists low and almost motionless.

7 arrange asked finest needed offer during
8 friend furnish indeed reading sound than
9 through ordered later annual around does

| 1 | 2 | 3 | 4 | 5 | 6 | 7 | 8 |

63D

NEED TO KNOW   **Goal:** To learn the author-date format for references   6 minutes

The writer of a report or term paper must give credit for any information (quotations, facts, or opinions) taken from other sources and used in preparing the report. Credit is given in several ways: parenthetical references, endnotes, and footnotes.

When parenthetical references are used, information about the source of the reference is keyed within parentheses in the body of the report. When possible, the reference is inserted before the ending punctuation. Otherwise, the reference is inserted as near as possible to the referenced material.

The **author-date format** is one form of parenthetical reference. The author-date format includes the author's last name and the year of publication, followed by a comma, and the page number: (Holmes 1987, 8). Information that is already given in the text (such as the author's name) is not repeated in the reference: "That was stated in Holmes' Reference Guide (1987, 10). If a specific page is not being referenced, include only the author's name and the date: (Holmes 1987).

63E

READ AND DO   **Goal:** To format and key author-date references   8 minutes

Read and study the following guidelines to determine the information needed for references keyed in the author-date format.

1. If a source has two authors, give both last names joined by the word *and*. (Brown and Clow 1986)
2. If a source has three or more authors, give the last name of one author followed by *et al.* (Turner et al. 1988)
3. When sources by two authors with the same last name are used, include the first name or initial in the reference to avoid confusion. (Conway, K. 1988)
4. When more than one work by the same author is used, give the title or a shortened version of the title after the author's name. (Barnett, Reports, 1988)

From the following sources, key the references in the author-date format.

Carter, Gary, and John Hough, Jr. 1987. A Dream Season. San Diego: Harcourt Brace Jovanovich, Publishers.

Hollander, Phyllis, and Zander Hollander. 1986. Amazing but True Sports Stories. New York: Scholastic, Inc.

Hollander, Zander. 1986. Complete Handbook of Pro Basketball 1986. New York: NAL Penguin, Inc.

Sirvoff, Seymour, Steve Hirdt, and Peter Keidt. 1987. The 1987 Elias Baseball Analyst. New York: Collier-Macmillan Publishing Company.

63F

APPLICATION: REPORTS   **Goal:** To key page 1 of a multiple-page report   18 minutes

File name: L63F   Key page 1 of this report. Use your name as the author. Save this document for use in 64E when the rest of the document will be keyed.

CUE: Leave a 1-inch bottom margin.

THE CONFIDENT TEST TAKER

Tests are a part of life at every age. Elementary students take achievement tests. Senior high school students take college entrance exams. College students take employment tests. Professional adults take examinations as they climb the career ladder. Most people take dozens of tests during their lifetimes, but they still "freeze" at the mere thought of a test. Is it possible to overcome this terrible fear of taking tests?

As with many things, the greatest fear of taking tests comes from the unknown. Understanding the nature of tests may be the first step in approaching a test confidently. Testing styles most often fall into these three categories: tests that

(Continued next page)

8D
KEYBOARD PRACTICE

Key each line 3 times.

DS after each group of lines.

Goal: To practice proper keystroking   10 minutes

1 few sat was wag were fate drag wade dare
2 kin oil ink nil look join junk link hook
3 heir also worn usual jangle island shelf
4 fee fund her how join late loss lot rent
5 we are; we will; we want; we think that;

8E
SELF-CHECK

Read each statement.

On a sheet of paper, handwrite the statement number and indicate whether the statement is true or false.

Check your answers in Appendix B.

Goal: To review good keyboarding techniques   8 minutes

1. After pressing the return/enter key, continue keying without pausing.
2. Space twice after a period in an abbreviation.
3. Keep your hands resting on the keyboard for support.
4. Always pause after releasing the shift key.
5. Space once after a period at the end of a sentence.
6. As you reach for the left shift key, your other fingers should not be in home-key position.
7. In keyboarding, every 5 strokes (characters or spaces) equal 1 word.
8. A 50-character line contains 8 "words."

8F
TECHNIQUE TIMING

Review proper arm position.

Then take two 2-minute timings.

Goal: To improve keyboarding techniques   12 minutes

Let your hands hang loosely at your sides. Hold your arms close to, but not touching, your body.

Bend your arms at the elbows without changing the position of your upper arms. If you can't place your fingers comfortably on the home keys, move your chair forward or backward.

(Continued next page)

63A

WARMUP

Key each line twice.

DS after each pair of lines.

Frequently misspelled words

Goal: To strengthen keyboarding skills   5 minutes

```
1 surprise transferred pursue acknowledgment wholly beneficial
2 To her surprise, we transferred so we could pursue the task.
3 The acknowledgment he gave is wholly beneficial to everyone.
```

| 1 | 2 | 3 | 4 | 5 | 6 | 7 | 8 | 9 | 10 | 11 | 12 |

63B

ACCURACY PRACTICE

DS after each group of lines.

Goal: To build keyboarding accuracy   5 minutes

Take a 2-minute accuracy timing on the lines in 63A. Repeat the timing. Try to improve your accuracy.

Checkpoint: Did you improve your accuracy?

63C

LANGUAGE ARTS

Read the rule in the box at the right.

Then key each numbered sentence, supplying underscoring where needed.

Check your work with the key in Appendix A.

Goal: To review use of the underscore   8 minutes

> Underscore titles of books, magazines, newspapers, movies, plays, and television series. Underscore all words, spaces, and punctuation marks that are part of the title itself. When working from printed material, underscore titles shown in italics.
>
> **Examples:**
>
> Her best book, <u>Cats: An Owner's Guide</u>, was excerpted in the <u>Boston Daily</u>. His play, <u>A Time to Laugh</u>, was not reviewed in <u>Newsreport</u>.

1. The textbook we will use is Business and the Law.
2. He borrowed my copy of the book The Origin of Words.
3. I subscribe to three of the most popular magazines: Newsreport, Quest, and Sports Afield.
4. Jane sold three freelance articles to Campers on Vacation.
5. My favorite movie, Star Vision, is on television tonight.
6. Their uncle wrote scripts for many television series, including the series The Golden Days.
7. Our Time is the play our theater group will produce.
8. Money Talks is a funnier play than Signs of the Times.
9. The Wall Street Record has informative articles.
10. Did you get the August issue of Dancer's News?

Key each line once. If you finish before time is called, start again.

DS after each timing.

Review the correct hand position for making reaches with your fingers.

Then take three 2-minute timings.

Key each line once. If you finish before time is called, start again.

DS after each timing.

1 John wants work at two in the afternoon.
2 I do not go along with the higher rents.
3 Joe thought the letter was sent in June.
4 Let the student find the food she needs.

Reach to the keys with your fingers; do not move your entire hands.

1 Lorna told Hal to sell the auto to Oran.
2 widow sure during foil girls worn learns
3 J. L. Jewel urged her to take the train.
4 keel soon seen door feel noon sheet root
5 I want to sing. Uri wants to sing also.

LESSON 9

9A
WARMUP

Key each line twice.

DS after each pair of lines.

Goal: To strengthen keyboarding skills   5 minutes

1 the of to and in for we that is this our
2 of the; in the; to the; for the; on the;
3 it is; with the; of our; and the; it is;
4 I want to. He is here. Just tell Jude.

| 1 | 2 | 3 | 4 | 5 | 6 | 7 | 8 |

9B
TECHNIQUE TIMING

Take two 2-minute timings on each group of lines.

DS after each timing.

Goal: To improve keyboarding techniques   10 minutes

Key easy letter combinations more rapidly. Slow down to key difficult letter combinations.

1 like had his work use two than who their
2 when take new do should other there send
3 due line then wish those sure here shall
4 In this; I want; In our; I would; Is it;

(Continued next page)

62C

NEED TO KNOW

Refer to the illustration at the right as you read about the format to use for the continuing pages of unbound reports.

Goal: To learn to format continuing pages of an unbound report   6 minutes

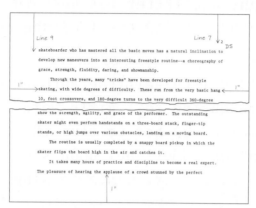

Continuing page of an unbound report

The second and all remaining pages of the report body, called **continuing pages,** are keyed in the same format as page 1.

1. Side margins: 1 inch.
2. Top margin: 1 inch.
3. Page number: Keyed on line 7, two spaces/columns before the right margin. Set a tab so that the numbers on all pages of your report will align.
4. Body of the report: Begins on line 9 and is DS.
5. Bottom margin: 1 inch.

62D

PROJECT PREVIEW

File name: L62D

DS

SM: 1″

Key as much of page 2 as you can in 5 minutes.

If you finish before time is called, start again.

Ignore misstrokes.

Goal: To key page 2 of an unbound report   7 minutes

Line 7 ↓   2   DS

When you key a report, try to avoid "widow" and "orphan" lines. A widow line is the first line of a paragraph keyed on the bottom of a page. An orphan line is the last line of a paragraph keyed at the top of a continuing page. Key at least two lines of a paragraph at the bottom of a page, and key at least two lines of a paragraph at the top of a new page.

62E

SELF-CHECK

Key the statement number and your answer: True or False.

Check your answers in Appendix B.

Goal: To review the format for unbound reports   5 minutes

1. The bottom margin of each full page should be at least 1 inch.
2. Single space the continuing pages of a report.
3. A report title is keyed in all caps.
4. The author's name is keyed with initial caps.
5. Side margins for unbound reports should be equal in width.
6. The body of a report should be double spaced.

62F

APPLICATION: REPORTS

Goal: To key page 2 of an unbound report   17 minutes

CUE: Key the page number on line 7.

Continue the report in 61F.

Take two 2-minute timings.

Keep your arms in correct position: arms slightly forward of your body and elbows close to, but not touching, your body.

5 into would further where note list until

6 sent own high life total first shall few

7 last within week offer while long thinks

8 One of; Is the; I will; It was; It will;

9C
NEW-KEY ORIENTATION

1. Locate the new key on the keyboard chart and on your keyboard.
2. Practice the first line. Watch your finger reach to the new key and return to home-key position.
3. Take two 1-minute technique timings on the second line. Goal: Eyes on copy.
4. Take a 2-minute technique timing on the third line. Goal: Eyes on copy.

Goal: To learn the location of Ⓟ Ⓒ and right ⌞SHIFT⌟ 16 minutes

P Practice the reach to Ⓟ with the **sem** finger. Keep your other fingers in home-key position.

1 ;p; ;p; ;p ;p ;p ;p ;p ;p ;p ;p ;p ;p ;p

2 up; pat lap; pal tape; wipe soap please;

3 pet pen past pep pug proper prior praise

, Practice the reach to Ⓒ with the **k** finger. The **j** finger may lift slightly, but your other fingers should remain in home-key position.

4 k,k k,k k, k, k, k, k, k, k, k, k, k,

5 kits, kids, kin, ink, rink, ring, kings,

6 life, like, hike, sit, seek, sake, fits,

SHIFT Practice the reach to the right shift key with the **sem** finger. Keep your other fingers in home-key position.

7 Sos Sos So So So So So So So So So So So

8 To Ron; Red; Sal; Fred; Dawn; Dean; Sue;

9 Run There Find Take Dear Send All We Eat

9D
KEYBOARD PRACTICE

Key each line 3 times.

DS after each group of lines.

Goal: To practice proper keystroking 11 minutes

1 Send the letter to Susan, the president.

2 Take an airplane to Dallas on the first.

3 The site of their new deal is Salt Lake.

(Continued next page)

call up a calculator, verify the figures, and continue keying your document. There's no need to have a calculator on your desk.

Some desktop software packages also include a powerful search feature. This special feature enables you to search your electronic phone directory by name, address, or telephone number. By using this search feature, you could prepare a mailing list of all your customers within a designated area code.

Many new software packages also include a spell checker. The spell checker searches a document for words that are misspelled or not in its dictionary. When the program finds a word it does not recognize, it stops searching and waits for you to make a correction or confirm that the word is okay.

Like any software, desktop packages vary greatly in their capabilities. For example, some calculator programs offer only four basic math functions—addition, subtraction, multiplication, and division. Others include more advanced functions such as percentages and square roots. Before you buy a desktop package, decide which functions you will need and use most often. Then, determine which program meets your needs.

Just think how your desk would look without all the accessories that clutter it. If you are like most people, however, you will soon find other "accessories" to put on your desk.

LESSON 62

Margins: Default or 1"
Spacing: SS or default   Tab: ¶

62A
WARMUP

Goal: To strengthen keyboarding skills   5 minutes

Key each line twice. DS after each pair of lines.

Speed
Accuracy
Number/Symbol

1 The oversight by the auditor held in spite of your findings.
2 A rough ghost brought a weighty gherkin to a ghoulish fight.
3 The "Tri-Wool" carpet sold for $1,568.99 less a 5% discount.

| 1 | 2 | 3 | 4 | 5 | 6 | 7 | 8 | 9 | 10 | 11 | 12 |

62B
GOAL WRITING

Goal: To measure timed-writing progress   10 minutes

DS or default.

Take two 3-minute goal writings.

If you finish before time is called, start again.

Record your speed and accuracy.

	1'	3'
In the future, our jobs may require us to be more	10	3
creative. As technology improves, computers will do more of	22	7
the routine work that we now do. This will free us to apply	35	12
more of our creative abilities to our jobs.	43	14
Employers will place more value on thinking skills,	54	18
such as the ability to make sound judgments and the capacity	66	22
to use creative thinking to solve problems. Employees may	78	26
find that they will be able to make more decisions and take	90	30
on additional responsibility. To prepare for the future, we	102	34
need to improve our skills in creative thinking.	112	37

AWL
5.7

Key each line 3 times.

DS after each group of lines.

4 Tell Paul to plan their trip to Newport.
5 Please take George, Dean, Helga, and Ed.
6 Please stop in San Jose and Los Angeles.
7 S. J. South and F. L. West are the ones.
8 Andrew worked with John throughout June.
9 We need a repair order for that printer.
10 Sell planes to all persons at this site.

9E
TECHNIQUE TIMING

Take a 2-minute timing on each group of lines.

Key each line once. If you finish before time is called, start again.

DS after each timing.

Goal: To improve keyboarding techniques 8 minutes

Keep your other fingers in home-key position as you make the reaches to the shift keys.

1 F. Freddie, K. Karl, S. Sarah, A. Arthur
2 We hope to hear that Red is now at work.
3 Washington, Florida, Illinois, Tennessee

Avoid pauses when shifting for capitals by using a one-two count.

4 Pat said that Andrew sent this in April.
5 E. Edward, J. Johnson, T. Tessie, L. Lee
6 Idaho Falls, Atlanta, Logan, West Jordan

Reach to the keys with your fingers, not your hands.

7 She is sending us two letters for Lorna.
8 She hopes we plan to send Nedra to town.
9 Let us know when the order gets to Kate.

LESSON 10

Margins: Default or 1" (12 pitch, 12-90; 10 pitch, 10-75)
Spacing: SS or default

10A
WARMUP

Key each line twice.

DS after each pair of lines.

Goal: To strengthen keyboarding skills 5 minutes

1 paid following where full general period
2 Regarding Life Total Will Past Write Set
3 As the, I hope, That I, To take, The new
4 We will not see Jane; Paul will see her.

| 1 | 2 | 3 | 4 | 5 | 6 | 7 | 8 |

61D
KEYBOARD COMPOSITION

DS or default.

Key as much as you can in 6 minutes.

Do not correct errors.

Goal: To compose at the keyboard   8 minutes

Choose one sentence to complete. Use the sentence as the beginning of a short paragraph.

1. If I could live anywhere in the world, I would choose . . .
2. If I could afford any car, it would be . . .
3. If I could afford any house to live in, it would look like . . .
4. If I could talk with the President for one hour, I would say . . .

61E
READ AND DO

Goal: To learn where to end a page   6 minutes

When keying documents of more than one page, you should generally leave a 1-inch bottom margin on each full page.

Some electronic typewriters and software enable you to use commands to set either the number of lines to be keyed on a page or the number of lines or inches to be left for the bottom margin. A signal or screen prompt may tell you when you have reached the last line on which you can key.

Other typewriters have page-end indicators. As you near the bottom of a standard-size page, the markings on the page-end indicator show you how many lines or inches remain on the page.

Determine how to set the page length or bottom margin, or how to use the page-end indicator for your equipment.

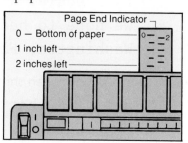

Use the page-end indicator to determine how many lines may be keyed to leave a 1-inch bottom margin.

61F
APPLICATION: REPORTS

Goal: To key page 1 of a two-page report   18 minutes

File name: L61F   DS   SM: 1"   Key page 1 of this two-page report. Save the document for use in 62F.

> **CUE:** Leave a 1-inch margin at the bottom of the page.

SMART DESKTOP ACCESSORIES
(Your Name)

Think of the many accessories that most office workers keep on their desks. A calendar, a calculator, a phone directory, note paper, pencils, and pens are just a few of the essential items that immediately come to mind.

Now think of how many times each of these items is used in the course of a day. A telephone call prompts a note on the calendar; an expense report requires the use of a calculator; a call to a client may require the phone directory. These are

routine tasks that almost every office worker performs many times each day.

Today there is a better, more efficient way to perform many of these same tasks. "Smart" desktop software programs for microcomputers offer an easy-to-use alternative to a cluttered desk. Picture the following situation. You are using word processing software on a microcomputer to key a lengthy report. Then, the telephone rings. Usually you would have to stop and search your desk for a pen and a message pad. Not anymore! By pressing a few keys on the computer, you can call up an electronic message board or calendar on which you can key the message. When you are done, you can return to your document by again pressing one or two keys. If, while you are keying the report you need to verify any financial information included in the report, you can quickly

(Continued next page)

10B
TECHNIQUE TIMING

Take two 2-minute timings on each group of lines.

Key each line once. If you finish before time is called, start again.

DS after each timing.

Goal: To improve keyboarding techniques   10 minutes

Do not pause while keying. Try to keep the carrier/cursor moving.

1 With this, Then the, There are, The past
2 When the, As there, And the, For we know
3 We heard Ralph and Frank are interested.

Keep your eyes on the textbook copy as you press the right shift key.

4 Done Weep Going Group Did Sell Right The
5 Glad Gone Show Thanks Field Find Whether
6 Where Fill Gear Dot Fiddle Row Sand Wish

Checkpoint: Did you remember to use the **sem** finger on the shift key?

10C
NEW-KEY ORIENTATION

1. Locate the new key on the keyboard chart and on your keyboard.
2. Practice the first line. Watch your finger reach to the new key and return to home-key position.
3. Take two 1-minute technique timings on the second line. Goal: Eyes on copy.
4. Take a 2-minute technique timing on the third line. Goal: Eyes on copy.

Goal: To learn the location of Ⓜ Ⓒ and Ⓠ   16 minutes

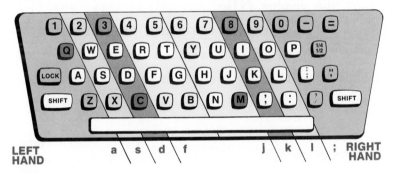

 Practice the reach to Ⓜ with the **j** finger. Keep your other fingers in home-key position.

1 jmj jmj jm jm jm jm jm jm jm jm jm jm jm
2 jam mud maps met mad moms from time some
3 most memo meet must form same month mail

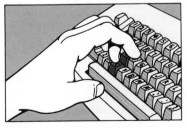

Practice the reach to Ⓒ with the **d** finger. The **f** finger may lift slightly, but your other fingers should remain in home-key position.

 4 dcd dcd dc dc dc dc dc dc dc dc dc dc dc
5 cod cad cot cuts cups cow such deck once
6 course call stock cash cost local office

(Continued next page)

61A
WARMUP

Key each line twice.
DS after each pair.

"ite" combinations

Goal: To strengthen keyboarding skills   5 minutes

```
1 finite kite bite site mite white item infinite dynamite site
2 This item has an infinite value in eliminating the termites.
3 Stalagmite and stalactite are made of calcite and aragonite.
```

| 1 | 2 | 3 | 4 | 5 | 6 | 7 | 8 | 9 | 10 | 11 | 12 |

61B
SPEED PRACTICE

Take a 20- or 15-second timing on each line. If you complete a line in the time allowed, go on to the next one.

Goal: To build keyboarding speed   5 minutes

		GWAM
	20"	15"

```
1 Jane wants to take her tests today.              21  28
2 The vendor files are on the first shelf.         24  32
3 Clay has chosen the south wing of the chapel.    27  36
4 Visitors to that airline pay for their major meal.  30  40
5 The workers are expected to be at their desks by eight.  33  44
```

| 1 | 2 | 3 | 4 | 5 | 6 | 7 | 8 | 9 | 10 | 11 |

61C
LANGUAGE ARTS

Read the rule in the box at the right.

Then key each numbered sentence, supplying quotation marks where needed.

Check your work with the key in Appendix A.

Goal: To review use of quotation marks   8 minutes

> Place quotation marks around the titles of articles, speeches, book chapters, songs, poems, and episodes of a television series.
>
> **Examples:**
>
> Kaye Clark wrote "Word Processing for Today" for the new magazine.
> His talk, "The Nature of an Expert System," was intriguing.
> The special series, "My Town," aired on Saturday.

1. Maria's favorite song is Somewhere My Love.
2. The title of the first chapter is My Childhood.
3. Robert Frost's poem Birches is one of my favorites.
4. Her speech about animal rights was titled Give a Hoot.
5. One segment of the news program was titled Dirty Air, Dirty Water.
6. I read his article, Success the Easy Way.
7. He wrote Chapter 1, In the Beginning, in one morning.
8. My poem, A Ray of Hope, is published in that anthology.
9. The Clean Machine: Car Maintenance is the title of her speech.
10. The chorus sang There Is Sunshine.

Practice the reach to Ⓠ with the **a** finger. Keep your other fingers in home-key position. Keep your wrist from moving up and down as you strike Ⓠ.

7 aqa aqa aq aq aq aq aq aq aq aq aq aq aq
8 aqua quit quips queen quick squid quarts
9 quota squad quote request quart requires

10D
KEYBOARD PRACTICE

Key each line twice.

DS after each pair of lines.

Goal: To practice proper keystroking   11 minutes

CUE: Speed up for easy-to-key letter combinations.

1 One of the quiet men will want to march.
2 Marge would like Que to sign the letter.
3 From the first, Carl did his work right.
4 Dick will ship our order within a month.
5 Quinn appreciates the time that I spent.
6 Right now is the time to finish the set.
7 Carl and the squad canceled the meeting.
8 Mara called them to help with the quilt.
9 Carole and Antonio canceled the meeting.
10 Marcia can collect all amounts due soon.

10E
TECHNIQUE TIMING

Take a 2-minute timing on each group of lines.

Key each line once. If you finish before time is called, start again.

DS after each timing.

Goal: To improve keyboarding techniques   8 minutes

Keep your wrist from turning outward as you strike Ⓒ with the **d** finger.

1 continue contain consult consist consent
2 complain computation comprise completion
3 conduct companies conclude comment costs

Keep your **sem** finger in home-key position as you reach for Ⓜ.

4 making manner market master matter means
5 might among home mammoth him making seem
6 more them make from claim flame cream me

Keep your wrist from turning outward as you strike Ⓠ.

7 conquers quorum squelch quoted squanders
8 squirt squash squirm squint squid square
9 liquid quotas sequel sequin unique squaw

60F

Goal: **To key a one-page unbound report** 7 minutes

File name: L60F

DS

SM: 1"

Key as much of page 1 as you can in 5 minutes.

Use your name as the author's name.

If you finish before time is called, start again.

Ignore misstrokes.

Line 13 ↓ A COMPUTER IN EVERY HOME? DS

Author's Name TS

Just a few years ago, the idea of having a computer in every home would have been labeled "ridiculous." Yet computers are now able to perform many household tasks that once could be done only by people.

Today, home computers are used to regulate the temperature of a room, to turn lights on and off, and to control home security systems. Through electronic communications made available with home computers, people can shop, pay bills, access reference services, or make airline and hotel reservations without having to leave their homes. Even the familiar telephone has been changed by computers. Now there are telephones enabling callers to reach frequently called persons simply by speaking their names into the receiver.

60G

APPLICATION:
REPORTS

Goal: **To key a one-page unbound report** 14 minutes

File name: L60G   DS   SM: 1"

CUE: Center and key the title on line 13.

THE IMPORTANCE OF APPEARANCE
(Your Name)

Perhaps you have heard this saying: "First impressions are lasting ones." When you prepare a report, you can make that first impression a favorable one by putting the right amount of effort and care into the preparation of the report. A first impression is formed by the report's appearance.

An acceptable and recognized format is necessary when you prepare a report. Side, top, and bottom margins should frame the finished work so that the report has an attractive appearance. Spacing within the report should be consistent with a recognized style manual.

A clean, white, high-quality paper should be selected for the report. If you are using a microcomputer, use both a printer and paper of better quality than you might use for ordinary jobs.

Once you have keyed your report, proofread it carefully. If you use a typewriter, proofread the text before you remove the paper from the typewriter. If you use a microcomputer, proofread the screen text before you print a hard copy. Proofread the hard copy also.

Correct all misstrokes and errors in context. Use your dictionary to verify spellings of which you are not certain. When in doubt, use a reference guide or style manual to verify the rules of punctuation and grammar. Your completed report should be attractive and free of errors.

Reinforcement

11A
WARMUP

Key each line twice.

DS after each pair of lines.

Goal: To strengthen keyboarding skills   5 minutes

1 much since cost could school price squid
2 with this, and that, we do not, could we
3 Please see, We would like, Let them know
4 Colorado, California, Montana, Minnesota

| 1 | 2 | 3 | 4 | 5 | 6 | 7 | 8 |

11B
TECHNIQUE TIMING

Take a 2-minute timing on each line.

DS after each timing.

Goal: To improve keyboarding techniques   14 minutes

Keep your eyes on the textbook copy as you press the right shift key.

1 Dealer Cash Summer Agent Electric Remain
2 Catalogs Estate Standard Getting Showing
3 Fiji Quick Works Super Doctor True Equal

Reach to the keys with your fingers; do not move your whole hand.

4 Union Indian Orion Point Junior Kiwi Leo
5 Million Nine Heritage Unique Image Often
6 Post Judge Kitchen Lock Music New Herald

11C
KEYBOARD PRACTICE

Key each line 3 times.

DS after each group of lines.

Goal: To practice proper keystroking   10 minutes

CUE: Keep your eyes on the textbook copy as you operate the shift keys.

1 Claims South Lands Hear Funds North West
2 To take, We would like for our, She will
3 Senator Jepson will come to Idaho Falls.
4 Finance Congress Lake East Commerce Risk
5 President Sims went to East High School.
6 Ohio, Oregon, Utah, and Iowa acquiesced.
7 Marta will go to Toronto or to Montreal.

TECHNIQUE
TIMING

DS or default.

Take two 2-minute
timings. Work on
improving the tech-
nique shown.

Goal: **To improve keyboarding techniques**   5 minutes

Keep your eyes on the copy as you key this paragraph.

One way to use time efficiently is to organize
your day. Make a list of what you want to accomplish.
Working from your list, decide which tasks are the most
important, and begin with the task that has top priority.
Whenever possible, complete one task before you begin
another. This will give you a sense of achievement.

Go to the beginning of the paragraph as quickly as you can. Proofread and
correct as many misstrokes as possible.

60D ━━━━━━━━━

NEED TO KNOW

Refer to the illustra-
tion at the right as
you read the instruc-
tions for keying an
unbound report.

Goal: **To learn the format for page 1 of an unbound report**   5 minutes

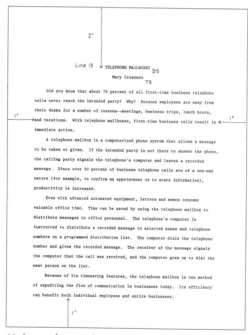

Unbound report

An **unbound report** is usually short,
and the pages are not stapled or hole
punched.

1. Side margins: 1 inch.
2. Top margin: 2 inches.
3. Bottom margin: 1 inch.
4. Title: Centered in all caps on line 13.
5. Author name: Centered and keyed
   with initial caps a DS below the title.
   (If a report has a title page, the author's name appears on the title page
   instead of here.)
6. Body of the report: Begins a TS after
   the author's name and is keyed DS.

Software Alert: If changes in line spacing
are difficult or impossible to make with
your software, follow the format your
teacher suggests, or make the following
changes: Key the title on line 12; DS and
key the author's name; then QS and key
the body.

The format for the continuing pages of
an unbound report is shown in 62C.

60E ━━━━━━━━━

SELF-CHECK

Key the statement
number and your an-
swer: True or False.

Check your answers in
Appendix B.

Goal: **To review the format for page 1 of an unbound report**   4 minutes

1. The title of a report is keyed with initial caps.
2. The author's name is keyed in all caps.
3. A DS is left between the title and the author's name.
4. The side margins for unbound reports are equal in width.
5. The body of a report should be single spaced.
6. The title of an unbound report is keyed on line 13.

11D

NEED TO KNOW

Goal: To learn how to use word scales   6 minutes

You can use word scales to determine your keyboarding speed. Keyboarding speed is measured in gross words a minute, or GWAM. To determine your GWAM:

1. Count the number of *complete* lines you keyed.
2. Multiply that number by the number of "words" in the line. The number of words in a line is the last number shown in the bottom word scale.
3. If you didn't finish a line, use the bottom word scale to determine the number of words keyed.
4. Add the number of words for the incomplete line (Step 3) to the number of words for the complete lines (Step 2). The total of the two represents your GWAM for 1 minute.

To save time, word scales that list cumulative GWAM, line by line, are provided. These word scales are printed to the right of the copy. To determine GWAM with this kind of scale, find the cumulative word count in the side word scale for the last complete line you keyed. Then, using the bottom word scale, determine the number of words keyed in any incomplete line. Add these two numbers; the answer is your 1-minute GWAM.

If you are timed for longer than 1 minute, you can still use the 1-minute scales to figure your GWAM. Simply divide the word count you get using the 1-minute scales by the number of minutes in the timing. If you keyed 60 words in 3 minutes, for example, your GWAM is 20 ($60 \div 3 = 20$).

11E

SELF-CHECK

Goal: To review word scale use   5 minutes

Use the illustration to answer the questions.

On a sheet of paper, handwrite the number of the question and your answer.

Check your answers in Appendix B.

```
                                                      1'
                                                      ──
 1 To do the job right, we need their help.     8
 2 He would like to share the results soon.    16
 3 She got the letter concerning the order.    24
 4 Call the department as soon as possible.    32
   |   |   |   |   |   |   |   |   |
       1   2   3   4   5   6   7   8
```

1. If you key all of line 1, what is your GWAM?
2. If you key all four lines, what is your GWAM?
3. If you key all of line 1 and up through **th** in the word *the* in line 2, what is your GWAM?
4. If you key lines 1, 2, and 3 and up through the space after the word *department* in line 4, what is your GWAM?

11F

TECHNIQUE TIMING

Goal: To improve keyboarding techniques   10 minutes

Take two 2-minute timings.

Return/enter when you see R/E. If you finish before time is called, start again.

DS after each timing.

Keep your eyes on the textbook copy as you return/enter.

Please send the letter. R/E   See me soon. R/E We need their help. R/E I am going to Chicago. R/E With luck, we will finish soon. R/E The check was mailed. R/E Please write. R/E Let us know what we should do. R/E The order was damaged.

(Continued next page)

JOB 2 ———————— Using the appropriate correction method for your equipment, make the following changes in JOB 1. Proofread carefully and make any necessary corrections.

Paragraph 1

1. "some years" to "many years"
2. "is not said" to "is not used"
3. "critical" to "valuable"
4. "failure and success" to "success and failure"

Paragraph 2

1. "person" to "friend"——in all instances
2. "think positive." to "THINK POSITIVE!"

LESSON 60

60A
WARMUP

Goal: To strengthen keyboarding skills   5 minutes

Key each line twice. DS after each pair of lines.

Speed   1 Yes, your parents may visit the four camps during the movie.
Accuracy   2 The vibrant Bavarians in Beverly braved the bevy of bovines.
Number/Symbol   3 The correct items are $24.67 or 15.67% and $12.65 or 78.34%.

| 1 | 2 | 3 | 4 | 5 | 6 | 7 | 8 | 9 | 10 | 11 | 12 |

60B
GOAL WRITING

DS or default.

Take two 3-minute goal writings.

If you finish before time is called, start again.

Record your speed and accuracy.

Goal: To measure timed-writing progress   10 minutes

	1'	3'
Is it any wonder that the dog occupies a position of	11	4
honor in our homes?	15	5
Dogs display remarkable adaptability. They serve as	26	9
sled dogs, hunting dogs, guard dogs, and seeing-eye dogs, to	38	13
name just a few of their abilities. During wartime dogs	49	16
have served faithfully on the battlefield. They have been	61	20
taught to swim and to herd schools of fish to the beach.	72	24
Stories abound of dogs who have alerted their blind masters	84	28
to pending danger, thus saving lives. The dog is a truly	96	32
incredible creature and has indeed earned a place of honor.	108	36

1' | 1 | 2 | 3 | 4 | 5 | 6 | 7 | 8 | 9 | 10 | 11 | 12 |
3' | 1 | 2 | 3 | 4 |

AWL
5.7

Take a 2-minute timing on each group of lines.

Key each line once. If you finish before time is called, start again.

DS after each timing.

Do not pause between letters or words. You should begin to key some letter combinations more quickly.

1 We do not think we will order the goods.
2 We look forward to seeing the president.
3 We would appreciate an answer in August.
4 I am sure the department will help them.

Reach to the keys with your fingers, not your hands.

5 The students went to see the production.
6 When she hears the tone, she must speak.
7 His uncle wanted to see the photographs.
8 Take the sample and use it during April.

LESSON 12

12A
WARMUP

Key each line twice.

DS after each pair of lines.

Goal: To strengthen keyboarding skills 5 minutes

1 The office is open. We want to see Jed.
2 The information is what Jo asked to see.
3 main range truck union file charges come
4 Trucking Charging Coming Clearing Filing

| | 1 | 2 | 3 | 4 | 5 | 6 | 7 | 8 | |

12B
TECHNIQUE TIMING

Take two 2-minute timings on each group of lines.

Key each line once. If you finish before time is called, start again.

DS after each timing.

Goal: To improve keyboarding techniques 10 minutes

Keep all other fingers in home-key position as you reach to the left shift key with the **a** finger. Release the shift key quickly.

1 Montana Utilities; Mutual Insurance Inc.
2 Northwest Petroleum Plant; Louisiana Oil
3 Northern Illinois Products; North Kansas

Keep all other fingers in home-key position as you reach to the right shift key with the **sem** finger. Release the shift key quickly.

4 Christmas Shop; South Dakota Coal Center
5 Eastern; Southern; Western; Southeastern
6 California Storage Area; Austin Electric

59F

READ AND DO

Goal: To learn about page layout   5 minutes

With typewriters and some software, you must establish document formats, or **page layouts,** before you key a document. Other software requires you to select page layouts before you print a document.

Make the following page layout changes for use in the next activity, 59G.

a. Left margin: 1 inch (10 pitch, 10; 12 pitch, 12).
b. Right margin: 1 inch (10 pitch, 75; 12 pitch, 90). If your software requires you to specify the number of characters or inches in the line, use 6.5 inches (10 pitch, 65 characters; 12 pitch, 78 characters).
c. Top margin: 1 inch (6 lines).
d. Bottom margin: 1 inch (6 lines).
e. Line spacing: DS or 2.
f. Page length: 54 lines.

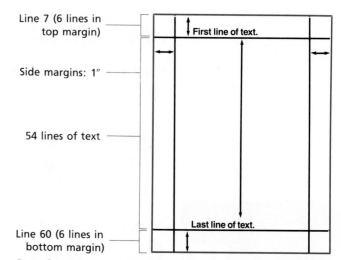

Line 7 (6 lines in top margin)

Side margins: 1"

54 lines of text

Line 60 (6 lines in bottom margin)

First line of text.

Last line of text.

Page layout

The illustration shows the page layout for all of these settings.

59G

APPLICATION: UNBOUND REPORT

Goal: To key a report page   18 minutes

JOB 1

File name: L59G

Key the paragraphs.

E T Do not remove your paper from the typewriter. Go on to Job 2.

M Save the document for use in Job 2.

    Some years ago a popular book encouraged people to say to each other: THINK POSITIVE! While the saying is not said as often today, it is still true that a positive attitude is one of the most critical habits you can develop now in preparing for your future. You may have several more years of education ahead of you; you may be looking forward to your first job. In either case, a good attitude may be the difference between failure and success.

    You too can become a positive thinker. Think of a person who has a positive attitude. Isn't it fun to be with that person? Doesn't that person make you feel better when things are not going well? Develop the habit of saying "I'll do better next time" when you have not done well.

    Above all, think positive.

(Continued next page)

12C
NEW-KEY ORIENTATION

1. Locate the new key on the keyboard chart and on your keyboard.
2. Practice the first line. Watch your finger reach to the new key and re-turn to home-key position.
3. Take two 1-minute technique timings on the second line. Goal: Eyes on copy.
4. Take a 2-minute technique timing on the third line. Goal: Eyes on copy.

Goal: To learn the location of Ⓑ Ⓨ and Ⓧ   16 minutes

Ⓑ Practice the reach to Ⓑ with the **f** finger. Keep your other fingers in home-key position.

1 fbf fbf fb fb fb fb fb fb fb fb fb fb fb
2 fob fib bit bids rib jabs both been best
3 business board bill blue book banks burn

Ⓨ Practice the reach to Ⓨ with the **j** finger. Keep your other fingers in home-key position.

4 jyj jyj jy jy jy jy jy jy jy jy jy jy jy
5 yours yoyo joy jay gym many myth yes hay
6 years yearly you yard yellow yield young

Ⓧ Practice the reach to Ⓧ with the **s** finger. The **a** finger may lift slightly. Your other fingers should remain in home-key position.

7 sxs sxs sx sx sx sx sx sx sx sx sx sx sx
8 six axe lax exits next oxen taxed exists
9 next tax index mix mixed mixture nix fix

12D
KEYBOARD PRACTICE

Key each line 3 times.

DS after each group of lines.

Goal: To practice proper keystroking   7 minutes

1 bake bacon baker ball balm banker barber
2 yard year youth young yours yonder yield
3 noxious next latex axial pixel exquisite

12E
TECHNIQUE TIMING

Take a 1-minute tim-ing on each line.

DS after each timing.

Goal: To improve keyboarding techniques   8 minutes

Do not pause while keying. Try to keep the carrier/cursor moving.

1 be been but about best before being both
2 yam yes yield yokes yule yank yellow you
3 xylene fixture xeric extend xerosis exit

(Continued next page)

59C

LANGUAGE ARTS

Read the rule in the box at the right.

Then key each numbered sentence, supplying the correct word (*are*, *hour*, or *our*).

Check your work with the key in Appendix A.

Goal: To review use of *are, hour,* and *our*   8 minutes

are	Present tense form of the verb *to be*
hour	60 minutes
our	Possessive form of *we*

Examples:

In one <u>hour</u>, <u>our</u> committee members will present a final report. The <u>hour</u> is late, and <u>our</u> responsibilities <u>are</u> clear.

1. Most of the groups _____ sure to have an _____ in which to relax.
2. Can you have _____ final specifications ready for us in an _____?
3. They were told that _____ presentation could last for about an _____.
4. _____ task force will require the full _____ to provide a report.
5. _____ they going to require more than an _____ to check _____ work?
6. _____ software and _____ hardware _____ due to arrive here on May 8.
7. If you need an _____, _____ supervisors will see that you get it.
8. Frankly, _____ recommendations _____ kept confidential.
9. We must tell Rhonda that _____ decisions _____ not binding on her.
10. _____ you sure that _____ complete report can be ready in an _____?

59D

SELF-CHECK

DS or default.

Key the statement number and your answer: True or False.

Check your answers in Appendix B.

Goal: To review proofreader's marks   6 minutes

1. Use ⌿ to indicate that a letter, word, or sentence is to be inserted into the copy.
2. Use # to indicate that a space should be added to copy.
3. Use ≡ under a letter to indicate that the letter should be capitalized.
4. Use ⊐ to indicate that copy should be moved to the left.
5. Use ∧ to indicate that a letter, word, or sentence is to be deleted from the copy.
6. When keying the word <u>schedule</u>, you would capitalize every letter in the word.
7. Use ⊏ to indicate the beginning of a new paragraph.
8. Use ∿ to indicate a change in the order of the copy.
9. When ⊃ follows a letter, you should insert a period.
10. Use ⁀ to indicate that a double space should be left.

59E Ⓜ

NEED TO KNOW

Goal: To learn about express cursor moves   3 minutes

To move the cursor directly to the beginning or ending of a document, page, or line, use **express cursor moves.**

A command or a combination of keystrokes is used for each of these express cursor moves. For example, one program uses the Code + Arrow (directional key) to move the cursor to the beginning of a page. Another program uses CTRL B to move the cursor to the beginning of a document.

Determine the commands for express cursor moves for your software.

Return to home-key position after making the reach to the new keys.

4 The best broker is the brother of Brent.

5 Yes, you may yearn for the yellow yacht.

6 Rex is an expert on exports from Mexico.

12F
GOAL WRITING

Take two 1-minute goal writings.

Key each line once. If time allows, start again.

Determine your GWAM.

Goal: To measure timed-writing progress   4 minutes

CUE: Key at a pace that is comfortable for you.

1'

1 Rex Yang is concerned about the new job.   8

2 Please explain that print queue to them.   16

3 We can bill them if they keep the goods.   24

| 1 | 2 | 3 | 4 | 5 | 6 | 7 | 8 |

LESSON
13

Margins: Default or 1"
Spacing: SS or default

13A
WARMUP

Key each line twice.

DS after each pair of lines.

Goal: To strengthen keyboarding skills   5 minutes

1 member hand try welcome air men box firm

2 I would like, We feel, I would be, It is

3 January; July; February; August; October

4 Thank you for the order; we are pleased.

| 1 | 2 | 3 | 4 | 5 | 6 | 7 | 8 |

13B
TECHNIQUE TIMING

Take a 2-minute timing on each group of lines.

Key each line once. If time allows, start again.

DS between timings.

Goal: To improve keyboarding techniques   5 minutes

Strike each key with a quick, sharp stroke.

1 exceed excellent excess exhibit existing

2 equality questionnaire require equipment

3 early yearly yield yourself youths yeast

Keep your other fingers in home-key position as you reach to [q] and [x].

4 I will try a quick stop on my next trip.

5 The quests for that extra exhibit ended.

6 The sixth technique is an excellent one.

UNIT 6

Unbound Reports

Your keyboarding skills may be used to prepare a variety of reports for personal or business purposes. In this unit, you will learn one format for preparing reports. Once you have mastered this format, you will easily learn other report formats.

UNIT OBJECTIVES

In this unit, Lessons 59–70, you will:

1. Increase your keyboarding speed and accuracy.
2. Format and key reports in unbound format.
3. Key parenthetical references in the author-date format.
4. Format and key short and long quotations.
5. Key reference and title pages for unbound reports.
6. Assemble the parts of a report in correct order.

ELECTRONIC CONCEPTS

express cursor moves (p. 141)   temporary indent (p. 154)
page layouts (p. 142)

LESSON
59

Margins: Default or 1"
Spacing: SS or default Tab: ¶

59A
WARMUP

Key each line twice.

DS after each pair of lines.

Frequently misspelled words

Goal: To strengthen keyboarding skills 5 minutes

1 pursue acknowledgment beneficial argument appearance fulfill
2 Their desire to pursue an acknowledgment memo is beneficial.
3 The argument about appearance will fulfill the requirements.

| 1 | 2 | 3 | 4 | 5 | 6 | 7 | 8 | 9 | 10 | 11 | 12 |

59B
ACCURACY PRACTICE

DS after each group of lines.

Goal: To build keyboarding accuracy 5 minutes

Take a 2-minute accuracy timing on the lines in 59A. Repeat the timing. Try to improve your accuracy.

Checkpoint: Did you improve your accuracy?

13C
NEW-KEY ORIENTATION

1. Locate the new key on the keyboard chart and on your keyboard.
2. Practice the first line. Watch your finger reach to the new key and return to home-key position.
3. Take two 1-minute technique timings on the second line. Goal: Eyes on copy.
4. Take a 2-minute technique timing on the third line. Goal: Eyes on copy.

Goal: To learn the location of Ⓥ and Ⓩ   12 minutes

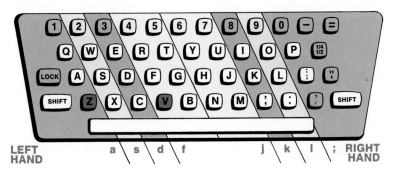

 Practice the reach to Ⓥ with the **f** finger. Keep your other fingers in home-key position.

1 fvf fvf fv fv fv fv fv fv fv fv fv fv fv
2 five cave vain rave vet ever haven every
3 give move above vine view ever vow haven

 Practice the reach to Ⓩ with the **a** finger. The **s** finger may lift slightly, but your other fingers should remain in home-key position.

4 aza aza az az az az az az az az az az az
5 zap fez zoo lazier zero zone dozen graze
6 zest zigzag zoom zip zinc zippers zodiac

13D
KEYBOARD PRACTICE

Key each line 3 times.

DS after each group of lines.

Goal: To practice proper keystroking   6 minutes

1 With great zeal, Victor studied zoology.
2 Virginia gave the zebra to the Zulu Zoo.
3 Vivian Zike spent five years at Zink Co.
4 Zobell Movers gave Dave Zemp seven days.
5 Zucchini existed for everybody to enjoy.

13E
NEED TO KNOW

Goal: To learn about tabs   3 minutes

To indent paragraphs efficiently and arrange text in columns, set tab stops. Then use the tab key (not the space bar) to move the carrier/cursor to the tab stop.

Operate the tab key with the finger closest to it. On most equipment, the tab key is on the left side of the keyboard and is operated by the **a** finger. Press the tab key quickly; then return the **a** finger to home-key position. Keep your other fingers on the home keys as you press the tab.

*Reach to the tab key with the **a** finger.*

4. ___ hunch is correct; Paula is the person ___ seeking.
5. ___ design was outstanding, and ___ presentation was superb.
6. ___ undoubtedly the best discussion leader in ___ section.
7. ___ estimates were close, and ___ projections were accurate.
8. After completing ___ reviews, you must return all ___ files.
9. ___ the best person, and ___ certain to get their votes.
10. Once ___ certified, ___ salary will increase.

58D

GOAL WRITING

DS or default.

Take two 3-minute goal writings.

If you finish before time is called, start again.

Record your speed and accuracy.

Goal: To measure timed-writing progress   10 minutes

	1'	3'
Many people now believe that the criteria for personal	11	4
success go beyond having a lot of money, a big home, and a	23	8
luxury car. More and more people strive for goals that are	35	12
harder to measure in terms of dollars, such as good health	47	16
and close bonds to family and friends.	55	18
Perhaps this shift in values has occurred because	65	22
financial success has become easier to attain. Since more	77	26
people now have college degrees, more people have the	87	29
ability to earn a big salary. When people feel financially	99	33
secure, they can take the time to pursue other goals.	110	37

1' | 1 | 2 | 3 | 4 | 5 | 6 | 7 | 8 | 9 | 10 | 11 | 12 | AWL
3' | 1 | 2 | 3 | 4 | 5.7

58E

KEYBOARD COMPOSITION

DS or default.

Key as much as you can in 5 minutes.

Do not correct errors.

Goal: To compose at the keyboard   7 minutes

Choose one sentence to complete, and use it as the beginning of a short paragraph.

1. The most influential person in my life is ___ because . . .
2. My favorite season of the year is ___ because . . .
3. My favorite kind of book is ___ because . . .
4. The career that I have selected is ___ because . . .
5. My greatest dream is ___ because . . .

58F

KEYBOARD PRACTICE

DS or default.

Key the paragraph three times. If time allows, start again.

Proofread your copy.

Identify misstrokes.

Goal: To practice proper keystroking   12 minutes

Sunlight contains ultraviolet light that damages the skin. Those who have fair skin may lie in the sun for hours, hoping to acquire a healthy, golden tan. But without the frequent use of a suntan lotion to block ultraviolet rays, a sunburn followed by peeling usually results.

13F

READ AND DO   **Goal:** To learn to indent paragraphs   7 minutes

Beginning with Lesson 14, suggested tab settings will be shown in the color band in the lesson opener. The most common tab setting will be "Tab ¶." This symbol (¶) stands for paragraph indent. The first line of a paragraph is usually indented 5 spaces.

Equipment with Default Tabs

Many electronic typewriters and most software have default tabs (preset tab stops) every so many spaces. For example, tab stops may be preset every 5 or 8 spaces. Use the default settings when possible.

1. Determine the default settings for your equipment.
2. Using the tab key or command, move the carrier/ cursor to the first default tab stop.
3. Begin keying the paragraph in 13G at this point.

Equipment without Default Tabs

Before you can set tabs, you must clear any tab stops that are already set.

1. Determine the appropriate method for clearing tabs on your equipment (see *About Your Equipment* in the front of this textbook).
2. Then clear all tab stops and press return.
3. Space over 5 spaces and set a tab stop; then, press return.
4. Press the tab key to check the tab setting. If the tab is correct, begin keying the paragraph in 13G at this point.

13G

KEYBOARD PRACTICE   **Goal:** To practice proper keystroking   6 minutes

DS or default.

Tab: ¶ or default.

Key the paragraphs. If time allows, start again.

CUE: Use the tab to indent paragraphs.

Thank you for your recent order and letter of explanation.

We will ship your order in one week if the strike is over. We cannot assure shipment any sooner.

Please let us know at your earliest convenience whether you prefer the items to be shipped by overnight express.

13H

GOAL WRITING   **Goal:** To measure timed-writing progress   6 minutes

Take two 2-minute goal writings.

Key each line once. If time allows, start again.

Determine your GWAM.

CUE: Key at a pace that is comfortable for you.
                                                                1'

1 Please send the letters to him tomorrow.   8
2 We want their business to buy our goods.   16
3 She will be able to mail the order soon.   24
4 Dan and I will go to the city next week.   32

| 1 | 2 | 3 | 4 | 5 | 6 | 7 | 8 |

57F
KEYBOARD COMPOSITION

DS or default.

Key as much as you can in 5 minutes.

Do not correct errors.

Goal: To compose at the keyboard   6 minutes

Choose one sentence to complete, and use it as the beginning of a short paragraph.

1. My favorite sport is ___ because . . .
2. The person whom I most admire is ___ because . . .
3. The most important quality that a person can have is ___ because . . .
4. The most difficult task that I ever had was to ___ because . . .
5. The most interesting class that I have ever taken was ___ because . . .

LESSON 58
Skill Building

Margins: Default or 1"
Spacing: SS or default   Tab: ¶

58A
WARMUP

Key each line twice. DS after each pair.

"ize" combinations

Goal: To strengthen keyboarding skills   5 minutes

```
1 recognizes economize systematizes generalize size synthesize
2 We realize you will subsidize, standardize, and finalize it.
3 I apologize; we failed to publicize the sizes of the prizes.
```
| 1 | 2 | 3 | 4 | 5 | 6 | 7 | 8 | 9 | 10 | 11 | 12 |

58B
SPEED PRACTICE

Take two 1-minute timings on each sentence. Try to increase your speed on the second timing.

Goal: To build keyboarding speed   7 minutes

```
                                                             1'
1 When convenient, please send us the marketing study you did.  12
2 Christmas is the work period when she does not want to work.  24
3 She does not have the authority to do the analysis you want.  36
```
| 1 | 2 | 3 | 4 | 5 | 6 | 7 | 8 | 9 | 10 | 11 | 12 |

58C
LANGUAGE ARTS

Read the rule in the box at the right.

Then key each numbered sentence, supplying the correct word (*your* or *you're*).

Check your work with the key in Appendix A.

Goal: To review use of *your* and *you're*   9 minutes

> **your**   Possessive form of *you*
> **you're**   Contraction for *you are*
>
> **Examples:**
>
> You're absolutely sure that you made your reservation in July?
> Is your friend, Dr. Williams, the one you're writing about?

1. If ___ sure about ___ decision, then return ___ report to me.
2. When you get ___ jacket back, you will be fortunate indeed.
3. When ___ through with ___ notes, please give them to Sue.

(Continued next page)

14A

WARMUP

Key each line twice.

DS after each pair of lines.

Goal: To strengthen keyboarding skills   5 minutes

1 If you have any questions, write to him.
2 Have Jody Pinckle bring me five quizzes.
3 Give your ideas to Gene, the supervisor.
4 Enclosed is a form; please mail it soon.

| 1 | 2 | 3 | 4 | 5 | 6 | 7 | 8 |

14B

READ AND DO

Goal: To learn about line endings   6 minutes

Beginning in this lesson, the drill lines contain 50 characters. For the remaining activities in this lesson, set your side margins as follows:

12 pitch, 2" (24-78); 10 pitch, 1½" (15-70)

Equipment with Auto Return/Word Wrap

With **automatic return** or **word wrap**, any word that is too long to fit within a set line length is automatically moved to the next line. When using auto return or word wrap, press return/enter only at the end of a paragraph or at the end of a short line.

Activate auto return or word wrap by using the appropriate key or command. In the next activity, do not press return/enter at the end of each line. Instead, press return/enter only at the end of each timing.

Equipment without Auto Return/Word Wrap

On equipment without auto return or word wrap, a margin signal sounds as copy nears the end of a line. This signal may be either a beep or a bell. When you hear the signal, you decide how much more copy you can key before you return. If you are unable to complete a word before the margin locks, use the margin release to finish the word.

The margin release enables you to key beyond the right margin. You may also use the margin release to move outside the left margin.

In the next activity, return at the end of every line. Listen for the margin signal as you approach the end of a line.

14C

TECHNIQUE TIMING

Take two 2-minute timings.

DS after each timing.

Goal: To improve keyboarding techniques   15 minutes

Release the left and right shift keys quickly and return your **a** and **sem** fingers to home-key position.

1 I am sure; At this time; You will find; Along with
2 Do not hesitate; You will be; This company; I have
3 Enclosed is a; He would be; We believe; As soon as

(Continued next page)

Take a 1-minute timing on each line. Work on improving the technique shown.

DS after each timing.

Keep the carrier/cursor moving. Do not pause between words.

4 Please take this quiz; then, file the results in the folder.
5 My high score on the analysis portion of the quiz amazes me.
6 There is the computer. It analyzes scores from the quizzes.

Keep your eyes on the textbook copy.
Repeat lines 4–6.

57D
COMPARISON COPY

DS or default.

Take two 3-minute timings on each paragraph.

Try to increase your speed on the second timing.

Goal: To build speed on a variety of copy   14 minutes

	1'	3'
Since one out of eight jobs is connected to world	10	3
trade, an understanding of other cultures is imperative.	22	7
For example, Asian business people do not use first names,	33	11
even at what seem to be social gatherings. In Arab	44	15
cultures, good etiquette demands that one stand close	55	18
to the speaker--as close as one foot away.	63	21

1' | 1 | 2 | 3 | 4 | 5 | 6 | 7 | 8 | 9 | 10 | 11 | 12 |
3' | 1 | 2 | 3 | 4 |

	1'	3'
Germans say "thank you" as a polite form of refusal.	12	4
In Mexico, keeping a client waiting for a half hour is the	25	8
normal way of doing business. In India, unemployment is so	39	13
high that employing a multitude of people is more important	52	17
than being cost-effective. International trade truly	63	21
demands special understanding.		

57E
LANGUAGE ARTS

Read the rule in the box at the right.

Then key each numbered sentence, supplying the correct word (*their, there,* or *they're*).

Check your work with the key in Appendix A.

Goal: To review use of *their, there, they're*   8 minutes

> **their**   Possessive form of *they*
> **there**   In that place; opposite of *here*
> **they're** Contraction for *they are*
>
> **Examples:**
>
> <u>Their</u> reason for leaving so early was to arrive <u>there</u> on time.
> <u>They're</u> taking a cab <u>there</u> because they lost <u>their</u> car keys.

1. ____ planning a visit to Houston to inspect ____ property.
2. ____ are four students who have completed ____ reports.
3. Randy should arrive at ____ house about sundown on Wednesday.
4. If ____ going to stop ____ first, they should leave earlier.
5. ____ group was selected because ____ the most qualified.
6. ____ are three reasons ____ returning ____ refunds to us.
7. ____ going to take some aluminum cans ____ for recycling.
8. He thinks that ____ idea to start the project is a good one.
9. Why can't they wait ____ turn? ____ not showing courtesy.

Take two 2-minute
timings on each
group of lines.

DS after each timing.

Sit in proper position at the keyboard.

4 I can ask her to amend the provisions of the bill.
5 I do not yet know the source of their information.
6 I was confident that the inquiry would come to me.

Space between words without pausing.

7 you identify left windows try questions is certain
8 told reasons core requirements zealous authorities
9 can clarify very positive new medicine our contact

14D
GOAL WRITING

Goal: To measure timed-writing progress   6 minutes

Take two 2-minute
goal writings.

Key each line once. If
time allows, start
again.

Determine your
GWAM.

CUE: Key at a pace that is comfortable for you.

1'

1 They handle the problems that the city gives them. 10
2 Eight of the girls want to go on both world tours. 20
3 Dixie wants to work with the endowment fund again. 30
4 The amendment is the right one to help their firm. 40

| 1 | 2 | 3 | 4 | 5 | 6 | 7 | 8 | 9 | 10 |

14E
NEED TO KNOW

Goal: To learn to identify misstrokes   6 minutes

All people who use keyboards make misstrokes. The important thing is to be able to find the misstrokes and correct them. Initially, you will need to identify the kinds of misstrokes that you make. Study the four kinds of misstrokes in the example to learn what some of the common kinds of misstrokes are.

Omitted Letter(s) (Plese) let us know; he (migt) write Jack.
Omitted Word(s) The member(s the) board were all there.
Added Letter(s) Please let (use) know; he might (writes) Jack.
Added Word(s) The members of the (of the) board were all there.

14F
KEYBOARD PRACTICE

Goal: To practice proper keystroking on handwritten copy   6 minutes

Key each line twice.

DS after each pair of
lines.

1 If you are able, please come; however, call first.
2 Ford Zoo is open; you are invited to go with them.
3 F. J. Rogerson, of course, will do the conducting.
4 We plan to attend. We hope they will also attend.

UNIT 5

Skill Building

The activities in this unit offer you an opportunity to concentrate on developing your keyboarding skills—good techniques and higher levels of speed and accuracy.

UNIT OBJECTIVES

In this unit, Lessons 57–58, you will:

1. Improve your keyboarding techniques.
2. Increase your keyboarding speed.
3. Improve your keystroking accuracy.

LESSON 57

Skill Building

Margins: Default or 1″
Spacing: SS or default   Tab: ¶

57A
WARMUP

Key each line twice.

DS after each pair.

Frequently misspelled words

Goal: To strengthen keyboarding skills   5 minutes

```
1 mortgage familiar receipt receive sincerely similar probably
2 You will probably receive a receipt on the mortgage by mail.
3 He looks familiar yet similar to a man he sincerely admired.
```

| 1 | 2 | 3 | 4 | 5 | 6 | 7 | 8 | 9 | 10 | 11 | 12 |

57B
ACCURACY PRACTICE

DS after each group of lines.

Goal: To build keyboarding accuracy   5 minutes

Take a 2-minute accuracy timing on the lines in 57A. Repeat the timing. Try to improve your accuracy.

Checkpoint: Did you improve your accuracy?

57C
TECHNIQUE TIMING

Tabs: every 15 spaces

Take two 2-minute timings. Tab from column to column. Repeat if time allows.

Goal: To improve keyboarding techniques   12 minutes

Quickly return to home-key position after pressing the tab key.

```
1 acquisition      criticism        privilege
2 alignment        curriculum       proceed
3 argument         defendant        prominent
```

(Continued next page)

**TECHNIQUE
TIMING**

DS or default.

Tab: ¶ or default.

Take two 2-minute
timings.

If time allows, start
again.

Goal: To improve keyboarding techniques   6 minutes

Return to home-key position after tabbing to indent paragraphs.

Our new plans for the company include the
purchase of a site for a storage building.
With your help, we are quite sure we can handle
any problems that might arise.
Please let us know by return mail whether you
will be available.

LESSON 15

Reinforcement

Margins: Default or 1"
Spacing: SS or default   Tab: ¶

15A
WARMUP

Key each line twice.

DS after each pair of
lines.

Goal: To strengthen keyboarding skills   5 minutes

1 We shall; We may; At our; You were; Please let us;
2 practical, possession, parallel, pamphlet, fulfill
3 If you have the information we need, please phone.
4 council put quality why accept never juror thought

| 1 | 2 | 3 | 4 | 5 | 6 | 7 | 8 | 9 | 10 |

15B
**TECHNIQUE
TIMING**

Take a 2-minute tim-
ing on each line.

DS after each timing.

Goal: To improve keyboarding techniques   20 minutes

Release the shift keys quickly and return fingers to home-key position.
1 The curriculum is easy. His criticism is helpful.
2 The taxes are deductible. Your procedure is good.
3 Analyze the grammar. Help with the new alignment.

Reach to the keys with your fingers, not your hands.
4 file page shipment hearing times labor lines paper
5 manager store things health sale enough hand found
6 changes doing entire least title air final men box

Keep your eyes on the textbook copy as you return/enter.
7 eight emblem handle end eye field firm fish handle
8 visual which wish visible wit world via with worth
9 rich profit right rising quantity rocks row signal

56A
GOAL WRITING

Warm up on 53A for 5 minutes.

DS or default.

Take two 3-minute goal writings.

If you finish before time is called, start again.

Record your speed and accuracy.

Goal: To measure timed-writing progress   15 minutes

	1'	3'
Many stores are using computer terminals that allow	11	4
customers to pay for their purchases with a debit card. A	22	7
debit card is used the same way that cash is used except for	35	12
one difference: the money never leaves the bank.	44	15
The debit card is inserted into a terminal that is	55	18
directly linked to the bank where the customer has an	66	22
account. The customer's special code number is entered	77	26
along with the purchase amount. At that exact moment, the	89	30
amount of the purchase is deducted from the customer's	100	33
account and added to the store's account.	108	36

1'	1	2	3	4	5	6	7	8	9	10	11	12	AWL
3'	1			2			3			4			5.7

56B
PRODUCTION MEASUREMENT

Goal: To measure formatting skills   35 minutes

JOB 1

File name: L56B1   DS   Center vertically and horizontally.

Hawaiian Luau
Lomi Lomi Salad
Chicken Hekkaka
Yams Wailea
Poi
Fresh Pineapple Spears
Tropical Fruit Punch

JOB 2

File name: L56B2   DS   Spaces between columns: 12   Center vertically and horizontally.

Statue of Liberty Dimensions

Height from heel to head	111 feet
Length of hand	16 feet
Width of mouth	3 feet
Length of nose	4 feet

JOB 3

File name: L56B3   DS   Spaces between columns: 8   Center vertically and horizontally.

RESIDENT AND NONRESIDENT COLLEGE EXPENSES

Tuition	$1,336.00	$5,962.50
Books and Supplies	357.00	357.00
Activity Fees	280.50	280.50
Room and Board	2,790.75	2,790.75
Clothing	363.37	363.37
Medical	270.50	270.50
Personal	209.75	209.75
Transportation	217.00	647.50
Utilities	103.53	103.53

15C
GOAL WRITING

Take two 2-minute goal writings.

Key each line once. If time allows, start again.

Determine your GWAM.

Goal: To measure timed-writing progress   6 minutes

CUE: Key at a pace that is comfortable for you.

1'

1 The girls will handle the problems with the signs. 10
2 Our auditors told them about the penalty problems. 20
3 The land at the downtown site is not right for us. 30
4 She owns the land where they want to build a home. 40

| 1 | 2 | 3 | 4 | 5 | 6 | 7 | 8 | 9 | 10 |

15D
NEED TO KNOW

Goal: To learn to identify misstrokes   5 minutes

Extra Space — The (nex t) order will reach (you   in) August.

No Space — I checked (theorder;) the goods (arehere.)

Misstroke — Please (wrote) us if you need (informarion).

Transposition — Take (em) to the leaders of his (gruop) now.

E T Strikeover — I am (familar) with the study (the) wrote.

15E
KEYBOARD PRACTICE

Key each line twice.

DS after each pair of lines.

Goal: To practice proper keystroking on handwritten copy   8 minutes

1 As a prominent person, she was very helpful to us.
2 Every defendant lost the argument about procedure.
3 We hope that keyboarding is in the new curriculum.
4 Her criticism was definite and very helpful to us.
5 The new tax assignment showed their keying skills.
6 Yes, I helped analyze the apparent grammar errors.
7 He is your liaison with Beneficial Life Insurance.
8 My note about the interference benefited everyone.

15F
TECHNIQUE TIMING

DS or default.

Tab: ¶ or default.

Take two 2-minute timings.

If you finish before time is called, start again.

Goal: To improve keyboarding techniques   6 minutes

Keep your eyes on the textbook copy as you operate the tab.

We are operating on the theory that you will be able to spend a week with us this month.

If you are not able to change your plans, be sure to let us know by Monday. We can then work out a more convenient time.

55D

TECHNIQUE
TIMING

DS

Left margin: 10 (10
pitch); 18 (12 pitch)

Take two 3-minute
timings.

Goal: To improve keyboarding techniques   8 minutes

Dec Tabs: **E** 15, 31, 51, 74 (10 pitch); 23, 39, 59, 82 (12 pitch)
　　　　　M 7, 22, 42, 65
Regular Tabs: **T** Every 19 spaces

1	1,200	13.34	286.57	106,723
2	500	29.05	93.74	4,895
3	5,600	6.84	340.02	298,456
4	800	23.85	587.99	734,902
5	8,900	45.62	470.87	482,731
6	3,100	57.13	4.63	5,614
7	2,700	8.71	725.48	543,547
8	400	72.82	67.27	67,812

55E

APPLICATION:
TABLES

Goal: To center and key tables   22 minutes

JOB 1

File name: L55E1   DS   Center vertically and
horizontally.

Telephone Manners

Answer promptly and speak clearly

Use a friendly voice

Identify yourself

Speak directly into the phone

Be courteous

Refer to the caller by name

Take messages accurately

End calls pleasantly

JOB 2

File name: L55E2   DS   Spaces between columns: 10
Center vertically and horizontally.

Great Bodies of Water

Pacific Ocean	65 million square miles
Atlantic Ocean	33 million square miles
Indian Ocean	28 million square miles
Arctic Ocean	5 million square miles

JOB 3

File name: L55E3   DS   Spaces between columns: 6
Center vertically and horizontally.

SNOW CARNIVAL ACTIVITIES AND FEES

Ice Sculpting	9 a.m.	$10.00
Ski Jump Competition	9 a.m.	5.00
Snowmobile Race	11 a.m.	5.00
Freestyle Competition	1 p.m.	5.00
Treasure Hunt on Skis	2 p.m.	12.00
Three-Legged Race	3 p.m.	5.00
Hot Dog Skiing	3 p.m.	10.50
Cross Country Race	3 p.m.	5.00
Bathtub Race	4 p.m.	6.50
Bobsled Rides	4 p.m.	6.00
100-Meter Race	5 p.m.	5.00
250-Meter Race	5 p.m.	5.00
Mad Hatter's Ball	8 p.m.	15.00
Winter Banquet	9 p.m.	20.00
Torchlight Parade	11 p.m.	2.00

16A
WARMUP

Key each line twice.

DS after each pair of lines.

Goal: To strengthen keyboarding skills   5 minutes

1 page correspondence directly discussed next family
2 dependent implement questionnaire attendance label
3 He will receive a questionnaire at the restaurant.
4 I believe that Zeke benefited from our attendance.

| 1 | 2 | 3 | 4 | 5 | 6 | 7 | 8 | 9 | 10 |

16B
TECHNIQUE
TIMING

Take a 3-minute timing on each group of lines.

Key each line once. If time allows, start again.

DS after each timing.

Goal: To improve keyboarding techniques   11 minutes

Shift for capital letters with a one-two count.

1 He believes that; You will develop; Your reference
2 At the restaurant; She can describe; The label was
3 Our liaison is; Her dependents are; They benefited

Keep your elbows at your sides and your arms parallel to the keyboard.

4 Address the correspondence to the female advisors.
5 Label the report for all in the department to see.
6 We discussed the possibility of attending classes.

Strike the space bar with a quick, down-and-in motion.

7 lines dozen six lot proper ten terms near tell try
8 hand level once using found item major bring doing
9 also body civic ivory end goals soap visual rising

16C
GOAL WRITING

Take two 2-minute goal writings.

Key each line once.

If time allows, start again.

Determine your GWAM.

Goal: To measure timed-writing progress   5 minutes

CUE: Key at a pace that is comfortable for you.

1′

1 The general public will qualify for the insurance.   10
2 They will handle the problems as their civic duty.   20
3 You should consult them before you visit the site.   30
4 Neither one of them is capable of driving the car.   40

| 1 | 2 | 3 | 4 | 5 | 6 | 7 | 8 | 9 | 10 |

Reinforcement

55A
WARMUP

Key each line twice.
DS after each pair.

"nd" combinations

Goal: To strengthen keyboarding skills   5 minutes

```
1 mend index kindest fund indicate under beyond sender amended
2 Andy and Wanda handle blunders and bungles under the tundra.
3 And we understand that Amanda can handle a second-hand sale.
```

| 1 | 2 | 3 | 4 | 5 | 6 | 7 | 8 | 9 | 10 | 11 | 12 |

55B
SPEED PRACTICE

Take two 30-second
timings on each sen-
tence. Try to increase
your speed on the
second timing.

GWAM = 1' GWAM × 2

Goal: To build keyboarding speed   5 minutes

1'

```
1 Their disks did not come in the mail for almost four months.   12
2 Some of our eight workers are to do their share of the work.   24
3 She sits to the right of the penalty box near our neighbors.   36
4 August is the month when most customers make their payments.   48
```

| 1 | 2 | 3 | 4 | 5 | 6 | 7 | 8 | 9 | 10 | 11 | 12 |

55C
LANGUAGE ARTS

Read the rule in the
box at the right.

Then key each num-
bered sentence, sup-
plying the correct
word (*to, too,* or
two).

Check your work with
the key in Appendix A.

Goal: To review use of *to, too, two*   10 minutes

to	Used before a verb to indicate the infinitive form In the direction of (preposition)
too	In addition to; excessive (adverb)
two	The sum of one plus one (noun)

Examples:

Let's go <u>to</u> lunch; I've made reservations for <u>two</u> at LeTour's.
Franklin and Bryan are much <u>too</u> busy <u>to</u> participate this time.

1. For the past five weeks, I have worked much ___ long each day.
2. Jon said that he, ___, went ___ Florida for ___ weeks in April.
3. If you are ___ tired ___ work, try one or ___ days of vacation.
4. In about ___ or three months, Debbie will travel ___ Rome.
5. Pam said she will need at least ___ chances ___ pass that test.
6. ___ of the supervisors took much ___ long getting the results.
7. The ___ operators had ___ learn a lot about the equipment.
8. If the batter is ___ thin, the cookies will be flat and dry, ___.
9. Martha, Frank, and Lauren want ___ go ___ the play with us.
10. Jonathan said that he, ___, wanted ___ weeks off in September for his
trip ___ Hawaii.

16D
NEED TO KNOW   **Goal: To learn how to identify misstrokes**   6 minutes

Proofreading, or finding misstrokes, is as important as keying accurately. You must be able to find your errors before you can correct them.

In the last two lessons you learned the most common kinds of misstrokes. From now on, identify your misstrokes when directed to do so.

After you complete a timed writing, you need to proofread your keyed text for misstrokes. Use the following guidelines when you are asked to record your speed and accuracy rates. (Practice proofreading using Activity 16C.)

1. Count only one misstroke per word. That is, if a word has two or more misstrokes in it, count the word only once as one misstroke.

2. Treat the spacing and punctuation that follow a word as part of the word. If the spacing or punctuation after a word is incorrect, count the word as a misstroke.

Display Screen Copy

1. Proofread the copy on your display or screen.
2. Identify and record on a separate sheet of paper any words that have misstrokes.

Paper Copy

1. Proofread the copy on your paper.
2. Circle any word in which there is a misstroke. Circle the entire word, not just the letter or space that was keyed incorrectly.

16E
KEYBOARD PRACTICE   **Goal: To practice proper keystroking**   15 minutes

Key each line 3 times.

DS after each group of lines.

1 quaint quart Quaker liquid request require quizzes
2 zero dizzy dozens frozen zoom zoological lazy whiz
3 extra next except exempt excessive exit text exams
4 brand brass brazier Brazil brave brag brace breaks
5 populate popular popcorn population poppy populace
6 action appear artist actual although always amount
7 beginning beacon bought brought bitten better best
8 relax ravine realize recipe recite remedial remain
9 description decision disagree deter definite delay

16F
TECHNIQUE TIMING   **Goal: To improve keyboarding techniques**   8 minutes

DS or default.

Tab: ¶ or default.

Take two 3-minute timings.

If time allows, start again.

Reach to the keys with your fingers, not your hands.

In reference to your questionnaire, I believe you need to label the sections. In my judgment, the heading you use should describe each section.

I also recommend that you try to give better directions at the beginning. If the directions are not clear, you might be disappointed with the responses you receive.

54D
PROJECT PREVIEW

Goal: To key a table that contains decimals   5 minutes

File name: L54D

Use the margins and dec tabs set in 54C.

Key as much as you can in 5 minutes. If you finish, start again.

line 26 ↓ NEW VIDEO RELEASES ᴛꜱ

TV Advertising	108 minutes	$135.50 ᴅꜱ
Newspaper Ads	45 minutes	72.50 ᴅꜱ
Store Displays	120 minutes	215.00 ᴅꜱ
Sales Techniques	57 minutes	165.60 ᴅꜱ
Packaging for Sales	92 minutes	105.75 ᴅꜱ
Use of Color	28 minutes	65.00 ᴅꜱ
Use of Animation	18 minutes	29.50

54E
APPLICATION: TABLES

Goal: To center and key tables   25 minutes

JOB 1

File name: L54E1

DS

Spaces between columns: 10

Center vertically and horizontally.

CUE: Set dec tabs as appropriate.

Texas Population Mix and Growth, 1980–1990

Asian	0.32 million residents	174.0% growth
Black	2.02 million residents	18.2% growth
Hispanic	4.34 million residents	45.3% growth
White	12.77 million residents	14.1% growth
Other	1.80 million residents	55.0% growth

Checkpoint: Did you set dec tabs where appropriate?

JOB 2

File name: L54E2   DS   Spaces between columns: 12
Center vertically and horizontally.

World's Highest Points

Kilimanjaro	19,343.3 feet
Vinson Massif	16,864.2 feet
Mount Everest	29,027.6 feet
Mount Kosciusko	7,309.7 feet
Mount Elbrus	18,510.2 feet
Mount McKinley	20,320.1 feet
Mount Aconcagua	22,833.8 feet

JOB 3

File name: L54E3

Key 54D, making these changes:

1. Arrange the new video releases in alphabetical order.
2. SS
3. Spaces between columns: 8

Checkpoint: Is your job centered vertically and horizontally?

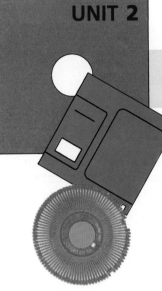

UNIT 2

Number and Symbol Keys

Now that you have learned to key the alphabetic keys by touch, you are ready to become acquainted with the rest of the keyboard. While you continue to improve your skills on the alphabetic keys, you will learn to use the number and symbol keys.

UNIT OBJECTIVES

In this unit, Lessons 17–32, you will:

1. Increase your keyboarding speed and accuracy.
2. Key the number keys by touch.
3. Key the most frequently used symbol keys by touch.
4. Improve keystroking techniques.
5. Locate additional machine parts and use them correctly.
6. Use various machine parts efficiently.
7. Figure your speed on 3-minute timed writings.
8. Continue to identify misstrokes.
9. Use correction techniques to correct misstrokes.

ELECTRONIC CONCEPTS

cursor movement keys (p. 51)	editing (p. 56)	insert (p. 56)
delete (p. 56)	embedded command (p. 49)	memory (p. 53)

LESSON 17

Margins: Default or 1"
Spacing: SS or default   Tab ¶

17A
WARMUP

Key each line twice.
DS after each pair.

Identify misstrokes.

Goal: To strengthen keyboarding skills   5 minutes

```
1 bone, win, snow, wind, hit, cane, van, shoe, rain,
2 maker; moral; youth; silver; fiber; meals; chairs;
3 feast loop text lion rare loom tested lump careers
4 This is a good time of day to sit alone and dream.
  |  1  |  2  |  3  |  4  |  5  |  6  |  7  |  8  |  9  |  10  |
```

54A
WARMUP

Key each line twice.

DS after each pair of lines.

Frequently misspelled words

Goal: To strengthen keyboarding skills   5 minutes

1 occasionally category dependent omitted preferred possession
2 Occasionally, the housing category is dependent on old data.
3 He omitted the fact that I preferred to maintain possession.

| 1 | 2 | 3 | 4 | 5 | 6 | 7 | 8 | 9 | 10 | 11 | 12 |

54B
ACCURACY PRACTICE

DS after each group of lines.

Goal: To build keyboarding accuracy   5 minutes

Take a 2-minute accuracy timing on the lines in 54A. Repeat the timing. Try to improve your accuracy.

Checkpoint: Did you improve your accuracy?

54C
READ AND DO

Goal: To learn how to set decimal tabs   7 minutes

Columns of numbers that contain decimals are usually aligned at the decimal point. Many electronic typewriters and microcomputers have a **decimal tab (dec tab)** feature that automatically aligns numbers at the decimal point.

E M *Electronic Typewriters/Microcomputers*

1. Determine the procedure for setting and clearing decimal tabs for your equipment/software.
2. Determine the key line for the table that you will be keying.
3. Set a dec tab at the decimal position for each column of numbers containing decimals. For any column in which a dec tab is going to be set, space in the necessary spaces/columns to set the dec tab at the correct position.
4. Set a dec tab at the first space after the whole number for columns of numbers without decimals or numbers followed by words (e.g., 91,000 square feet).
5. Set a regular tab for a column that contains words alone or words followed by numbers (such as a date—March 31, 1992).

T *Typewriters*

If you are using an electric typewriter or equipment without the decimal tab feature, begin by determining the key line. Then, set regular tabs for keying all columns, including columns of numbers. Space forward or backward from the tab to align the numbers at the decimal.

Use the key line below to set margins, dec tabs, or regular tabs for the Project Preview in 54D. Leave 6 spaces between columns.

```
LM                                    Dec            Dec
                                      Tab            Tab  RM
     Packaging for Sales123456108minutes123456$135.50
```

17B
TECHNIQUE TIMING

Take a 1-minute timing on each line.

DS after each timing.

Goal: To improve keyboarding techniques   8 minutes

Reach to the keys with your fingers, not your hands.

1 chair maps eight owns widow rich profit firm panel
2 They will market his system in about eight months.
3 quiet zenith xylophone quest zone next quiz xyster

Keep your eyes on the copy as you key.

4 room hello borrow beet lesson better fellow rubber
5 The new bookkeeper is a former employee from here.
6 My car engine overheated on the way to work today.

17C
NEW-KEY ORIENTATION

1. Locate the new key on the keyboard chart and on your keyboard.
2. Practice the first line. Watch your finger reach to the new key and return to home-key position.
3. Take two 1-minute technique timings on the second line. Goal: Eyes on copy.
4. Take a 2-minute technique timing on the third line. Goal: Eyes on copy.

**Goal: To learn the location of and **   12 minutes

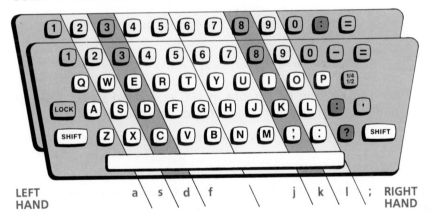

LEFT HAND   a \ s \ d \ f \   j \ k \ l \ ;   RIGHT HAND

Practice striking the : with the **sem** finger. On some keyboards, you have to press the left shift key while striking the :. If so, quickly release the shift key and return the **a** finger to home-key position. *Space twice after a colon used as a mark of punctuation.*

1 ;:; ;:; ;: ;: ;: ;: ;: ;: ;: ;: ;: ;:
2 Dear Sir: Dear Ms. Turner: as follows:
3 Dear David: To: From: Date: Subject:

Practice the reach to ? with the **sem** finger while pressing the left shift key. Quickly release the shift key and return the **a** finger to home-key position. *Space twice after a question mark at the end of a sentence.*

4 ;?; ;?; ;? ;? ;? ;? ;? ;? ;? ;? ;? ;?
5 Are they? Is she? Is it? Why? Where?
6 Can she? Will they? Why not? Are you?

53C

GOAL WRITING

DS or default.

Take two 3-minute goal writings.

If you finish before time is called, start again.

Record your speed and accuracy.

Goal: To measure timed-writing progress   10 minutes

	1'	3'
Long before the days of pen and paper, people relied on	11	4
the use of common objects to communicate and record	22	7
information. For centuries, shepherds kept bags of pebbles	34	11
to keep count of the herd. If an animal was sold or lost, a	46	15
pebble was tossed out. Pebbles were added as the herd grew	58	19
in number. Another means of recording significant events	70	23
during these ancient times was the carved stick. On a	81	27
calendar stick, for example, days were represented by a	92	31
notch and weeks were indicated with a groove.	101	34

AWL	5.7

53D

PROOFREADING PRACTICE

DS

Goal: To practice the use of proofreader's marks   10 minutes

CUE: Review proofreader's marks in 40C, 41D, 42C.

Key the paragraphs in 49C at a rapid speed. Then proofread your copy carefully, marking all corrections with proofreader's marks.

Key a final copy of the paragraphs from your rough-draft copy.

53E

APPLICATION: TABLES

Goal: To center and key tables   15 minutes

JOB 1

File name: L53E1   DS   Spaces between columns: 10
Center vertically and horizontally.

Special Events for June

June Social	Junior Huff and Puff
Newcomers' Welcome	Kids in the Kitchen
Dinner for Dad	Fun in the Sun
Hammer and Nails	Kids' Band
Heyday Cookout	Miniature Golf
Penny Carnival	Olympics in the Park
Afternoon Aerobics	Time for Tykes
Kids' Story Time	Children's Hoe-down
Children's Museum	Country Bake-off
Morning Jog	Field Races
Puppet Palace	Pets on Parade
Horribles Parade	Sight and Sound

JOB 2

File name: L53E2   DS   Spaces between columns: 8
Center vertically and horizontally.

Electric Appliances

radio	microwave	refrigerator
oven	tape recorder	dryer
dishwasher	toaster	television
washer	stereo	water heater
lamp	typewriter	printer
range	clock	video recorder
food processor	iron	microcomputer

17D
KEYBOARD PRACTICE

Key each line 3 times.

DS after each group of lines.

Goal: To practice proper keystroking   9 minutes

CUE: Leave two spaces after the colon and the question mark.

1 Are these they: enclosure, similar, and separate?
2 Can you spell these words: maintenance, employee?
3 Is calendar right? Are library and license right?
4 He spelled enterprise; then he spelled bookkeeper.
5 Did you rekey: eligible, canceled, and mortgages?

Checkpoint: Did you remember to space correctly after all punctuation?

17E
TECHNIQUE TIMING

Take a 1-minute timing on each line.

DS after each timing.

Goal: To improve keyboarding techniques   4 minutes

Do not pause while keying. Keep the carrier/cursor moving.

1 Will Chuck attend? Will he write? Will he speak?
2 Spell these words: calendar, embarrass, mortgage.
3 He reached a decision: namely, he wouldn't do it.

Checkpoint: Did you leave two spaces after the colon and question mark?

17F
READ AND DO

Goal: To learn to operate the backspace key   6 minutes

*Strike the backspace key with the **sem** finger*

The **backspace key** is located at the far right on the top row. The backspace key moves the carrier/cursor back one space each time it is pressed. On some electronic typewriters and microcomputers, the backspace key (labeled **delete** or with a left arrow) deletes charac-

ters as you move back through text. Follow these steps to learn to operate the backspace key.

1. Move your carrier/cursor to the left margin.
2. Key: at end
3. With the **sem** finger, press the backspace key four times. Notice how the carrier/cursor moves back to **d**, then to **n**, then to **e**, and finally to the blank space between the two words. (These letters may be deleted by your equipment.)
4. Strike Ⓣ. Rekey the letters end, if they were deleted. The two words at end are now the word attend.
5. Return/enter and repeat steps 1–4.

JOB 2

File name: L52E2   DS   Spaces between columns: 8
Center vertically and horizontally.

Information Processing Terms

character printer	input
cursor	peripherals
daisy wheel	document
facsimile	global search
output	memory
format line	integrated software
graphics	laser printer
spreadsheet	voice message
database	software
dot-matrix printer	electronic calendar
merge	wraparound
scroll	hard disk
menu	modem
dec tab	mouse
network	monitor
headers	footers

JOB 3

File name: L52E3   SS   Spaces between columns: 6
Center vertically and horizontally.

CUE: Use correct spacing after titles.

Animal Group Terminology

Troop of kangaroos	Leap of leopards
Crash of rhinoceri	Mute of hounds
Drove of cattle	Skulk of foxes
Herd of elephants	Trip of goats
Kindle of kittens	Nest of rabbits
Band of gorillas	Brood of chicks
Pride of lions	Gam of whales
Colony of ants	Gang of elks
Clowder of cats	Litter of pigs
Sounder of swine	Pack of wolves
Sleuth of bears	Pod of seals
Charm of finches	Drift of hogs
Drove of sheep	String of ponies

Checkpoint: Did you use correct spacing after the title?

LESSON 53

Margins: Default or 1"
Spacing: SS or default   Tab: ¶, Center

53A
WARMUP

Goal: To strengthen keyboarding skills 5 minutes

Key each line twice. DS after each pair of lines.

Speed 1 Yes, the girls wish they could spend the entire day with us.
Accuracy 2 More than likely the kennel on the knoll had an iron kettle.
Number/Symbol 3 Four quarts, 1 gallon, and 3.785 liters are identical terms.

| 1 | 2 | 3 | 4 | 5 | 6 | 7 | 8 | 9 | 10 | 11 | 12 |

53B
KEYBOARD COMPOSITION

Use each of the words listed at the right in a complete sentence.

Do not correct errors.

Goal: To compose at the keyboard 10 minutes

1. exercise
2. daily
3. vacations
4. reading
5. cold

6. imagination
7. payday
8. reward
9. taxes
10. warmup

GOAL WRITING

DS or default.

Take two 2-minute goal writings.

Key at a pace that is comfortable for you.

If time allows, start again.

Determine your GWAM.

Goal: To measure timed-writing progress   6 minutes

```
                                                            1'
        Computers are playing a role of importance in      9
all our lives.  Computers are used in car engines,         20
robots, home appliances, and even toys and games.          29
        They are used in hospitals, banks, airports,       39
and stores.  They may even be found in many of our         49
homes today.                                               51
                                                           AWL
|   1   |   2   |   3   |   4   |   5   |   6   |   7   |   8   |   9   |   10   |   5.7
```

LESSON 18

Margins: Default or 1"
Spacing: SS or default   Tab ¶

18A
WARMUP

Key each line twice. DS after each pair of lines.

Identify misstrokes.

Goal: To strengthen keyboarding skills   5 minutes

1 Jane is apt to fix the torn flap if she can do it.
2 That omission was not noticeable to Zelda Jackson.
3 Key these words: bud, dual, eye, name, body, won.
4 Is she the one? What did they say? Will they go?

```
|   1   |   2   |   3   |   4   |   5   |   6   |   7   |   8   |   9   |   10   |
```

18B
TECHNIQUE TIMING

Take a 3-minute timing on each group of lines.

If time allows, start again.

DS between timings.

Goal: To improve keyboarding techniques   8 minutes

Keep your eyes on the copy as you key.

1 Robert was a member of the National Computer Club.
2 The truck Sara drives is from Auto Central Trucks.
3 Sports events will be broadcast by National Radio.
4 Vince had an idea that he sold to Joy Toy Company.

Use a one-two count when shifting for capitals.

5 President Prescott was nominated during September.
6 The voters had lunch at the Happy Days Restaurant.
7 Mrs. Jenkins told Sheila to study harder each day.
8 Our school, Mission Park North, won many trophies.

52C

Goal: To learn how to format tables   5 minutes

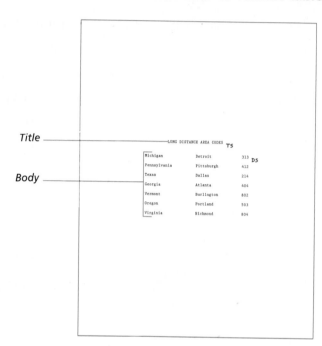

Title

Body

Tables are frequently used in reports, letters, and memos to present a large amount of information in a small amount of space.

1. Center tables vertically and horizontally on the page.
2. Center and key the title in all caps. TS after the title.
3. Format the body of the table in columns. SS or DS the body.
4. Center the columns horizontally, leaving equal space between columns—usually 6-8 spaces.
5. Align columns of words on the left. Align columns of figures on the right or at the decimal points.

Software Alert: If changes in line spacing are difficult or impossible to make with your software, quadruple space (QS) after the heading or title.

52D

TECHNIQUE TIMING

Goal: To improve keyboarding techniques   8 minutes

Keep your eyes on the copy as you tab from column to column.

Left margin: 10 (10 pitch); 18 (12 pitch)

Tabs: Every 19 spaces

Take two 3-minute timings.

1 acquisition	criticism	grammar	prejudice
2 alignment	curriculum	grateful	privilege
3 analyze	deductible	height	procedure
4 apparent	defendant	helpful	proceed
5 argument	definite	hopeful	prominent

52E

APPLICATION: TABLES

Goal: To center and key tables   22 minutes

JOB 1

File name: L52E1

DS

Spaces between columns: 6

Center vertically and horizontally.

American Indians

Navjo	Blackfoot	Shoshone	Arapahoe
Chippewia	Cheyenne	Siuox	Seminole
hopi	Pawnee	apache	Choctaw
Zuni	Mohawk	Ue	winnebago
Haidae	papago	Yuuok	Kark
Cherokee	Creek	Shawnee	chickasaw

(Continued next page)

18C
NEW-KEY ORIENTATION

1. Locate the new key on the keyboard chart and on your keyboard.
2. Practice the first line. Watch your finger reach to the new key and re-turn to home-key position.
3. Take two 1-minute technique timings on the second line. Goal: Eyes on copy.
4. Take a 2-minute technique timing on the third line. Goal: Eyes on copy.

Goal: To learn the location of ⦿ and ⊖   12 minutes

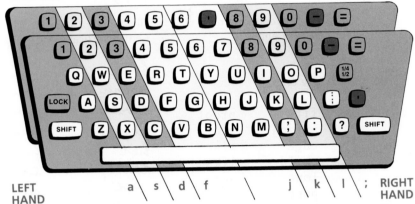

LEFT HAND   a s d f   j k l ;   RIGHT HAND

  KEYBOARD 1: Practice the reach to ⦿ with the **sem** finger. Keep your other fingers in home-key position. *Do not space before or after the apostrophe.*

1 ;'; ;'; ;' ;' ;' ;' ;' ;' ;' ;' ;' ;'
2 it's she's you're can't aren't shouldn't
3 dog's won't isn't Bob's who's Ken's he's

KEYBOARD 2: Practice the reach to ⦿ with the **j** finger while pressing the left shift key. Quickly release the shift key and return the **a** finger to home-key position. *Do not space before or after the apostrophe.*

4 j'j j'j j' j' j' j' j' j' j' j' j' j'
5 won't don't she's can't shouldn't you're
6 car's Vic's hadn't Pat's I'm she's Que's

  Practice the reach to ⊖ with the **sem** finger. Keep your other fingers in home-key position. Do not lift your wrist as you strike ⊖. *Do not space before or after the hyphen.*

7 ;-; ;-; ;- ;- ;- ;- ;- ;- ;- ;- ;- ;-
8 up-to-date seven-page four-way well-read
9 quiet-hand tried-and-true month-by-month

18D
KEYBOARD PRACTICE

Key each line twice.

DS after each pair of lines.

Goal: To practice proper keystroking   6 minutes

1 easy-to-read paper; weren't you; Polly's E-Z Print
2 Jo's and Bob's sales quotas are do-or-die efforts.
3 The red-faced woman is Kate's part-time secretary.
4 Fred's ready-to-print copy solved Paul's problems.
5 Acme's year-end sale features Vi's no-iron shirts.

JOB 2

File name: L51G2   DS   Spaces between columns: 6
Determine the key line. Center vertically and horizontally.

CUE: Clear tabs before setting new ones.

check	book	fire	proof
leader	ship	nation	wide
trust	worthy	edge	wise
bird	house	child	like
care	fully	lone	some
over	confident	post	script
smoke	stack	home	made
hour	glass	camp	ground
sketch	book	horse	shoe
hay	wire	note	book

Checkpoint: Did you use the key line to determine the margins and tab stops?

JOB 3

File name: L51G3   SS   Spaces between columns: 8
Center vertically and horizontally.

busy	busier	busiest
rough	rougher	roughest
lovely	lovelier	loveliest
happy	happier	happiest
hot	hotter	hottest
thin	thinner	thinnest
sad	sadder	saddest
merry	merrier	merriest
happy	happier	happiest
fat	fatter	fattest
strong	stronger	strongest
tall	taller	tallest

LESSON 52

Margins: Default or 1"
Spacing: SS or default   Tab: ¶, Center

52A

WARMUP

Key each line twice.
DS after each pair.

"gh" combinations

Goal: To strengthen keyboarding skills   5 minutes

1 neighborhoods through though thoughts troughs naughty caught
2 Ghent ghost ghastly knight laugh rough high highland brought
3 The right knights brought the light to the old neighborhood.

| 1 | 2 | 3 | 4 | 5 | 6 | 7 | 8 | 9 | 10 | 11 | 12 |

52B

SPEED PRACTICE

Take two 2-minute timings on each paragraph. If you finish before time is called, start again. Try to increase your speed on the second timing.

Goal: To build keyboarding speed   10 minutes

	1'	2'
She is the eighth person to sign the proxy forms that	11	6
entitle me to be the new chairman of the board. That job is	23	12
one with rising problems for each member to think about.	34	17
The winter social kept her busy for about half of the	11	23
month. She spent the other half at the home of her son. I	23	29
did not visit with her or her girls about their work.	34	34

18E
READ AND DO

Do not space before or after a hyphen.

A dash is two hyphens. Do not space between the hyphens or before and after the dash.

Goal: To learn correct spacing for hyphens and dashes   7 minutes

Key these sentences using correct spacing around hyphens and dashes.

1 The up-to-date report--as you know--was completed.
2 His hat--an out-of-date style-- was not attractive.
3 Your two-page memos have been found-- to my relief.
4 Mr. Frye-- the mild-mannered diplomat-- met Marilyn.
5 That day-- Monday--is a happier-than-ever occasion.

18F
READ AND DO

Goal: To learn to key in all capital letters   5 minutes

To key a series of letters or words in all capital letters (ALL CAPS), use the **caps lock** or **shift lock key.** On some software, ALL CAPS is a special command.

1. Press the caps/shift lock key (usually to the left of Ⓐ), or use the ALL CAPS command.
2. Key: FBLA meeting, releasing the caps/shift lock

key or ending the ALL CAPS command before keying meeting.
4. Key: YOUR NAME, pressing and releasing the caps/ shift lock key or beginning and ending the ALL CAPS command where necessary.

18G
TECHNIQUE TIMING

DS or default.

Take two 3-minute timings.

If time allows, start again.

Goal: To improve keyboarding techniques   7 minutes

Do not pause as you move from one paragraph to the next.

Rather than cancel the NACSE meeting, we held it in the UACSE library. The summary is enclosed.

The none-too-competent committee attended the meeting. New employees did not.

LESSON
19

Margins: Default or 1"
Spacing: SS or default   Tab ¶

19A
WARMUP

Key each line twice. DS after each pair of lines.

Identify misstrokes.

Goal: To strengthen keyboarding skills   5 minutes

1 Can he handle the problem if she is not with them?
2 The jury--as you predicted--did high-quality work.
3 Vice President Oveson's all-steel desk isn't here.
4 Sue's reason--and mine also--has to do with money.

| 1 | 2 | 3 | 4 | 5 | 6 | 7 | 8 | 9 | 10 |

51E

APPLICATION: KEY LINE

File name: L51E

Determine the longest line in each column.

Identify and format the key line.

Leave 8 spaces between columns.

Goal: To prepare a key line to use in centering columns   3 minutes

incredible	responsible	possible
convertible	sensible	legible
flexible	susceptible	feasible
visible	terrible	divisible
audible	compatible	credible
accessible	combustible	dirigible
deductible	negligible	edible
impossible	tangible	fallible

Note the position where your typewriter carrier stopped, or keep the document on your screen for use in 51F.

51F

READ AND DO

Goal: To learn how to use the key line to format columns   6 minutes

Key line from 51E

LM   Tab   Tab   RM

convertible12345678responsible12345678divisible

1. Set a left margin or a tab setting for the first column.

E T *Typewriters*

Set the left margin at the point where your carrier stopped in 51E. This is the beginning of Column 1, the position where you will key the *c* of *convertible*.

 Microcomputers

Note the column/space where the left edge of the key line begins. Set your left margin at this point, if your equipment allows. If not, set your left margin at printing. Column 1 starts at *c* of *convertible*.

2. From the position where column 1 begins, move the carrier/cursor forward once for each character in the first column of the key line, including the 8 spaces

to be left between columns. Set a tab for the *r* of *responsible*. Column 2 begins at this point. (Note: You may need to write down the tab settings as you space in from the left.)

3. From the tab stop for column 2, move the carrier/cursor forward once for each character in the second column of the key line plus 8 spaces. Set a tab for the *d* of *divisible*. Column 3 begins at this point.

4. Space to the first space after the *e* in *divisible*. Set the right margin at this point. Your margins and tabs are now set.

5. Check the centering of the key line. If you are using a typewriter, check to see if the left and right margins appear to be equal. On a microcomputer, compare your key line with the margin markers on the ruler/format line.

51G

APPLICATION: COLUMNS

JOB 1

File name: L51G1

DS

Goal: To center columns vertically and horizontally   18 minutes

Key the columns in 51E. You have already selected the key line and determined your margins and tab stops. Determine the starting line to center the columns vertically.

Checkpoint: Does your job appear centered on the page?

(Continued next page)

19B
TECHNIQUE TIMING

Take two 2-minute timings.

Key each line once. Repeat if time allows.

Goal: To improve keyboarding techniques   5 minutes

Keep your eyes on the textbook copy.

```
1 To:  From:  Date:  Subject:  Dear Vic:  Cal:  Tex:
2 Is he here?  Will she go?  Will he sing?  Why not?
3 can't won't didn't couldn't shouldn't doesn't it's
4 One car-care firm--Sav-Mor Auto--was self-insured.
5 WYSIWYG stands for:  WHAT YOU SEE IS WHAT YOU GET.
```

> **Checkpoint:** Did you look up fewer times on the second timing?

19C
NEW-KEY ORIENTATION

1. Locate the new key on the keyboard chart and on your keyboard.
2. Practice the first line. Watch your finger reach to the new key and return to home-key position.
3. Take two 1-minute technique timings on the second line. Goal: Eyes on copy.
4. Take a 2-minute technique timing on the third line. Goal: Eyes on copy.

Goal: To learn the location of " and -   12 minutes

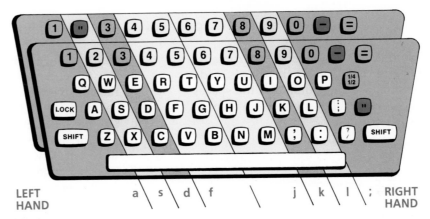

LEFT HAND   a \ s \ d \ f   j \ k \ l \ ;   RIGHT HAND

KEYBOARD 1: Practice the reach to " with the **sem** finger while pressing the left shift key. Keep your other fingers in home-key position. *Do not space between quotation marks and the text within them.*

```
1 ;"; ;"; ;" ;" ;" ;" ;" ;" ;" ;" ;" ;" ;"
2 "his" "were" "them" "she" "duty" "water"
3 an "A" the "word" his "truck" an "eater"
```

KEYBOARD 2: Practice the reach to " with the **s** finger while pressing the right shift key. Keep your other fingers in home-key position. *Do not space between quotation marks and the text within them.*

```
4 s"s s"s s" s" s" s" s" s" s" s" s" s" s"
5 "they" "new" "way" "stop" "stay" "asked"
6 a "cue" the "boy" their "goal" an "urge"
```

(Continued next page)

4. Ms. Whitworth replied, "I don't think ____ a suitable reason."
5. If George thinks ____ hectic now, he won't believe the tax season.
6. A weasel must find ____ way back home through a set of tunnels.
7. Because of ____ great popularity, the rally is held every year.
8. Rodgers asked whether ____ ever happened before at work.
9. ____ going to be one year before ____ time to buy a new car.
10. ____ too bad that Harry can't locate ____ original owner.

51C

ACCURACY PRACTICE

DS after each group of lines.

Goal: To build keyboarding accuracy   5 minutes

Take a 2-minute accuracy timing on the lines in 51A. Repeat the timing. Try to improve your accuracy.

> **Checkpoint:** Did you improve your accuracy?

51D

READ AND DO

Goal: To learn how to identify and format the key line   6 minutes

To center columns of information horizontally, begin by identifying the **key line.** The key line is made up of the longest line in each column and the spaces between columns. Use the following steps to identify and format the key line.

1. Prepare your machine.

E T *Typewriters*

a. Make sure your paper and the paper guide are at 0.
b. Set equal side margins.
c. Clear all tabs.
d. Return the carrier to the left margin.

M *Microcomputers*

a. Clear the screen.
b. Clear all tabs.
c. Move the cursor to the left edge of the screen.
2. Identify and format the key line.

Follow the appropriate steps for your equipment as you identify and format the key line for the example given in this activity.

Equipment with Auto Centering

1. Activate the auto centering function.
2. Enter the key line.

a. Key the longest line in column 1—*committee.*
b. Key the numbers *123456* (or tap the space bar six times)—the number of spaces to be left between columns 1 and 2.
c. Key the longest line in column 2—*privilege.*
d. Key the numbers 123456—the number of spaces to be left between columns 2 and 3.
e. Key the longest line in column 3—*beneficial.*
3. End auto centering and return/enter.

Equipment without Auto Centering

1. Enter the key line. Follow **a** through **e** of step 2 for equipment with auto centering.
2. Return several times.
3. Tab to center.
4. Move the carrier to the left once for every two characters in the key line.

committee	analysis	receipt
probably	privilege	judgment
foreign	truly	eligible
grateful	quantity	beneficial

Key line

committee123456privilege123456beneficial

KEYBOARD 1: Practice the reach to ⊖ with the **sem** finger while pressing the left shift key. Keep your other fingers in home-key position. For lines 8–9, key the word, backspace to the beginning of the word, and then underscore it. **Note:** If you have automatic word underscore or if you need a special command to underscore, skip lines 7–9 and go on to 19D.

7 ;_; ;_; ;_ ;_ ;_ ;_ ;_ ;_ ;_ ;_ ;_ ;_ ;_

8 I; were; no; yes; can; okay; joke; your;

9 zebras; questions; x-ray; Mexican; Zeda;

19D E M
READ AND DO
Goal: To learn to underscore using commands 5 minutes

E *Electronic Typewriters*

Some electronic typewriters have an **automatic underscore** feature. By pressing a key or using a special command, a word or a series of words is underscored automatically.

Determine the appropriate method to underscore for your equipment. Then follow these steps:

1. Key the following, inserting the appropriate underscore command: The Wall Street Journal.
2. Look at the line on your paper. It should appear as: The Wall Street Journal.

M *Microcomputers*

On some software packages, underscoring may require an **embedded command** to the printer. Begin the command before keying the first letter to be under-

scored, and end the command after the last letter to be underscored. The underscore may not show on your screen, but it will appear in the printed copy.

For example, text to be underscored may appear on the screen as: *Gone with the Wind*. However, the same line will print: Gone with the Wind.

Determine the appropriate method to underscore for your equipment. Then follow these steps:

1. Key the following, inserting the underscore commands at the beginning and end: The Wall Street Journal.
2. Look at your screen. Notice if the codes for the underscore appear.
3. When printed, the keyed line should appear as: The Wall Street Journal.

19E
KEYBOARD PRACTICE

Key each line twice.

DS after each pair of lines.

Goal: To practice proper keystroking 5 minutes

1 Michael said, "Yes, she will need a new car soon."
2 Janet will surely have to read Gone with the Wind.
3 Jared said, "The One-Minute Manager is the title."
4 The supervisor said, "Get this in the mail today."

19F
TECHNIQUE TIMING

DS or default.

Take two 2-minute timings.

If time allows, start again.

Goal: To improve keyboarding techniques 5 minutes

Reach with your fingers, not your hands.

1 Determine the part of speech needed for each word.
2 If a verb is necessary, affect is usually correct.
3 The word effect is appropriate if you need a noun.
4 Determine whether they should use the word affect.

APPLICATION:
COLUMNS

Goal: To key centered columns 17 minutes

JOB 1

File name: L50F1   DS   Left margin: 10 (10 pitch); 18 (12 pitch)   Tabs: Every 20 spaces   Center vertically.

78 dogs	about 78	789 more	8,889
98 birds	around 89	879 times	7,779
17 flies	inside 16	521 drums	5,156
34 cats	under 22	234 orders	3,324
23 snakes	over 43	432 books	4,233
65 ants	below 35	274 pens	6,918
93 mice	after 74	497 desks	9,438

JOB 2

File name: L50F2   DS   Left margin: 10 (10 pitch); 18 (12 pitch)   Tabs: Every 18 spaces   Center vertically.

admit	admitted	allot	allotted
commit	committed	compel	compeled
confer	conferred	control	controlled
dipel	dispelled	equip	equipped
excele	excelled	fit	fited
infer	infered	omit	omitted
permit	permitted	refer	referred

LESSON 51

Margins: Default or 1″
Spacing: SS or default   Tab: ¶, Center

51A

WARMUP

Goal: To strengthen keyboarding skills 5 minutes

Key each line twice.

DS after each pair of lines.

Frequently misspelled words

1 analysis license receipt necessary probably develop familiar
2 You are probably familiar with such necessary receipt forms.
3 In his analysis, he developed a theory of familiar licenses.

| 1 | 2 | 3 | 4 | 5 | 6 | 7 | 8 | 9 | 10 | 11 | 12 |

51B

LANGUAGE ARTS

Goal: To review use of *it's* and *its* 7 minutes

Read the rule in the box at the right.

Then key each numbered sentence, supplying the correct word (*it's* or *its*).

Check your work with the key in Appendix A.

it's	Contraction of *it is* and *it has*
its	Possessive form of the pronoun *it*

Examples:

I think <u>it's</u> too bad Margaret's class ring has lost <u>its</u> stone.
If <u>it's</u> to be truly legal, <u>its</u> owner must first get a license.

1. Because of ____ value, the museum doubled ____ security.
2. Do you remember if ____ ever been awarded to their accountant?
3. A bird always makes ____ home in a relatively safe spot.

(Continued next page)

19G
NEED TO KNOW

Read the information at the right.

Goal: To learn how to use double word scales   3 minutes

Beginning with this lesson, you will take 3-minute goal writings. The word scales shown for the goal writing are double word scales; that is, they give GWAM (Gross Words A Minute) for both 1-minute and 3-minute timed writings. Look at the word scales in 19H. The 1-minute scales at the side and bottom of the goal writing are printed in red. The 3-minute scales are printed in black.

To determine your GWAM on 3-minute goal writings, use the 3-minute side and bottom word scales. First, find the cumulative word count in the 3-minute side word scale for the last complete line you keyed. Then, use the 3-minute bottom word scale to determine the number of words in any incomplete line. Add these two numbers to determine your 3-minute GWAM.

19H
GOAL WRITING

DS or default.

Take two 3-minute goal writings.

Key at a pace that is comfortable for you.

If time allows, start again.

Determine your GWAM.

Goal: To measure timed-writing progress   10 minutes

	1'	3'
Keying by touch means that you are capable of	9	3
striking the keys without looking at your fingers.	20	7
A distinctive trait of outstanding keyboarders is	30	10
their ability to key by touch.	36	12
You presently should be keying nearly all of	45	15
your work by touch. Seldom should you have to	54	18
glance at your fingers. Instances when you have	64	21
to look down should be few and far between.	73	24

1' | 1 | 2 | 3 | 4 | 5 | 6 | 7 | 8 | 9 | 10 | AWL
3' | 1 | 2 | 3 | 5.7

LESSON	
20	**Reinforcement**

Margins: Default or 1"
Spacing: SS or default   Tab ¶

20A
WARMUP

Key each line twice. DS after each pair of lines.

Identify misstrokes.

Goal: To strengthen keyboarding skills   5 minutes

1 The usual penalty paid by the audit firm is small.
2 The effect--as I predicted--was a four-page issue.
3 James said, "Wasn't one group affected--the NLRB?"
4 Its effects are two: one-day service and quality.

| 1 | 2 | 3 | 4 | 5 | 6 | 7 | 8 | 9 | 10 |

50B
GOAL WRITING

DS or default.

Take two 3-minute goal writings.

If you finish before time is called, start again.

Record your speed and accuracy.

Goal: To measure timed-writing progress   10 minutes

	1'	3'
For many of us, the telephone is a necessary evil. We	11	4
need the telephone at home and at work, but we pay a price.	23	8
Lost telephone messages, telephone tag, and missed telephone	35	12
calls are a constant source of wasted time and frustration.	47	16
A telephone answering machine is one solution to this	58	19
dilemma, but it also has a price. Many callers find the	70	23
machine impersonal and refuse to talk to it. To help the	81	27
caller, owners are using cleverly taped messages. The	92	31
caller is disarmed by the message and talks to the machine.	104	35

1' | 1 | 2 | 3 | 4 | 5 | 6 | 7 | 8 | 9 | 10 | 11 | 12 | AWL
3' | 1 | 2 | 3 | 4 | 5.7

50C
KEYBOARD COMPOSITION

Use each of the words or phrases listed at the right in a complete sentence.

Goal: To compose at the keyboard   7 minutes

1. printer
2. format changes
3. keyboard
4. accurate
5. corrections
6. software
7. concentration
8. computer
9. screen
10. discipline

50D
TECHNIQUE TIMING

DS

Left margin: 10 (10 pitch); 18 (12 pitch)

Tabs: Every 18 spaces

Key as many lines as you can in 4 minutes.

Goal: To improve keyboarding techniques   6 minutes

Use the tab key to move from one column to the next.

1 absence   concede   explanation   opportunity
2 pamphlet   familiar   occurrence   accessible
3 feasibility   parallel   consensus   accommodate
4 acquaintance practical   convenience   fulfill

50E
SELF-CHECK

Key the statement number and your answer: True or False.

Check your answers in Appendix B.

Goal: To review keying columns of information   5 minutes

1. Column format makes text easier to read.
2. When keying columns of information, key down each column before tabulating to the next column.
3. Clear all tab stops before setting new tab stops.
4. Space with the space bar to move to a new column.
5. Information is often keyed in columns because columns provide a more attractive format.
6. Press the tab clear key to set new tab stops.

20B

TECHNIQUE TIMING

Take two 2-minute timings on each group of lines.

If time allows, start again.

DS after each timing.

Goal: To improve keyboarding techniques   14 minutes

Keep your eyes on the copy as you key hyphens and dashes.

1 I will advise you when our open-stock sale begins.
2 Our advice--and it is advice only--is to sell now.
3 I advise you to seek high-level advice from Jones.

Keep wrists low, but not touching the keyboard.

4 The jeep is serviceable, but it needs maintenance.
5 That license is similar, but it has been canceled.
6 The bookkeeper sent this mortgage to that library.

Key easy stroke combinations rapidly; slow down for difficult combinations.

7 manual method nature road save checks machines its
8 teachers told worked brought code enjoyed valuable
9 informed indeed move persons release accounts late

| 1 | 2 | 3 | 4 | 5 | 6 | 7 | 8 | 9 | 10 |

20C E M

NEED TO KNOW

Goal: To learn about cursor movement   3 minutes

Most equipment has **cursor movement keys** that are usually labeled with arrows. Other equipment may vary.

Determine the cursor movement keys or commands that enable you to move the cursor on your equipment.

20D

LANGUAGE ARTS

Read the rule in the box.

Then key the sentences, underlining all common nouns.

Check your work with the key in Appendix A.

Goal: To review rules for capitalization   6 minutes

A common noun names a person, place, thing, or idea in a general class. A common noun is not capitalized unless it begins a sentence.

Examples:

The teacher and students were completely surprised.
The new computers, printers, and software are in that room.

1 The concert was well attended.
2 The children played games and broke balloons.
3 Do you plan to attend the seminar with Nancy?
4 He spoke to the attorney and to Judge Blackburn.
5 Baseball and dancing are her favorite activities.

49F

TECHNIQUE TIMING

DS

Left margin: 10 (10 pitch); 18 (12 pitch)

Tabs: Every 19 spaces

Take two 2-minute timings.

Goal: To improve keyboarding techniques   6 minutes

Anchor the *s* finger when reaching for the tab key.

1	absence	consensus	fulfill	parallel
2	analyze	curriculum	grammar	privilege
3	benefited	dependent	judgment	recommend
4	calendar	embarrass	license	similar
5	competent	exaggerate	occurrence	supersede

49G

APPLICATION: COLUMNS

Goal: To key centered columns   15 minutes

JOB 1

File name: L49G1   DS   Left margin: 10 (10 pitch); 18 (12 pitch)   Tabs: Every 19 spaces   Center vertically.

farther	further	peace	piece
lean	lien	reality	realty
miner	minor	scene	seen
defer	differ	vary	very
incite	insight	precede	proceed
lessen	lesson	quiet	quite
overdo	overdue	shear	sheer

JOB 2

File name: L49G2   DS   Left margin: 10 (10 pitch); 18 (12 pitch)   Tabs: Every 20 spaces   Center vertically.

32	3015	52	26721
41	2977	86	39443
59	4369	91	50309
62	5820	43	78612
47	3941	24	91821
89	7353	75	63592
72	1802	98	67103

JOB 3

File name: L49G3

Key the information given in the Project Preview, 49E, SS. Center the information vertically.

LESSON 50

50A

WARMUP

Goal: To strengthen keyboarding skills   5 minutes

Key each line twice. DS after each pair of lines.

Speed 1 The auditor may have the right form by the end of the month.
Accuracy 2 In my opinion, the slope operator was cropping the top crop.
Number/Symbol 3 One square foot is equivalent to 929.030 square centimeters.

| 1 | 2 | 3 | 4 | 5 | 6 | 7 | 8 | 9 | 10 | 11 | 12 |

**KEYBOARD
PRACTICE**

Key each line 3 times.

DS after each group
of lines.

Goal: To practice proper keystroking   8 minutes

CUE: Use correct spacing after punctuation marks.

1 Do you think the best gymnast is Jon, Cal, or Lee?
2 Is F. K. Simmons here? What about Ray M. Western?
3 We are finished. They can do the report tomorrow.
4 Tell Harris to see me; I will advise him properly.
5 Who won? Who lost? I don't know; ask the others.

20F

READ AND DO

Do not space be-
tween quotation
marks and the
text within them.

When quotation
marks follow
punctuation, use
the spacing that
applies to the
punctuation.

Goal: To learn the spacing before and after quotation marks   4 minutes

Key these sentences using the correct spacing around quotation marks.
1 He said, "I will." "I am unable to go," she said.
2 "The plan of action," he said, "is to do the job."
3 Joe said, "Get the job done." I did what I could.
4 "Buy low; sell high," said Sue. "That's my rule."

20G

**TECHNIQUE
TIMING**

Take two 2-minute
timings on each
group of lines.

DS after each timing.

Goal: To improve keyboarding techniques   10 minutes

Key handwritten copy without pausing.
1 Michelle is proficient in keying handwritten copy.
2 Twenty people made their last-minute reservations.
3 The blue-gray suit looks better than the rust one.
4 Is the up-to-date summary of your meeting concise?

Reach to the keys with your fingers, not your hands.
5 He delivered an excellent presentation to brokers.
6 How did you plan to get to the late meeting place?
7 Were you able to key more quickly the second time?
8 The reservations have already been made for Ronda.

49C

GOAL WRITING

Goal: To measure timed-writing progress 10 minutes

DS or default.

Take two 3-minute goal writings.

If you finish before time is called, start again.

Record your speed and accuracy.

		1'	3'
When considering acquiring a pet, take care to select		11	4
a pet that is appropriate for your lifestyle.		20	7
The kind of residence you live in and where you live		31	10
should influence the kind of pet you consider. For		41	14
instance, the size of your home should be a determining		53	18
factor in deciding the size of dog that you select.		63	21
Another factor in selecting a pet is the time allotted		74	25
to it. If you are gone extensively, you should understand		86	29
that dogs suffer from loneliness, whereas cats might not.		97	32

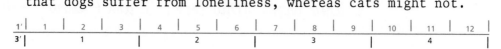

```
1'| 1  | 2  | 3  | 4  | 5  | 6  | 7  | 8  | 9  | 10  | 11  | 12  |   AWL
3'|       1        |        2       |        3        |       4        |   5.7
```

49D

NEED TO KNOW

Goal: To learn how to key columns of information 4 minutes

Information is often arranged in column format. Columns provide a more attractive format and make the copy easier to read.

E T *Typewriters*

1. Set the paper guide at 0.
2. Clear all tab stops.
3. Set equal side margins.
4. Move the carrier to the required tab positions and set tab stops.
5. Tab across the page to make sure all tabs are set correctly.
6. Press the return key as many times as necessary to move down to the starting line of the document.
7. Key the information across the page. Use the tab key to move from one column to the next.

M *Microcomputers*

1. Move cursor to first column/space on screen.

2. Clear all tab stops, using the procedure for your software.
3. Set new tab stops. The two most common methods of setting tab stops are:
   a. Access the **ruler/format line** that is displayed across the top or the bottom of the screen. Move the cursor to the first desired tab position. Press the appropriate key for setting tabs (usually the tab key or the letter **T**). Repeat this procedure to set the remaining tab stops.
   b. Give the tab set command. When the prompt asks for a column number, key the column number for the first tab setting. Repeat this procedure to set the remaining tab stops.
4. Press return/enter to move the cursor to the line on which the document is to begin.
5. Key the information across the page. Use the tab key to move from one column to the next.

49E

PROJECT PREVIEW

Goal: To key columns of words 5 minutes

DS

Left margin: 10 (10 pitch; 18 (12 pitch)

Tabs: Every 19 spaces

Key as much as you can in 3 minutes.

line 13 ↓	Tab→	Tab→	Tab→
careful	envelope	necessary	supersede
category	equipped	noticeable	temporary
committee	equivalent	occasion	thorough
comparative	exaggerate	occurrence	omission
competent	excellent	withholding	yield

21A
WARMUP

Key each line twice.
DS after each pair.

Identify misstrokes.

Goal: To strengthen keyboarding skills   5 minutes

1 She said they wish to visit downtown and the lake.
2 Quinn said, "Has anyone read The Laughable Clown?"
3 Any one of the following will do: SE, SW, or SSW.
4 Is anyone's birthday on the same day as Cameron's?

| 1 | 2 | 3 | 4 | 5 | 6 | 7 | 8 | 9 | 10 |

21B
SPEED PRACTICE

Take a 20- or 15-second timing on each line. If you complete a line in the time allowed, go on to the next one.

Goal: To build keyboarding speed   5 minutes

	GWAM	
	20"	15"
1 Both rich men have the emblem.	18	24
2 Penalty times go with our problems.	21	28
3 Elvis got big profits for the ivory die.	24	32
4 The rigid auditor got the firm to lend daily.	27	36

| 1 | 2 | 3 | 4 | 5 | 6 | 7 | 8 | 9 |

21C
READ AND DO

Goal: To learn to correct misstrokes   6 minutes

Read the appropriate instructions for correcting on your equipment. Then, complete these steps:

1. At the left margin, key teh student.
2. Change teh to the.

Equipment with Display

Some equipment enables you to replace incorrect characters by keying over them. Other equipment requires you to delete the incorrect characters and then insert the corrections. Determine the appropriate procedure for your equipment or software.

Equipment with Correction Memory

Correction memory enables you to automatically correct errors made within memory. Backspace to the error, then press the **correction/cancel key** to delete incorrect characters. After you key the correct characters, press the **relocate key** (if available) to return the carrier to the next keying position.

Equipment with Correction Keys

Use the backspace key to move back to the error. Press the backspace correction key to delete the incorrect characters. Then, key the correct characters. On some equipment, you may have to strike over the incorrect characters to delete them.

Equipment without Correction Keys

Special correction paper or correction fluid may be used to correct misstrokes.

To use correction paper, position the carrier at the misstroke, place the correction paper over the misstroke, chalky/sticky side against the paper. Strike the incorrect character, remove the correction paper, backspace, and strike the correct character.

To use correction fluid, move the paper up, shake the bottle of fluid well, then *lightly* brush the fluid on the misstroke. When the correction is dry, return your paper to the correct position and key the correct character.

APPLICATION:
CENTERING

Goal: To center lines vertically and horizontally   22 minutes

JOB 1

File name: L48F1   DS

Key the example in 48D for which you determined the starting line. Center each line horizontally.

JOB 2

File name: L48F2   DS   Center the lines vertically and horizontally.

```
The Conservative Business Look

Navy, black, or dark gray suit or dress
White shirt or blouse
Red tie or scarf
Black or dark gray shoes
Dark socks or neutral hosiery
Neat, clean, and styled hair
Well-groomed nails
```

JOB 3

File name: L48F3   DS   Center the lines vertically and horizontally.

```
Ways to IMPROVE YOUR VOCABULARY
Play vocabulary games
Drill by using vocabulary crads
Use a thesaurus when you rite
Do crossword puzzels
KEEP a list of knew wrods as you read
use words in a sentence
Adde a new word to your vocabulary every
```

Checkpoint: Does your copy appear centered on the page?

LESSON

49

Margins: Default or 1"
Spacing: SS or default   Tab: ¶, Center

49A
WARMUP

Goal: To strengthen keyboarding skills   5 minutes

Key each line twice. DS after each pair of lines.

Speed
Accuracy
Number/Symbol

1 Paul may want to thank the printers for the time they spent.
2 The small, quiet squirrel squinted quite uniquely at a bird.
3 They cut the lumber into 10-foot lengths (6 3/4" x 10 3/4").

| 1 | 2 | 3 | 4 | 5 | 6 | 7 | 8 | 9 | 10 | 11 | 12 |

49B
ACCURACY
PRACTICE

DS after each group of lines.

Goal: To build keyboarding accuracy   5 minutes

Take a 2-minute accuracy timing on the lines in 49A. Repeat the timing. Try to improve your accuracy.

Checkpoint: Did you improve your accuracy?

21D
TECHNIQUE TIMING

Take two 3-minute timings on each group of lines.

DS after each timing.

Goal: To improve keyboarding techniques 14 minutes

Keep your eyes on the textbook copy.

1 Everyone--and I mean everyone--is welcome to come.
2 Key these words: we're, they're, you're, there's.
3 My gross-words-per-minute rate is "above average."
4 There is no such thing as a free lunch--TINSTAAFL.

Reach to the keys with your fingers; do not move your whole hand.

5 The Zealous Quest is Lexie Xavier's autobiography.
6 Why do we need to buy a state-of-the-art computer?
7 He asked, "Didn't I win?" I replied, "Who cares?"
8 Key five words: auto, lend, foam, rock, and pays.

21E
KEYBOARD PRACTICE

DS or default.

Key each line twice.
DS after each pair.

Repeat if time allows.

Goal: To practice proper keystroking 8 minutes

1 Buy two books: Principles of Health and The King.
2 Don't lose sight of their firm's annual objective.
3 Principal Hanson taught "botany principles" today.
4 "Yes, Red McGraw is loose again," said the warden.

21F
GOAL WRITING

DS or default.

Take two 3-minute goal writings.

Key at a pace that is comfortable for you.

If time allows, start again.

Determine your GWAM.

Goal: To measure timed-writing progress 10 minutes

	1	3'
Although rainfall is measured in several	8	3
ways, the most commonly used measuring instrument	18	6
is the rain gauge, which is a cylinder containing	28	9
a funnel on top and a narrow tube inside.	37	12
The total moisture collected by a network of	46	15
rain gauges at periods throughout the year is	55	18
used to compute the annual amount of moisture for	65	22
a region in a given year.	70	23

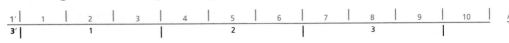

1' | 1 | 2 | 3 | 4 | 5 | 6 | 7 | 8 | 9 | 10 | AWL
3' | 1 | 2 | 3 | 5.7

48C

NEED TO KNOW   **Goal:** To learn about spacing between lines of text   6 minutes

Single-Spaced Lines	*Double-Spaced Lines*	*Triple-Spaced Lines*	*Quadruple-Spaced Lines*

Single-Spaced Lines

1 Denver Chorale ss
2 Spring Festival
3 May 5, 7:30 p.m.
4 Palace Theatre

When you SS, no blank lines are left between the keyed lines.

Double-Spaced Lines

1 Denver Chorale DS
2
3 Spring Festival
4
5 May 5, 7:30 p.m.
6
7 Palace Theatre

When you DS, one blank line is left between the keyed lines.

Triple-Spaced Lines

1 Denver Chorale TS
2
3
4 Spring Festival
5
6
7 May 5, 7:30 p.m.
8
9
10 Palace Theatre

When you TS, two blank lines are left between the keyed lines.

Quadruple-Spaced Lines

1 Denver Chorale QS
2
3
4
5 Spring Festival
6
7
8
9 May 5, 7:30 p.m.
10
11
12
13 Palace Theatre

When you QS, three blank lines are left between the keyed lines.

48D

READ AND DO   **Goal:** To learn how to center lines vertically   7 minutes

1   Open House
2
3   Saturday
4
5   December 5
6
7   1–5 p.m.
8
9   Aspen Room
10
11 Fallbrook Inn
12
13   Snowmass

1. Count the number of text and blank lines in the copy to be keyed at the left (1 blank line is left when you DS lines).

   13 lines used

2. Subtract the total number of used lines from 66.

   66
   −13 used lines
   53 unused lines (top/bottom margin)

3. Divide by 2. Disregard any fraction.

   53 ÷ 2 = 26 blank lines

4. Add 1 line. (The first line of text will be on line 27, leaving 26 blank lines for the top margin.)

   26 + 1 = 27 (first line of text)

5. Start keying on the 27th line from the top edge of the paper/screen.

E **M** *Electronic Typewriters/Microcomputers*

Remember to include the default top margin in the 27 lines.

48E

SELF-CHECK   **Goal:** To review line spacing   5 minutes

Key the statement number and your answer.

Check your answers in Appendix B.

1. When you DS lines of text, _____ blank line is left between the keyed lines.
2. When you QS lines of text, _____ blank lines are left between the keyed lines.
3. When you SS lines of text, _____ blank lines are left between the keyed lines.
4. When you TS lines of text, _____ blank lines are left between the keyed lines.
5. Always _____ after keying a title.
6. To vertically center a job containing 12 lines of text that are DS, begin keying on line _____.

22A
WARMUP

Key each line twice.
DS after each pair of lines.

Identify misstrokes.

Goal: To strengthen keyboarding skills   5 minutes

1 Rod may wish to pay for the visit when he is paid.
2 If they do lose the game, will anyone be affected?
3 Her advice is good; every one of them understands.
4 I can't dispute any one of the principal findings.

| 1 | 2 | 3 | 4 | 5 | 6 | 7 | 8 | 9 | 10 |

22B
ACCURACY PRACTICE

DS after each group of lines.

Goal: To build keyboarding accuracy   5 minutes

Take a 2-minute accuracy timing on the lines in 22A. Repeat the timing. Try to improve your accuracy.

Checkpoint: Did you improve your accuracy?

22C
GOAL WRITING

DS or default.

Take two 3-minute goal writings.

Key at a pace that is comfortable for you.

If time allows, start again.

Determine your GWAM.

Goal: To measure timed-writing progress   10 minutes

	1'	3'
Gold and silver were once the most common	9	3
forms of money. Today, however, money consists	18	6
mostly of paper money and coins.	25	8
Paper money itself has little value. People	34	11
accept the paper as a medium of exchange for work	44	15
or goods because they know that others will take	54	18
the paper in exchange for the things desired and	64	21
that the government will back the paper with gold.	74	25

1' | 1 | 2 | 3 | 4 | 5 | 6 | 7 | 8 | 9 | 10 | AWL
3' | 1 | | 2 | | 3 | | 5.7

22D
KEYBOARD PRACTICE

Key each line 3 times.

DS after each group of lines.

Goal: To practice proper keystroking   9 minutes

1 sit oak sod pen wit die rug and big the key handle
2 Do they have a problem if the auditor comes today?
3 Be sure that you sign your name on the right form.
4 than with that both held worn auto dual fish girls
5 Half of the boys went to the city in the new auto.

APPLICATION: CENTERING   **Goal: To key centered documents with headings**   15 minutes

JOB 1

File name: L47G1   DS   Start keying: Line 26
Center each line horizontally.

> **CUE:** Center and key the title in all caps. TS after the title.

Precautions for VDT Operators
Reduce glare from windows or lights
Change the tilt of the screen
Lower the height of the screen
Adjust your chair to a comfortable height
Position reference books close by
Take a break every two hours
Have your eyes examined annually

JOB 2

File name: L47G2   DS   Start keying: Line 27
Center each line horizontally.

Study procedures

Schedul*e* a regular time *#* to study

Be ___ fresh and ready *to* learn

Find a ~~nice~~ quiet place

Use *a* la*a*rge flat w*ro*k sur face

keep reference *materials* handy

Sum marize each sect*io*n read

> **Checkpoint:** Did you center and key the title in all caps with a TS after it?

Margins: Default or 1″
Spacing: SS or default: Tab: ¶, Center

48A
WARMUP

Key each line twice.
DS after each pair.

"tw" and "cc" combinations

Goal: To strengthen keyboarding skills   5 minutes

1 twist twine twinkle two twice twirl twelve twenty twig twang
2 soccer account occupied accounting eccentric accident occurs
3 Twirl around twins at twelve. Accept the accidental twinkle.

| 1 | 2 | 3 | 4 | 5 | 6 | 7 | 8 | 9 | 10 | 11 | 12 |

48B
SPEED PRACTICE

Take a 20- or 15-second timing on each line. If you complete a line in the time allowed, go on to the next one.

Goal: To build keyboarding speed   5 minutes

	GWAM
	20″ | 15″

1 Use single spacing for those memos.   21 \| 28
2 James is renting their ranch to the men.   24 \| 32
3 The third invention does not merit your time. 27 \| 36
4 Without question, he is a mature and famous coach. 30 \| 40

| 1 | 2 | 3 | 4 | 5 | 6 | 7 | 8 | 9 | 10 |

22E
NEED TO KNOW

Goal: To learn how to edit text   5 minutes

Editing is the process of making changes in text by inserting or deleting text.

Deleting Text

1. To **delete** unwanted text, move the cursor to where you want to begin deleting.
2. Using the appropriate delete key or delete command, delete all unwanted text. The text to the right automatically moves left to fill the space left by the deleted text.

Inserting Text

1. To **insert** new text, move the cursor to where you want to begin inserting.
2. Using the appropriate insert key or insert command, key the new text. The remaining text automatically moves right to allow for new text.
3. When you have finished inserting, use the appropriate key or command to end the insert mode.

22F
SELF-CHECK

Read each statement. On a sheet of paper, key the statement letter and indicate whether the statement is true or false.

Check your answers in Appendix B.

Goal: To review spacing rules   8 minutes

a. A dash is made by keying *hyphen, space, hyphen.*
b. Space once after a colon within a sentence.
c. When quotation marks follow punctuation, use the spacing that applies to the mark of punctuation.
d. Space once after a period that ends a sentence.
e. Space twice after a semicolon within a sentence.
f. Space once after a period within an abbreviation.

22G
TECHNIQUE TIMING

Take two 3-minute timings.

Key each line once. Repeat if time allows.

DS after each timing.

Goal: To improve keyboarding techniques   8 minutes

Keep your eyes on the textbook copy.

1 Paul asked, "Why?" "Because," replied his friend.
2 Can't we buy the EPROM chips from New-Age Systems?
3 Use this phrase: drip-dry, ready-to-wear clothes.
4 Sarah Norma Chris Kevin Fred Louis David Lars Rick

LESSON
23

Margins: Default or 1"
Spacing: SS or default   Tab ¶

23A
WARMUP

Key each line twice. DS after each pair of lines.

Identify misstrokes.

Goal: To strengthen keyboarding skills   5 minutes

1 The big quake did shake the car, but it held firm.
2 The devices--all four of them--have been patented.
3 He said, "I must read The Car--An Amazing Device."
4 The device is new; Jane devised it in record time.

| 1 | 2 | 3 | 4 | 5 | 6 | 7 | 8 | 9 | 10 |

47D

LANGUAGE ARTS

Key the sentences at the right. Apply rules of capitalization and word division as needed.

Review:

20D, 24E, 38C, 39C, 41B, 43D

Check your work with the key in Appendix A.

Goal: To review capitalization and word division rules   8 minutes

1. Ann green attends green valley community college.
2. On monday, april 15, richard dannon will speak here.
3. John works for educational computer systems of america, inc.
4. They work on all Holidays, even christmas and easter.
5. Their working hours are 9–5:30, monday through saturday.
6. My work at the Hospital will be finished in august.
7. The words *many, staff,* and *along* (can/cannot) be divided.
8. You (should/should not) divide the names of holidays.
9. You (should/should not) divide the names of people.
10. You (should/should not) divide a number.

47E

NEED TO KNOW

Refer to the illustration at the right as you read about the format for headings and titles.

Goal: To learn how to format headings and titles   3 minutes

A heading or **title** identifies the information that it introduces.

1. Center the heading or title horizontally.
2. Key the heading or title in all caps.
3. Triple space (TS) after the heading or title.
4. Double space (DS) or single space (SS) between the other lines as indicated in the directions.

Software Alert: If changes in line spacing are difficult or impossible to make with your software, quadruple space (QS) after the heading or title.

47F

PROJECT PREVIEW

File name: L47F

Center each line horizontally.

Key as much as you can in 5 minutes.

If you finish before time is called, TS and start again.

Goal: To key a centered project with a heading   7 minutes

Line 26↓ QUALITIES OF AN ENTREPRENEUR $_{TS}$

High need for achievement $_{DS}$

Self-sufficient $_{DS}$

Independent $_{DS}$

Natural or developed leadership qualities $_{DS}$

High level of energy $_{DS}$

Sound business judgment $_{DS}$

Honest

23B
TECHNIQUE TIMING

Take two 2-minute timings.

If time allows, start again.

DS after each timing.

Goal: To improve keyboarding techniques   5 minutes

Key easy stroke combinations rapidly; slow down for difficult ones.

1 Their office staff has already completed the exam.
2 Bob and Lynn are all ready to attend the meetings.
3 Jack is all ready to review the contract tomorrow.
4 Nedra, Michael, and Rex will already be in Dallas.
5 They will lose that game if we modify our offense.
6 If they can get away, they can join us for dinner.

23C
NEW-KEY ORIENTATION

1. Locate the new key on the keyboard chart and on your keyboard.
2. Practice the first line. Watch your finger reach to the new key and re-turn to home-key position.
3. Take two 1-minute technique timings on the second line. Goal: Eyes on copy.
4. Take a 2-minute technique timing on the third line. Goal: Eyes on copy.

Goal: To learn the location of **2** **3** and **4**   16 minutes

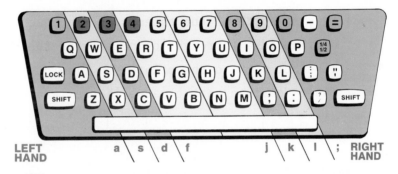

2 Practice the reach to **2** with the **s** finger. Keep the **f** finger anchored in home-key position.

1 s2s s2s s2 s2 s2 s2 s2 s2 s2 s2 s2 s2 s2
2 22; 22 sets; 22 sides; 222 sums; 22 sips
3 22 maps 222 lakes 222 fish 22 fields 222

3 Practice the reach to **3** with the **d** finger. Keep the **a** finger anchored in home-key position.

4 d3d d3d d3 d3 d3 d3 d3 d3 d3 d3 d3 d3 d3
5 33; 33 days; 33 dogs; 333 dimes; 33 dice
6 33 keys 33 autos 333 furs 333 clerks 333

4 Practice the reach to **4** with the **f** finger. Keep the **a** finger anchored in home-key position.

7 f4f f4f f4 f4 f4 f4 f4 f4 f4 f4 f4 f4 f4
8 44; 4 films; 44 facts; 44 fads; 444 furs
9 4 hands 44 men 444 firms 44 pens 44 rugs

Margins: Default or 1"
Spacing: SS or default: Tab: ¶, Center

47A
WARMUP

Key each line twice.
DS after each pair.

"st" combinations

Goal: To strengthen keyboarding skills   5 minutes

1 vast waste install best start stock cost instead assist east
2 Stan Vest still instructs the staff at State Street Storage.
3 The state contest's fastest student pianist was Stan Stoust.

| 1 | 2 | 3 | 4 | 5 | 6 | 7 | 8 | 9 | 10 | 11 | 12 |

47B
SPEED PRACTICE

Take two 30-second timings on each sentence. Try to increase your speed on the second timing.

GWAM = 1′ GWAM × 2

Goal: To build keyboarding speed   5 minutes

1′

1 Yes, in spite of the talents of the coach, they did not win.   12
2 Merlin did a thorough job of showing their findings to them.   24
3 Take her work to the printer to find out about the printing.   36
4 Their donation to the cause is the last one given this year.   48

| 1 | 2 | 3 | 4 | 5 | 6 | 7 | 8 | 9 | 10 | 11 | 12 |

47C
PRODUCTION TIMING

E M
Auto center

T
Tab: Center

Center each line horizontally.

Take two 3-minute timings.

If you finish before time is called, start again.

Goal: To improve techniques for centering copy   7 minutes

CUE: Key *a.m.* without spacing. Space once after the period following the *m.*

line 26 ↓ On Friday, October 15, DS

Visit and Browse DS

at the DS

Country Sampler Boutique DS

Grand Opening DS

9 a.m. to 6 p.m. DS

Willow Creek Clubhouse DS

5454 Ridge Road DS

Littleton, Colorado

23D
KEYBOARD PRACTICE

Key each line twice.

DS after each pair of lines.

Identify misstrokes.

Goal: To practice proper keystroking   8 minutes

1 Order us 2 books, 22 catalogs, and 22 price lists.
2 Please find 3 apples, 33 oranges, and 33 avocados.
3 Send 44 screws, 44 bolts, 44 nuts, and 44 washers.
4 Their numbers are 23, 24, 42, 43, 32, 34, and 234.
5 We want Nos. 22, 33, 44, 234, 432, 23, 24, and 43.
6 Please total these numbers: 23, 443, 323, and 34.

23E
READ AND DO

Do not space before or after a period used as a decimal point.

Do not space before or after a comma used to separate thousands or millions in numbers.

Do not space after a colon used to express time.

Goal: To learn the spacing with punctuation in numbers   6 minutes

Key these sentences using the correct spacing after the periods, commas, and colons.

1 In August, 2,343 cars, or 42.2 percent, were sold.
2 Janet Worth drove 233.33 miles by 4:33 p.m. today.
3 Patrick lives 2.2 miles from the railroad station.
4 John added the numbers 3.443 and 2.432 for Jackie.
5 The fire started at 2:43 a.m.; they arrived later.
6 By 2:43 p.m. Wednesday, they had sold 2,234 books.

23F
TECHNIQUE TIMING

Take two 2-minute timings on each group of lines.

DS after each timing.

Goal: To improve keyboarding techniques   10 minutes

Key without pausing. Try to keep the carrier/cursor moving.

1 Whenever you key numbers, check them for accuracy.
2 What percentage of each order did not get shipped?
3 She easily adjusted the stock numbers and amounts.
4 Total all the figures in the final amount columns.

Reach to the keys with your fingers, not your hands.

5 Our plant is exactly 23.3 miles from Kay's office.
6 Order 34 of Item No. 2234 and 42 of Item No. 3424.
7 Of 44,243 calls, 4.4 percent are made by 3:43 p.m.
8 Use these percent figures: 43.2, 32.4, and 324.3.

46E E M

READ AND DO **Goal:** To learn how to use an automatic centering function 6 minutes

In Lesson 45, you learned a manual method for centering words and lines horizontally. In this lesson, you will learn to use the **automatic centering** function to center text. If your equipment has an automatic (auto) centering function, follow these guidelines.

E Electronic Typewriters

1. Make sure the paper guide is at 0.
2. Insert a sheet of paper with the left edge at 0.
3. Set equal side margins.
4. Clear all tabs.
5. Activate the auto centering function. Follow the steps for auto centering on your equipment.
6. Key the text to be centered. If you make an error,

press the correction key and key the correct character or line again.
7. Press return/enter to print the centered text.

M Microcomputers

1. Move the cursor to the left side of the screen.
2. Enter the centering command. Follow the steps for auto centering on your equipment.
3. Key the text to be centered.
4. Enter the command to end centering.

If your equipment has an automatic centering function, use this function to key the remaining centering activities in this unit.

46F

APPLICATION: CENTERING **Goal:** To center horizontally and key lines 20 minutes

JOB 1

File name: L46F1 DS Start keying: Line 28
Center each line horizontally.

> **CUE:** Remember to include the default top margin in the 28 lines.

To write an effective letter

Get to the point

Give only the necessary details

Encourage a prompt response

Key the letter in correct format

Proofread the letter and correct errors

JOB 2

File name: L46F2 DS Start keying: Line 27
Center each line horizontally.

To get a promotion

Maintain a positive attitude

Perform work efficiently and productively

Assume responsibility

Listen effectively

Demonstrate flexibility

Continue your education

JOB 3

File name: L46F3 DS Start keying: Line 28
Center each line horizontally.

Job information sources include
Friends and relatives
Newspaper classified sections
Employment agencies
Direct inquiries
Job fairs

JOB 4

File name: L46F4 DS Start keying: Line 27
Center each line horizontally.

Career planning involves
Knowing your interests
Determining your aptitudes
Evaluating your skills and knowledge
Choosing a long-term goal
Selecting a short-term goal
Learning what education is needed

24A
WARMUP

Key each line twice.
DS after each pair of
lines.

Identify misstrokes.

Goal: **To strengthen keyboarding skills**   5 minutes

1 Eight firms wish to bid for the right to the land.
2 During the year just passed, we sold 443 new cars.
3 The council passed all 24 motions this past month.
4 On September 23, Brad's past-due account was paid.

| 1 | 2 | 3 | 4 | 5 | 6 | 7 | 8 | 9 | 10 |

24B
SPEED PRACTICE

Take two 2-minute
timings on the para-
graph. If you finish
before time is called,
start again.

Goal: **To build keyboarding speed**   5 minutes

The auditor is spending most of her time with
·us during the first half of the audit. If someone
asks, she says that she might finish the audit.

	1'	2'
	9	5
	20	10
	29	15

| 1' | 1 | 2 | 3 | 4 | 5 | 6 | 7 | 8 | 9 | 10 |
| 2' | 1 | | 2 | | 3 | | 4 | | 5 | |

24C
NEW-KEY ORIENTATION

1. Locate the new key
on the keyboard
chart and on your
keyboard.
2. Practice the first
line. Watch your
finger reach to the
new key and re-
turn to home-key
position.
3. Take two 1-minute
technique timings
on the second line.
Goal: Eyes on copy.
4. Take a 2-minute
technique timing
on the third line.
Goal: Eyes on copy.

Goal: **To learn the location of ⑦ ⑧ and ⑨**   16 minutes

LEFT HAND   a \ s \ d \ f   j \ k \ l \ ;   RIGHT HAND

Practice the reach to ⑦ with the **j** finger. Keep the **sem** finger
anchored in home-key position.

1 j7j j7j j7 j7 j7 j7 j7 j7 j7 j7 j7 j7 j7
2 7; 77 jokes; 777 jets; 7.77 jacks; 7,777
3 777 banks 77.7 lines 777 ways 7,777 days

(Continued next page)

46A
WARMUP

Goal: To strengthen keyboarding skills   5 minutes

Key each line twice. DS after each pair of lines.

Speed
Accuracy
Number/Symbol

1 The eight girls think they may go to the convention with us.
2 Theresa tried the three terrific tried-and-true typewriters.
3 He's sure Questions 36-40 are from Chapter 29 (pp. 481–508).

| 1 | 2 | 3 | 4 | 5 | 6 | 7 | 8 | 9 | 10 | 11 | 12 |

46B
GOAL WRITING

DS or default.

Take two 3-minute goal writings.

If you finish before time is called, start again.

Record your speed and accuracy.

Goal: To measure timed-writing progress   10 minutes

	1'	3'
Travelers often overlook the cost of money when they	11	4
are budgeting for a trip to a foreign country.	20	7
Initially, the tourist pays a fee when he or she	30	10
changes money into travelers' checks. When the tourist	41	14
reaches a foreign country, the tourist will then need to	53	18
convert the travelers' checks into the currency used in	64	21
that country. The fee for this conversion varies. A	75	25
hotel or a store will charge the largest fee. A bank or	86	29
a money exchange station will charge the smallest fee.	97	32

1'	1	2	3	4	5	6	7	8	9	10	11	12	AWL
3'		1		2		3		4					5.7

46C
TECHNIQUE TIMING

Take a 1-minute timing on each line.

DS after each timing.

Goal: To improve keyboarding techniques   4 minutes

Try to key the numbers as smoothly as you key the letters.

Key lines 1–3 in 31E.

46D
SELF-CHECK

DS or default.

Key the statement number and your answer: True or False.

Check your answers in Appendix B.

Goal: To review a manual method of horizontal centering   5 minutes

1. Use the same procedure for centering lines of text as you use for words.
2. Copy that is centered horizontally has equal side margins.
3. The center of standard-size paper is 40 when you are using 10 pitch.
4. Move left from center once for each character to be centered.
5. Move the carrier/cursor to the center before manually centering.
6. When centering the word *keyboarding,* do not move left a space for *g.*
7. The center of standard-size paper is 51 when you are using 12 pitch.

8 Practice the reach to 8 with the **k** finger. Keep the **sem** finger anchored in home-key position.

4 k8k k8k k8 k8 k8 k8 k8 k8 k8 k8 k8 k8 k8

5 8; 88 kites; 88 kinds; 8,888 kings; 88.8

6 888 uses 88.8 inches 888 lots 8,888 feet

9 Practice the reach to 9 with the **l** finger. Keep the **j** finger anchored in home-key position.

7 191 191 19 19 19 19 19 19 19 19 19 19 19

8 99; 9 lives; 999 lakes; 99.9 lots; 9,999

9 999 oaks 99.99 ft. 999 games 9,999 votes

24D
KEYBOARD PRACTICE

Key each line twice.

DS after each pair of lines.

Goal: To practice proper keystroking   7 minutes

1 Their numbers are 78, 79, 97, 98, 87, 89, and 789.

2 We want Nos. 77, 88, 99, 789, 987, 89, 79, and 98.

3 Help find these numbers: 7,789; 998; 878; and 89.

4 Can you add these numbers: 77, 789, 88, 789, 987?

5 Mail an order for 4 mats, 34 blanks, and 23 rings.

6 Be sure you buy 83 kits, 29 boxes, and 478 covers.

24E
LANGUAGE ARTS

Read the rule in the box.

Then key the sentences, supplying capitalization where needed.

Check your work with the key in Appendix A.

Goal: To review rules for capitalization   8 minutes

> Capitalize proper nouns. A proper noun names a specific person, place, or thing.
>
> **Examples:**
>
> The Smithsonian Institute is located in Washington, D.C.
> Please bill Amy Jones at the Executive Office Supply Company.

1 My friend susan will enter roosevelt high school.

2 His favorite teacher, ms. mason, speaks spanish.

3 The young man attends the u.s. air force academy.

4 The baxters will visit yellowstone national park.

5 Did you go to the sears tower in chicago?

6 The lorex corporation is in bellevue, washington.

7 Is your new address 32 rosecrans boulevard?

8 Basketball is popular at syracuse university.

9 Plays by william shakespeare will be featured.

b. Say to yourself *yb* and move the carrier/cursor to the left one space.

c. Say to yourself *oa* and move the carrier/cursor to the left one space.

d. Say to yourself *rd* and move the carrier/cursor to the left one space.

e. If a single character is left at the end of a word, do not move the carrier/cursor for that character.

ke yb oa rd

Move left   1 1 1 1

3. Begin keying the word *keyboard* at the point where the carrier/cursor is located.

4. Use the same procedure for centering lines of text. Move the carrier/cursor to the left once for every two characters in the line, including the spaces (#) to be left between words. For example:

ce nt er in g# li ne s

Move left 1 1 1 1 1 1 1 0

45F

APPLICATION: CENTERING

Press the return/enter key twice to DS these activities.

Center each word horizontally.

Goal: To center horizontally and key a list of words 20 minutes

JOB 1

File name: L45F1

CUE: Move the carrier/cursor to the left once for every two characters.

equipped

stationery

business

commitment

weight

occasionally

height

rigidity

mutinous

desirous

incision

JOB 2

File name: L45F2

CUE: Do not move the carrier/cursor for a single character left at the end of a line.

numeral

guess

foreign

omega

guidepost

consensus

ideal

license

forceable

detests

benefit

JOB 3

File name: L45F3

calendar

possession

accidentally

offering

impending

impression

category

JOB 4

File name: L45F4

environment

opportunity

government

guarantee

thorough

description

laboratory

Take two 2-minute timings on each group of lines.

Key each line once. If you finish before time is called, start again.

DS after each timing.

Goal: To improve keyboarding techniques   9 minutes

Keep your eyes on the textbook copy as you strike the number keys.

1 The latter figures, 3,243 and 23,324, are correct.
2 After selecting both 88 and 99, I like the latter.
3 Later in the day, they will deliver Order No. 382.
4 Flight 433 leaves too early; I'll take the latter.

Checkpoint: Did you look up fewer times on the second timing?

Don't let your wrists "bounce" as you reach to the top row.

5 23 dogs; 89 birds; 237 cats; 2,789 mice; 27 snakes
6 43 pens, 74 pencils, 984 papers, 72 books, 3 desks
7 Jane is 34; Dennis is 43; Elvira is 23; Mike is 2.
8 Order 2 apples, 4 bananas, 8 oranges, and 9 plums.

LESSON 25

Margins: Default or 1″
Spacing: SS or default   Tab ¶

Reinforcement

25A
WARMUP

Key each line twice. DS after each pair of lines.

Identify misstrokes.

Goal: To strengthen keyboarding skills   5 minutes

1 That lake is so clear that you can see the bottom.
2 Herb is the one who's there; whose name was heard?
3 Whose number does Que want--89, 28, 94, 39, or 27?
4 Who's going to referee: Beth, Tex, Zeke, or Fran?

| 1 | 2 | 3 | 4 | 5 | 6 | 7 | 8 | 9 | 10 |

25B
ACCURACY
PRACTICE

DS after each group of lines.

Goal: To build keyboarding accuracy   5 minutes

Take a 2-minute accuracy timing on the lines in 25A. Repeat the timing. Try to improve your accuracy.

Checkpoint: Did you improve your accuracy?

45C

TECHNIQUE TIMING

SM: Default or 1″

Body: Auto return or margin signal.

Take two 2-minute timings.

If you finish before time is called, start again.

Goal: To improve keyboarding techniques   5 minutes

Keep your eyes on the textbook copy.

    Monarch butterflies have colorful orange and black wings. They are an excellent example of what some might call the ultimate flying machine. With amazing precision, they use wind currents to fly thousands of miles south each fall. Even the most severe weather does not delay their travel.

45D

KEYBOARD COMPOSITION

Answer each question with a complete sentence.

Do not correct errors.

Goal: To compose at the keyboard   7 minutes

1. What is your one wish for the world?
2. What other cultures would you like to explore?
3. What is your best trait or quality?
4. What careers are good for people who enjoy mathematics?
5. What careers are good for people who enjoy writing?
6. What careers are good for people who enjoy working outdoors?
7. Why is good attendance important on the job?
8. What would be the most important considerations to you in choosing between two jobs?
9. How important would the personalities of your coworkers be to you in enjoying your job?

45E

READ AND DO

Goal: To learn a manual method of horizontal centering   8 minutes

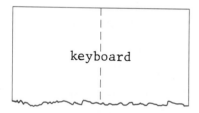

When text is centered horizontally, there is the same number of characters to the left and right of center.

    Some equipment has an automatic centering function; some does not. Because you may use equipment without an automatic centering function, you should learn to center text using a manual method. Follow these guidelines to center text horizontally using the manual backspace method:

1. Move the carrier/cursor to center.

E T *Typewriters*

a. Make sure the paper guide is at 0.
b. Set equal side margins.

c. Clear all tab stops.
d. Set a tab stop at center. The center of a standard size (8½″ × 11″) sheet of paper is 42 for 10 pitch and 51 for 12 pitch.
e. Tab to center.

M *Microcomputers*

a. Determine the center of the line. For example, if you have an 80-character/column display, the center is 40 characters from the left edge (column 41).
b. Use the space bar to move the cursor to the center of the line.
c. Set a tab stop at center.
2. Move the carrier/cursor to the left once for every two characters in the word *keyboard*. Do not key the word.
a. Say to yourself *ke* and move the carrier/cursor to the left one space.

(Continued next page)

25C
GOAL WRITING

DS or default.

Take two 3-minute goal writings.

Key at a pace that is comfortable for you.

If time allows, start again.

Determine your GWAM.

Goal: To measure timed-writing progress   10 minutes

	1'	3'

Advances in technology have changed the job market. Some fields of employment have been eliminated while others have been created.

What the world of work will be like in the years to come will depend on the changes in technology. When you select a career, try to choose one that will allow you some flexibility to meet the changes in technology.

	1'	3'
	9	3
	18	6
	27	9
	35	12
	44	15
	53	18
	63	21
	70	23

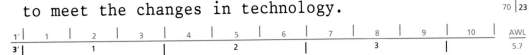

AWL 5.7

25D
KEYBOARD COMPOSITION

Key each word at the right, followed by a colon. Then key at least three words that rhyme with the word.

Goal: To compose at the keyboard   6 minutes

Example   Hair: bear, mare, care

1 Lawn   4 Key   7 Candy

2 Pen   5 Rope   8 Sky

3 Table   6 Book   9 Pad

25E
KEYBOARD PRACTICE

Key each line 3 times.

DS after each group of lines.

Identify misstrokes.

Goal: To practice proper keystroking   16 minutes

1 Call me if you're positive about Engine No. 83492.
2 Your 34-minute call was your second one that week.
3 If you're the one with No. 44-999, please call me.
4 File these numbers: 373-8993, 489-2398, 323-4892.
5 I'm not sure; but isn't the NARBT number 478-4293?
6 The part numbers are 434-782, 434-298, and 32-739.

25F
TECHNIQUE TIMING

Tab: ¶

Take three 2-minute timings.

For lines 1, 3, and 5, press the tab key.

Goal: To improve keyboarding techniques   8 minutes

Keep your eyes on the textbook copy as you use the tab.

1   We hope that they will attend.
2 We would like to hear from Ty soon.
3   Please let us serve them soon.
4 The department will open next week.
5   Enclosed are the eight copies.

Horizontal and Vertical Centering

The ability to center documents horizontally is an important aspect of document formatting. Most electronic typewriters and microcomputer software have automatic centering functions. However, if your equipment does not have an automatic centering function, you may center a document manually.

UNIT OBJECTIVES

In this unit, Lessons 45–56, you will:

1. Increase your keyboarding speed and accuracy.
2. Manually center words and lines of copy horizontally.
3. Center words and lines of copy using automatic (auto) centering.
4. Recognize single, double, triple, and quadruple spacing.
5. Center copy vertically on the page.
6. Prepare centered columns and tables.
7. Set and use decimal (dec) tabs.

ELECTRONIC CONCEPTS

automatic (auto) centering (p. 115)   column (p. 121)

decimal (dec) tab (p. 131)   ruler/format line (p. 121)

LESSON 45

Margins: Default or 1"
Spacing: SS or default   Tab: ¶, center

45A
WARMUP

Key each line twice.

DS after each pair of lines.

Frequently misspelled words

Goal: To strengthen keyboarding skills 5 minutes

```
1 psychology yield achievement category transferred possession
2 Their psychology should yield the very best in achievements.
3 That category is the one to which we transferred possession.
  |   1   |   2   |   3   |   4   |   5   |   6   |   7   |   8   |   9   |   10   |   11   |   12   |
```

45B
ACCURACY PRACTICE

DS after each group of lines.

Goal: To build keyboarding accuracy 5 minutes

Take a 2-minute accuracy timing on the lines in 45A. Repeat the timing. Try to improve your accuracy.

Checkpoint: Did you improve your accuracy?

Margins: Default or 1″
Spacing: SS or default   Tab ¶

26A
WARMUP

Key each line twice. DS after each pair of lines.

Identify misstrokes.

Goal: To strengthen keyboarding skills   5 minutes

1 A big fish toyed with the line but would not bite.
2 Lakeview's City Council will appeal to OSHA today.
3 Please take Max's counsel; you'll be glad you did.
4 Is Elaine Olson head of the Council of Publishers?

| 1 | 2 | 3 | 4 | 5 | 6 | 7 | 8 | 9 | 10 |

26B
NEW-KEY ORIENTATION

1. Locate the new key on the keyboard chart and on your keyboard.
2. Practice the first line. Watch your finger reach to the new key and re-turn to home-key position.
3. Take two 1-minute technique timings on the second line. Goal: Eyes on copy.
4. Take a 2-minute technique timing on the third line. Goal: Eyes on copy.

Goal: To learn the location of ① ⓪ and Ⓢ   16 minutes

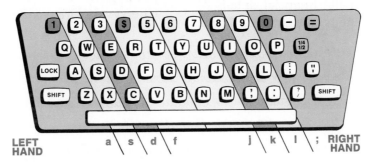

1 Practice the reach to ① with the **a** finger. Keep the **f** finger anchored in home-key position.

1 a1a a1a a1 a1 a1 a1 a1 a1 a1 a1 a1 a1 a1
2 1; 11 acts; 11 ads; 111 dozen; 1.11 days
3 11 spots 11.1 hours 1,111 paces 11 zones

0 Practice the reach to ⓪ (zero) with the **sem** finger. Keep the **j** finger anchored in home-key position.

4 ;0; ;0; ;0 ;0 ;0 ;0 ;0 ;0 ;0 ;0 ;0 ;0 ;0
5 0; 20 laws; 300 dots; 7,000 years; 4,020
6 200 boys 2,002 days 20.22 ft. 2,202 dogs

$ Practice the reach to the Ⓢ with the **f** finger while pressing the right shift key. Quickly release the shift key and return the **sem** finger to home-key position. *Do not space after the dollar sign.*

7 f$f f$f f$ f$ f$ f$ f$ f$ f$ f$ f$ f$ f$
8 $; $40; $788; $2.34; $33.97; $89.99; $42
9 $22 $4.00 $994 $3,782 $774 $2.94 $24,774

44B

PRODUCTION: MEASUREMENT

Goal: To measure formatting skills   35 minutes

JOB 1

Personal Business Letter   File name: L44B1

Mrs. Brenda Reynolds / Claims Manager / American States Insurance Group / 1102 Springfield Lane / Rockford, IL 61110 / I want to take this opportunity to thank you and your company for the help, both financial and psychological, you gave us during the recent hurricane. As we stared at our collapsed roof and virtually destroyed home, we felt devastated by the loss we had suffered. ¶ We soon discovered that we did not have to worry about the financial details of this loss. Your company stepped right in and took over. You wasted no time in sending an adjuster to inspect our house and in filing a claim for us. In a matter of hours, your company provided us with a check to cover our loss, and your adjuster was kind enough to recommend someone to whom we could turn to begin the process of rebuilding our home. ¶ My family and I were amazed at the personal, unselfish interest your company showed in our welfare. You may be sure that we will not forget the assistance your company gave us. / Sincerely / Ted Vaughn / 923 Cherryvale Drive / Beaumont, TX 77051

JOB 2

Business Letter
File name: L44B2

Letterhead/Envelope

Send to:

Mr. Steven R. Troeger
Trade Manager
National Trade Co.
5861 Farm Avenue
Hartford, CT 06156

Thank you for inquiring about our Electronic Meeting Board. To understand how this system works, imagine meeting rooms in several locations equipped with an Electronic Meeting Board and a television monitor. People in each location can send and receive visual images. As a person writes on a Meeting Board, an image appears on the television monitors at all locations. Participants at any location can alter that image by writing on or erasing their Meeting Boards.

This system increases the effectiveness of a teleconference by giving all participants the ability to draw and modify diagrams, charts, schedules, and other visual images when telecommunicators want to discuss an issue.

As we discussed, our sales representative will contact you next week to set a time for demonstrating the Electronic Meeting Board to you and your staff.

Sincerely

Russell Blackman
Teleconferencing Consultant

26C
KEYBOARD PRACTICE

Key each line 3 times.

DS after each group of lines.

Goal: To practice proper keystroking   8 minutes

1 The fourth item is 1,719; it isn't 1,123 or 1,411.
2 The final dates are May 20, May 30, and August 20.
3 The sums were $4, $84, $94, $34, $24, $74, and $4.
4 For $44, I'll get 10 books, 10 keys, and 10 exams.
5 Order 141 is for $144; 142 for $841; 143 for $941.

26D
KEYBOARD COMPOSITION

Answer each question with a single word.

Do not correct errors.

Goal: To compose at the keyboard   5 minutes

1 Do you own a dog?
2 During which month is your birthday?
3 Do you have dark hair?
4 What is your first name?
5 Have you read a book this month?
6 Do you have any sisters?

26E
GOAL WRITING

DS or default.

Take two 3-minute goal writings.

Key at a pace that is comfortable for you.

If time allows, start again.

Identify misstrokes.

Determine your GWAM.

Goal: To measure timed-writing progress   10 minutes

	1'	3'
The typewriter is not dead. The computer did	9	3
not bury it as many had said. Far from being	19	6
useless, the electronic typewriter is having	28	9
record sales. More than one million were sold in	38	13
a recent year in this country alone.	45	15
The electronic typewriter has many of the	54	18
best features of a personal computer, but it costs	64	21
much less than the personal computer.	71	24

AWL 5.7

26F
TECHNIQUE TIMING

Take a 2-minute timing on each group of lines.

DS between timings.

Goal: To improve keyboarding techniques   6 minutes

Use a one-two count when shifting for capitals.

1 Bob Lake cited Dr. Ira West at the August meeting.
2 The Loyal Order of Moose's meeting site is Denver.
3 "A Sight for Sore Eyes" is Jennifer Riley's title.

Keep your eyes on the textbook copy as you strike the hyphen.

4 Their glasses give you sight-of-the-future vision.
5 The all-important site is near the east-side park.
6 Those sights were not-to-be-forgotten experiences.

43F

SELF-CHECK

Choose the word or phrase that correctly completes each statement.

Key the statement number and your answer.

Check your answers in Appendix B.

Goal: To review letter parts   5 minutes

Answers: reference initials   Ladies and Gentlemen   writes
courtesy title   date   single spaced
open   double space   salutation
enclosure notation

1. The name used in the salutation of business letters usually consists of the addressee's ____ and last name.
2. With ____ punctuation, do not put a colon after the salutation.
3. When a letter is addressed to a company, an appropriate salutation to use is ____.
4. The ____ may be used to identify the person who prepared the letter.
5. Dear Mr. Scott is an example of a ____.
6. The first item in a business letter keyed on letterhead stationery is the ____.
7. The originator is the person who ____ the letter.
8. The body of a letter is ____.
9. In a block-format business letter, you usually ____ to indicate the beginning of a new paragraph.
10. The ____ indicates to the reader that something else was sent with a letter.

LESSON
44

Measuring Mastery

44A

GOAL WRITING

Warm up on 43A for 5 minutes.

DS or default.

If you finish before time is called, start again.

Record your speed and accuracy.

Goal: To measure timed-writing progress   15 minutes

	1'	3'
Do you believe that you are what you speak? Do you	11	4
think that people form opinions of you by listening to you?	23	8
How can you tell if you are sending the right oral messages?	35	12
Begin by listening to yourself. A tape recording of	46	15
your voice could reveal slurred words, poor grammar, slang	57	19
words, and fillers such as "you know" and "like."	67	22
Many celebrities testify that developing good speaking	79	26
habits played a key role in their success. Bad habits are	90	30
tough, but not impossible, to break.	98	33

1'	1	2	3	4	5	6	7	8	9	10	11	12	AWL
3'		1		2		3		4					5.7

27A
WARMUP

Key each line twice.
DS after each pair of
lines.

Identify misstrokes.

Goal: To strengthen keyboarding skills   5 minutes

1 That tall elm tree has been in our yard for years.
2 She will not venture forth without NASA's consent.
3 Here is the fourth in every case: 47, 37, 98, 21.
4 "Go forth in style," said Tex, "or go not at all."

| 1 | 2 | 3 | 4 | 5 | 6 | 7 | 8 | 9 | 10 |

27B
ACCURACY PRACTICE

DS after each group
of lines.

Goal: To build keyboarding accuracy   5 minutes

Take a 2-minute accuracy timing on the lines in 27A. Repeat the timing. Try
to improve your accuracy.

Checkpoint: Did you improve your accuracy?

27C
NEW-KEY ORIENTATION

1. Locate the new key
   on the keyboard
   chart and on your
   keyboard.
2. Practice the first
   line. Watch your
   finger reach to the
   new key and re-
   turn to home-key
   position.
3. Take two 1-minute
   technique timings
   on the second line.
   Goal: Eyes on copy.
4. Take a 2-minute
   technique timing
   on the third line.
   Goal: Eyes on copy.

Goal: To learn the location of ⑤ ⑥ and %   16 minutes

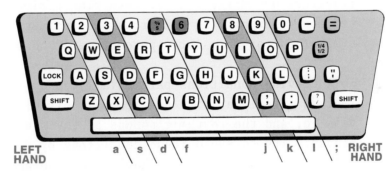

5 Practice the reach to ⑤ with the **f** finger. Keep the **a** finger
anchored in home-key position.

1 f5f f5f f5 f5 f5 f5 f5 f5 f5 f5 f5 f5 f5
2 5; 55 fires; 555 fans, 5,555 hats; 55.55
3 555 words 555.5 in. 5,555 ft. 55.55 yds.

6 Practice the reach to ⑥ with the **j** finger. Keep the **sem** finger
anchored in home-key position.

4 j6j j6j j6 j6 j6 j6 j6 j6 j6 j6 j6 j6 j6
5 6; 66 jobs; 66 jabs; 666 gaps; 66.6 rugs
6 666 titles 66.66 cm. 6,666 km. 666.66 m.

(Continued next page)

reasons. First, your firm has always been considered the most professional and reputable in Cedar Rapids. Second, I wish to pursue a career as a lawyer, and working in your firm would give me the opportunity to participate in the practical, day-to-day functions of a law office. ¶ My keyboarding skills are above average, 80 words a minute. My shorthand dictation speed is 120 words a minute. I have experience on three different word processors, and I have a working knowledge of legal databases. ¶ I will be in school this fall, but I am available for summer work. My telephone number is 770-1346. I am available to talk with you at your convenience. / Sincerely / (key your name and address)

JOB 2

Business Letter

File name: L43E2

Letterhead/Envelope

Send to:

Mr. Richard L. Koeppe
Reservation Agent
Astro Travel, Inc.
4362 Valley View Road
Dallas, TX 75234

From:

Evelyn Coughlin
District Manager

I am writing in response to your letter in which you ask for information about driving for extended time periods. I think you will find the following information helpful.

Travelers who drive for extended time periods should remember that driving and drowsiness do not mix. Fatigue is a major factor in a large percentage of road accidents.

Some driving conditions particularly conducive to drowsiness include a warm car with no fresh air circulation, no one to talk to, and the rhythmic sounds of the windshield wiper blades. Try to avoid these conditions by driving with your window open just a bit, by having someone accompany you, and by stopping for a rest at regular intervals.

Given normal driving conditions, you can drive about eight hours at a time, as long as you stop every couple of hours for a stretch and a walk. Of course, the most important way to fight fatigue is to get a good night's sleep the night before you travel.

Sincerely

Practice the reach to **%** with the **f** finger while pressing the right shift key. Quickly release the shift key and return the **sem** finger to home-key position. *Do not space before the percent sign.*

7 f%f f%f f% f% f% f% f% f% f% f% f% f% f%

8 %; 40%; 31%; 78%; 100%; 99%; 14.0%; 280%

9 7% and 8% and 3% and 90% and 20% and 10%

27D
KEYBOARD PRACTICE

Key each line 3 times.

DS after each group of lines.

Goal: To practice proper keystroking   8 minutes

1 What is the sum of 5 and 55 and 555 and 55 and 55?

2 Should Mina buy 66 lids, 66 bottoms, and 6 labels?

3 He gave chain discounts of 7%, 4%, and 3% to them.

4 About 56% of the Class of 1956 are at the meeting.

5 He is not sure whether 56 or 65 is the 50% figure.

27E
KEYBOARD COMPOSITION

Key the sentence number (followed by a period and two spaces). Then complete each sentence with a word or phrase that best completes it.

Do not correct errors.

Goal: To compose at the keyboard   6 minutes

1. The lighting in this room seems (dim, dark, bright, dull).
2. The temperature outside is (hot, cold, warm, cool).
3. When this class is over, I'm going to (have lunch, do homework, go home, take a test).
4. The last book that I read was (interesting, funny, challenging, suspenseful).
5. My last report was keyed on a(n) (microcomputer, electric typewriter, word processor, electronic typewriter).
6. The number that I have more difficulty keying is (1, 5, 7, 0).
7. My favorite color is (blue, yellow, green, red).
8. To correct my misstrokes, I (delete, erase, use correction paper, use correction fluid).

27F
TECHNIQUE TIMING

Take two 2-minute timings on each group of lines.

DS after each timing.

Goal: To improve keyboarding techniques   10 minutes

Key short words as words rather than as separate letters.

1 field and panel our which busy fit world pay usual

2 their air focus half cut girls via chair fit right

3 if eight down men signs an profit box six they for

Keep your eyes on the textbook copy.

4 She thinks the figures are 55%, 66%, 56%, and 65%.

5 56 men, 65 women, 556 miles, 665 fathoms, 565 days

6 On June 6, 55 orders were 65%, not 56%, completed.

43C
GOAL WRITING

DS or default.

Take two 3-minute goal writings.

If you finish before time is called, start again.

Record your speed and accuracy.

Goal: To measure timed-writing progress   10 minutes

	1'	3'
When a resume is prepared by a job seeker, a cover	10	3
letter should also be written. Many people are not aware	22	7
that the cover letter has as much importance as the resume.	34	11
They compose the cover letter quickly and carelessly, and	46	15
they wonder why they are never called for a job interview.	57	19
The cover letter is a sales letter. Its product is the	69	23
writer. The letter should highlight information on the	80	27
resume, ask for a specific job, and request an interview. A	92	31
good cover letter should capture the reader's interest.	103	34

```
1'|  1  |  2  |  3  |  4  |  5  |  6  |  7  |  8  |  9  | 10  | 11  | 12  |    AWL
3'|        1        |        2        |        3        |        4        |    5.7
```

43D
LANGUAGE ARTS

Read the rule in the box at the right.

Then key each numbered sentence, supplying capitalization where needed.

Check your work with the key in Appendix A.

Goal: To review rules for capitalization   5 minutes

Capitalize all important words in business names, names of organizations, institutions, schools, and clubs. Refer to the organization's letterhead for the preferred capitalization. Do not capitalize *the, and,* and *of* and other such words unless they are the first word of the business name.

Examples:

John Martinez is a recent graduate of Vincennes University.
I purchase most of my office supplies at The Paper Palace.

1. Annie has decided to attend clement college next year.
2. The needle in a haystack is my favorite needlepoint shop.
3. Tomorrow's concert will feature the boston city orchestra.
4. Elizabeth's attorneys are with post, czarnek, and pillar.
5. The omelets at the sunshine cafe are simply delicious.
6. Wendy has belonged to the daytona club for 15 years.
7. Our school tennis team practices at racquets unlimited.
8. The cheerleaders of westland university won the competition.
9. Golf practice is available year-round at pro golf, inc.
10. Don't overlook ye olde corner cafe in your search.

43E
APPLICATION: LETTERS

Goal: To prepare block-format letters   19 minutes

JOB 1

Personal Business Letter   File name: L43E1

Mrs. Antoinette Pantano / Attorney at Law / Haskins and Associates / 11 Bellaire Avenue / Cedar Rapids, IA 52402 / I am writing in re-sponse to your newspaper advertisement for a part-time clerk. The advertisement appeared in Sunday's Cedar Rapids Chronicle. ¶ I am interested in working for your law firm for two major

(Continued next page)

28A
WARMUP

Key each line twice. DS after each pair of lines.

Identify misstrokes.

Goal: To strengthen keyboarding skills   5 minutes

1 My job at home is to rake maple leaves every fall.
2 It's time for a quiz; we'll have it on January 15.
3 His book, The 13th Day, is in its fourth printing.
4 Bill said, "It's 23% profit on the $15.25 candle."

| 1 | 2 | 3 | 4 | 5 | 6 | 7 | 8 | 9 | 10 |

28B
SPEED PRACTICE

Take a 20- or 15-second timing on each line. If you complete a line in the time allowed, go on to the next one.

Goal: To build keyboarding speed   5 minutes

	GWAM	
	20″	15″
1 Firm goals are the right ones.	18	24
2 Analyze your goals to clarify them.	21	28
3 Anticipate changing goals as you mature.	24	32
4 A goal set for yourself ought to be exciting.	27	36

| 1 | 2 | 3 | 4 | 5 | 6 | 7 | 8 | 9 |

28C
GOAL WRITING

DS or default.

Take two 3-minute goal writings.

Key at a pace that is comfortable for you.

If time allows, start again.

Identify misstrokes.

Determine your GWAM.

Goal: To measure timed-writing progress   10 minutes

	1′	3′
Computer systems are made up of several	8	3
components: computer, keyboard, screen, printer,	18	6
and disk drive. The keyboard is used to enter	28	9
data into the computer. Data may be viewed on	37	12
the screen or sent to the printer. Data is	46	15
stored on floppy disks using the disk drive. A	55	18
computer system is useful only when you have	64	21
software that tells the computer what to do.	73	24

| 1′ | 1 | 2 | 3 | 4 | 5 | 6 | 7 | 8 | 9 | 10 | AWL |
| 3′ | | 1 | | 2 | | 3 | | 5.7 |

28D
KEYBOARD COMPOSITION

Key the sentence number (followed by a period and two spaces). Then complete each sentence with a short answer.

Goal: To compose at the keyboard   7 minutes

1. My favorite sport is ____.
2. If I could be anyone else, I would be ____.
3. One of the best books that I ever read was ____.
4. If I could visit any country in the world, I would visit ____.
5. I want to live in the city of ____.
6. My favorite animal is ____.

application, database management, value, format, validated, controlled vocabulary, free text, and autogeneration. ¶ This is a partial list of technical terms one might encounter in using an automated records management system. New terms appear daily; however, this list will provide your new employees with a basic understanding of some of the more frequently used records automation terms. / Sincerely / Eric Johnson / Automation Technician

Checkpoint: Did you remember to supply an appropriate salutation?

JOB 3

File name: L42E3

SM: 2"

Top margin: Line 13

Key this enclosure for JOB 1. DS except where otherwise indicated.

Review instructions in Appendix C for assembling a letter with an enclosure.

Yes, I am interested in receiving additional information about the KEY ID Security System. QS

Name

Position

Company Name

Street Address

City, State, ZIP Code

Telephone Number

Reinforcement

Margins: Default or 1"
Spacing: SS or default   Tab: ¶

43A
WARMUP

Goal: To strengthen keyboarding skills   5 minutes

Key each line twice. DS after each pair of lines.

Speed   1 If she is not being paid, she ought to get in touch with us.
Accuracy   2 The nimble, menial nomad condemned that modern nomenclature.
Number/Symbol   3 Type: #38 and (9%) and 15-lb. bag and 270 A-1 at $46/share.

| 1 | 2 | 3 | 4 | 5 | 6 | 7 | 8 | 9 | 10 | 11 | 12 |

43B
KEYBOARD COMPOSITION

Key the paragraphs, filling each blank with a word or a short phrase.

Do not correct errors.

Goal: To compose at the keyboard   6 minutes

My favorite hobby is ____. I enjoy my hobby most in the (mornings, afternoons, evenings) because this time of day seems ____. ____ and ____ are other people I know who enjoy this same hobby.

I spend about ____ hours each week on my hobby. If I could, I would like to spend ____ more hours on my hobby. But because I'm ____, I really don't have the time to spare.

**KEYBOARD
PRACTICE**

Key each line 3 times.

DS after each group
of lines.

Identify misstrokes.

Goal: To practice proper keystroking   13 minutes

1 These are contractions: it's, who's, I've, won't.
2 10 and 29 and 38 and 47 and 56 and 10568 and 29473
3 "Yes," said Wes, "we sell easy-to-clean products."
4 Guy's results are 71%, 109%, 204%, 367%, and 875%.
5 Who's head of these groups: UARP, UAORT, and UFT?
6 Part No. 56-328 is priced at $32.75 in lots of 12.
7 The Zealot costs $19.95; The Patriot costs $16.00.
8 What signs have you seen that they intend to move?

28F
**TECHNIQUE
TIMING**

Take two 2-minute
timings on each
group of lines.

DS after each timing.

Goal: To improve keyboarding techniques   10 minutes

Return to home-key position after striking each number or symbol key.
1 $29.00 $286.57 $1,067.23 $450.05 $293.74 $1,134.89
2 29% 13% 65% 50% 36.84% 23.85% 45.62% 14.76% 45.99%
3 The new retail prices are $9.95, $7.50, and $5.40.

Keep your eyes on the textbook copy.
4 The following were hired: Jones, Timm, and Smith.
5 The driver leaves promptly at 6:30 a.m., not 7:15.
6 The blank form should be sent to our other outlet.

**LESSON
29**

Margins: Default or 1"
Spacing: SS or default   Tab ¶

29A
WARMUP

Key each line twice.

DS after each pair of
lines.

Identify misstrokes.

Goal: To strengthen keyboarding skills   5 minutes

1 The pears will be ready to be picked by next week.
2 "The Personnel Department," said Vic, "wants her."
3 Personal Finance I is scheduled; Lane can take it.
4 About 30% bought personal copies at $23.75 apiece.

| 1 | 2 | 3 | 4 | 5 | 6 | 7 | 8 | 9 | 10 |

42D
ROUGH DRAFT

SM: Default or 1"

Read the copy. Then key the paragraphs making the changes indicated.

Proofread and correct all errors.

Goal: To key rough-draft copy   10 minutes

Telecommunications allows many home bound people, such as the disabled or those with children, to enter the work force. by conecting a personal computer to a telephone, a home bound person can work at home as effectively as as if sitting at a desk in a big office. Working at home has many advantages. the time, expense, and nuisance of commuting are eliminted. No special robe is required. One can create one's own hours and one's own working conditions. and for those who perfer solitude, there are no interruptions or noise from co workers.

42E
APPLICATION: LETTERS

JOB 1

File name: L42E1

Letterhead/Envelope

Key an envelope in OCR format.

Send to:

Mr. Jerold Hunter
Security Director
Data Exel, Inc.
548 Eisenhower Avenue
Lincoln, MI 48742

From:

Joe Tamburella
Sales Director

Goal: To key block-format business letters with envelopes   25 minutes

We are proud to introduce our new KEY DI Security System. This system provides and additional level of protcetion for high-security areas. For employees to gain access to secured areas, they must insert the KEY D card and enter a three- or four-digit personal number identification. The system recognizes an incorrect code and sounds an alrm after three attempts. should an intruder force an auntorized cardholder to enter a secure area, the cardholder can relay a special code to the centeral controller. This special code silently alerts security personnel of an unauthorized entry. Please return the enclosed card for more information.

Checkpoint: Did you key an Enclosure notation?

JOB 2

File name: L42E2   Letterhead/Envelope

CUE: Key an envelope in OCR format.

Ms. Marcia Berry / Records Manager / Brigham Abel, Inc. / 723 Woodlawn Drive / Detroit, MI 48233 / Like most technical subjects, records automation has its own vocabulary. One must become familiar with the jargon to communicate with people who are involved in records management. ¶ Although people may use different words to express the same idea, the following are some of the frequently used terms in records automation: automated records system, record, fields,

(Continued next page)

29B
TECHNIQUE TIMING

Take two 2-minute timings on each group of lines.

DS after each timing.

Goal: To improve keyboarding techniques   10 minutes

Keep other fingers in home-key position as you use the shift keys.

1 Within Before Sales September Product Long Provide
2 District Include Doctor Student Purchase Financial
3 Enough Changes Center Morning Giving Title Serving

Keep hands and arms quiet; keep wrists low but hands not resting on the machine.

4 On Tuesday, April 14, Mr. James will come to town.
5 Yes, Christmas Day is next Wednesday, December 25.
6 The winter sale is at Manhattan Sporting Goods Co.

| 1 | 2 | 3 | 4 | 5 | 6 | 7 | 8 | 9 | 10 |

29C
NEW-KEY ORIENTATION

1. Locate the new key on the keyboard chart and on your keyboard.
2. Practice the first line. Watch your finger reach to the new key and return to home-key position.
3. Take two 1-minute technique timings on the second line. Goal: Eyes on copy.
4. Take a 2-minute technique timing on the third line. Goal: Eyes on copy.

Goal: To learn the location of) (and /   16 minutes

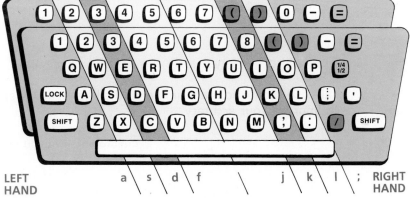

LEFT HAND   a s d f   j k l ; RIGHT HAND

KEYBOARD 1: Practice the reach to) with the **sem** finger while pressing the left shift key. Keep the **j** finger anchored in home-key position. *Do not space before the*).

1 ;); ;); ;) ;) ;) ;) ;) ;) ;) ;) ;) ;)
2 1) I will; 2) you are; 3) he, she, it is
3 1) one 2) three 3) five 4) seven 5) nine

KEYBOARD 2: Practice the reach to) with the **l** finger while pressing the left shift key. Keep the **j** finger anchored in home-key position. *Do not space before the*).

1 1)1 1)1 1) 1) 1) 1) 1) 1) 1) 1) 1) 1) 1)
2 1) I will; 2) you are; 3) he, she, it is
3 1) one 2) three 3) five 4) seven 5) nine

(Continued next page)

41H
APPLICATION: ENVELOPES

Goal: To key envelope mailing addresses in OCR format   7 minutes

Key an envelope for each of the addresses in 41F. Refer to 41G for correct placement.

LESSON
42

42A
WARMUP

Key each line twice.

DS after each pair of lines.

"al" combinations

Goal: To strengthen keyboarding skills   5 minutes

1 although always all altogether fall call sale mall calm lamp
2 Although the lamp would always fall, the male remained calm.
3 Clap after all the pals call the tall, pale males from Yale.

| 1 | 2 | 3 | 4 | 5 | 6 | 7 | 8 | 9 | 10 | 11 | 12 |

42B
ACCURACY PRACTICE

DS after each group of lines.

Goal: To build keyboarding accuracy   5 minutes

Take a 2-minute accuracy timing on the lines in 42A. Repeat the timing. Try to improve your accuracy.

Checkpoint: Did you improve your accuracy?

42C
NEED TO KNOW

Goal: To learn proofreader's marks   5 minutes

Proofreader's marks are used to indicate corrections or changes in copy. Refer to the table here to learn what each mark means, how to use it, and what the corrected copy looks like.

Mark	Meaning	Example	Corrected Copy
/	lower case	many People were	many people were
⊐	move right	You will find	You will find
⊏	move left	⌷ You will find	You will find
¶	paragraph	lawn.¶ There are three	lawn. There are three
stet	let stand	I am, ~~however,~~ glad	I am, however, glad

KEYBOARD 1: Practice the reach to (with the **l** finger while pressing the left shift key. Keep the **j** finger anchored in home-key position. *Do not space between parentheses and the copy enclosed within them.*

4 l(l l(l l(l(l(l(l(l(l(l(l(l(l(

5 (late); (aunt); (label); (after); (labs)

6 (1) per (2) ago (3) its (4) let (5) many

KEYBOARD 2: Practice the reach to (with the **k** finger while pressing the left shift key. Keep the **j** finger anchored in home-key position. *Do not space between parentheses and the copy enclosed within them.*

4 k(k k(k k(k(k(k(k(k(k(k(k(k(k(

5 (late); (aunt); (label); (after); (labs)

6 (1) per (2) ago (3) its (4) let (5) many

Practice the reach to / with the **sem** finger. Keep all other fingers in home-key position. *Do not space before or after the diagonal.*

7 ;/; ;/; ;/ ;/ ;/ ;/ ;/ ;/ ;/ ;/ ;/ ;/ ;/

8 and/or; he/she/it; true/false; they/them

9 add 1/2, 2/3, 3/8, 11/13; subtract 5/16;

29D
KEYBOARD PRACTICE

Key each line 3 times.

DS after each group of lines.

Goal: To practice proper keystroking   8 minutes

1 My construction project (Green Acres) is finished.

2 Kim (my foreman) and Earl (your foreman) are gone.

3 The store has spring/summer and fall/winter sales.

4 Two words (it's/its) were correct 95% of the time.

5 Which of the discounts (17% or 18%) do you prefer?

6 She could key the reports and/or file the letters.

| 1 | 2 | 3 | 4 | 5 | 6 | 7 | 8 | 9 | 10 |

29E
KEYBOARD COMPOSITION

Key the question number (followed by a period and two spaces) and a short answer.

Do not correct errors.

Goal: To compose at the keyboard   5 minutes

1. What do you like to do in your spare time?
2. What brand of keyboard are you using?
3. Where do you usually study?
4. Where do you plan to spend your next vacation?
5. In your opinion, what is the most important world issue?
6. For your "ideal" career, what skills will you need most?
7. If you could make one change in your routine, what would you change?

Example
```
MS ALMA ELKINS
VICE PRESIDENT
SUNSHINE INC
ONE BART SQUARE
BOSTON MA 02164
```

Key these mailing addresses in OCR format. TS between the mailing addresses.

CUE: Use the caps/shift lock key or all caps command to key all caps.

1 Mr. Ronald Filene
Marketing Consultant
Stone and Rodgers, Inc.
4906 Orchard Street
Wichita, KS   67209

2 Mr. James Ross
Attorney at Law
Williams, Markham, and Jones
3402 Arapaho Avenue
Tacoma, WA   98401-5113

3 Mrs. Melody Burns
Office Manager
Heritage Consultants
759 Monroe Avenue West
White Plains, NY   10601

4 Ms. Rosemary Kehr
Assistant Director
Cottonwood Enterprises
6702 Oakwood Road
Jackson, MS   39431

41G
NEED TO KNOW

Goal: **To learn how to key envelopes in OCR format**   5 minutes

Use a No. 10 envelope with its mailing address keyed in OCR (Optical Character Recognition) format for business correspondence. Many businesses use envelopes with their return addresses printed in the upper left corner.

The mailing address on the envelope should be the same as the inside address of the letter.

Ⓜ Before you begin, make these changes in default settings: set the top margin and the left margin at 0.

The following steps for keying envelopes are the same for all equipment.

1. If a plain envelope is used, key the return address in the upper left corner. Position 2 lines down from the top and 3 spaces from the left edge of the envelope/screen.
2. Position the mailing address as follows: Top margin: 2½ inches (line 15) from the top edge of the envelope/ screen. Left margin: 4 inches (40 spaces for 10 pitch; 48 spaces for 12 pitch) from the left edge of the envelope/screen.
3. Key the SS lines of the address in all capital letters. Use no punctuation except for the hyphen in the nine-digit ZIP Code.
4. Key the city, two-letter state abbreviation, and ZIP Code on the same line. Leave 2 spaces between the state abbreviation and the ZIP Code.

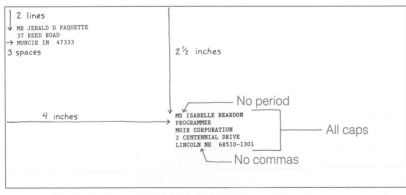

No. 10 envelope in OCR format

TECHNIQUE
TIMING

Goal: To improve keyboarding techniques 6 minutes

Reach to the keys with your fingers, not your hands.

Take two 2-minute timings.

If time allows, start again.

DS after each timing.

1 Send me $25 (and not a penny more) on November 15.
2 The new rate ($10.50/hour) went into effect today.
3 Sales for three months (May-July) were 15% higher.
4 For $655, I can purchase most (about 75%) of them.
5 By 9:15 (or was it earlier?), about 85% were sold.

Checkpoint: Did you use the correct spacing with the symbols?

LESSON
30
Reinforcement

Margins: Default or 1"
Spacing: SS or default   Tab ¶

30A
WARMUP

Goal: To strengthen keyboarding skills 5 minutes

Key each line twice. DS after each pair of lines.

Identify misstrokes.

1 His new car will go very fast when it is tuned up.
2 "The greens complement the yellows," added Quimby.
3 The roof--costing $245,000--complements the house.
4 Complimentary donations are these: $67, $68, $40.

| | 1 | 2 | 3 | 4 | 5 | 6 | 7 | 8 | 9 | 10 | |

30B
SPEED PRACTICE

Goal: To build keyboarding speed 5 minutes

Take two 1-minute timings on each paragraph. If you finish before time is called, start again.

	1'	2'
They want to have the name of the person who	9	5
did the body work on your car. They think they	19	9
can get a discount if they use the same person who	29	15
did your body work.	33	16
She spent most of her time visiting her son.	9	21
You might know that he lives on the island most of	19	26
the year and works for a downtown firm that lets	29	31
him work at home.	33	33

1'| 1 | 2 | 3 | 4 | 5 | 6 | 7 | 8 | 9 | 10 |
2'| 1 | 2 | 3 | 4 | 5 |

41C

SPEED PRACTICE

Goal: To build keyboarding speed 8 minutes

Take two 1-minute timings on each sentence. Try to increase your speed on the second timing.

1'
—
1 Six busy neighbors man this boat for a pair of cheap owners. 12
2 The sign and the emblem in the coal field got the work done. 24
3 Both of those fishermen got blue shoes for their movie work. 36

| 1 | 2 | 3 | 4 | 5 | 6 | 7 | 8 | 9 | 10 | 11 | 12 |

41D

NEED TO KNOW

Goal: To learn proofreader's marks 4 minutes

Proofreader's marks are used to indicate corrections or changes in copy. Refer to the table here to learn what each mark means, how to use it, and what the corrected copy looks like.

Mark	Meaning	Example	Corrected Copy
≡	capitalize	keep	Keep
		keep	KEEP
∼	change the order	have you	you have
		mircocomputer	microcomputer
∧	insert a comma	pause your	pause, your
⊙	insert a period	equipment Keep	equipment. Keep

41E

ROUGH DRAFT

Goal: To key rough-draft copy 9 minutes

SM: Default or 1"

Read the copy. Then key the paragraphs making the changes indicated.

Proofread and correct all errors.

Most people will put off doing an unpleasant tasks. However, if you frequently put off tasks and craete more misery for yourself by putting them off than by doing them, you've got a problem with procrastination. With a little effort and insight can you cure your problem.

first, take a look at why you put things off. If the job is so big that the task overwhelms you, break the job down into manageable chunks. If you fear failure, than realize that if you don't do the job, you are certin to fail and even if you do fail, will the failure be so bad? When you do a task, reward yourself!

41F

READ AND DO

Goal: To learn to key envelope mailing addresses in OCR format 5 minutes

Key mailing addresses on envelopes in OCR (Optical Character Recognition) format. OCR format uses all capital letters and leaves out all marks of punctuation. That is, periods are not used with abbreviations or initials; commas are not used between the cities and states. However, a hyphen is used with ZIP-Plus, the nine-digit ZIP Code.

(Continued next page)

30C
GOAL WRITING

DS or default.

Take two 3-minute goal writings.

Key at a pace that is comfortable for you.

If time allows, start again.

Identify misstrokes.

Determine your GWAM.

Goal: To measure timed-writing progress   10 minutes

	1′	3′

    Travel agents need to have good sales skills
and be able to do detail work under pressure.
    It is often difficult to get jobs as travel
agents because so many qualified people apply for
each job opening.   In addition to receiving a
salary or a commission, a travel agent often gets
bonuses from many airlines.   The bonuses may
include cash, free trips, and prizes.

1′	3′
9	3
18	6
27	9
37	12
48	16
57	19
66	22
73	24

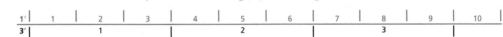

AWL
5.7

30D
TECHNIQUE TIMING

Take a 2-minute timing on each group of lines.

Then take a 1-minute timing on the lines for the technique that needs the most improvement.

DS after each timing.

Goal: To improve keyboarding techniques   6 minutes

Make the reaches with the fingers rather than the entire hand.

1 Write $40 and 50% and $60 and 70% and $80 and 90%.
2 (1/3), (2/3), (3/4), (4/5), (5/6), (1/10), (12/13)
3 She won in 1979, 1980, 1982, 1984, 1986, and 1987.

> **Checkpoint:** Were you able to keep your hands from moving up and down while keying?

Key short words as words rather than as separate letters.

4 the can he of year to copy and letter order in all
5 you when we their for may such your these that new
6 our have me two on with most thank than them other

30E
READ AND DO

> Do not space before or after the diagonal in a "made" fraction.
>
> Leave a space between a whole number and a "made" fraction.

Goal: To learn the spacing with "made" fractions   7 minutes

Key these sentences using the correct spacing with the diagonal and before a "made" fraction.

1 What is the sum of 14 1/2, 1/4, 2 1/3, and 2 1/12?
2 He used 1 1/2 times the amount of salt called for.
3 She tried to add 1/2, 2/3, 3 1/2, 3/4, and 2 5/16.
4 The rate was 16 3/4 percent, but she wrote 16 1/2.
5 The new substance contains 2 1/2 times more water.

JOB 2

File name: L40F2   Letterhead

Ms. Ashley McElreath / Marketing Manager / Data Processing, Inc. / 2600 Sheffield Street / Detroit, MI 48503 / (supply salutation) / We continually strive to keep our customers informed about what is happening in technology. Consequently, we have this bit of information for you regarding the graphics you generate. ¶ Once you enter information into your computer, you have three ways to obtain a hard copy: printers, plotters, and graphic cameras. ¶ Printers produce graphics the same way newspapers produce a photograph, by breaking the image into tiny dots. Every graphics printer makes its image with dots. Of course, the more dots that can be used to create a given image size, the better the quality. After all, even photographs are made of small dots of silver created by light falling on the film. To the eye, photographic images appear solid. ¶ The enclosed brochure illustrates some of the graphics generated by our new OP LASER 7000. If you would like to have a demonstration, call me at (303) 773-1634. / Sincerely / James P. Smith / Office Products Manager / Enclosure

LESSON 41

Margins: Default or 1"
Spacing: SS or default   Tab: ¶

41A
WARMUP

Key each line twice. DS after each pair.

"tri" combinations

Goal: To strengthen keyboarding skills   5 minutes

```
1 trial contrite trill intricate triple tribute trick tribunal
2 She was twice tricked by the trio in the trifling tribunals.
3 The Tri-City Electric District tried to trim electric rates.
```

| 1 | 2 | 3 | 4 | 5 | 6 | 7 | 8 | 9 | 10 | 11 | 12 |

41B
LANGUAGE ARTS

Read the rule in the box at the right.

Then key each numbered sentence, supplying capitalization where needed.

Check your work with the key in Appendix A.

Goal: To review rules for capitalization   7 minutes

> Capitalize days of the week, months of the year, and holidays.
>
> **Examples:**
>
> The new office will be open on Mondays, Tuesdays, and Thursdays.
> This year Thanksgiving falls on Thursday, November 25.

1. My letter dated march 29 contained some inaccurate information.
2. We plan to open our new office on wednesday, may 15.
3. We are open for business tuesday through friday.
4. We are closed on monday, may 25, for memorial day.
5. Our big clearance sale takes place on the monday after new year's day.
6. July 4 is also known as independence day.
7. We will be open on weekends after labor day.
8. I don't like to work on saturday or sunday.
9. When I work on christmas, I get paid double time.

30F
KEYBOARD COMPOSITION

Key each sentence and the phrase that best completes it.

Do not correct errors.

Goal: To compose at the keyboard   5 minutes

1. I like to be with people who are (a lot of fun, serious when studying, enthusiastic about athletics).
2. My favorite way to spend a rainy day is (reading a book indoors, working on my hobbies, talking to friends).
3. One creature that I do not want to encounter is (an alarmed snake, a frenzied shark, an angry dragon).
4. My best friend is (sincere, a good worker, honest).
5. My favorite part of fall is (the crunching of the leaves, watching football games, picking and eating apples).

30G
KEYBOARD PRACTICE

Key each line twice.

DS after each pair of lines.

Identify misstrokes.

Goal: To practice proper keystroking   7 minutes

1 The checks are for $3.87, $9.21, $2.06, and $3.54.
2 Invoice No. 29387 was discounted at 3 1/2 percent.
3 The dates are May 15, May 18, May 23, and June 30.
4 The I.D. numbers were 519-34-8441 and 540-40-7995.
5 If he adds 13 5/8 to 21 3/4, he should get 35 3/8.

30H
TECHNIQUE TIMING

Take two 2-minute timings.

DS after each timing.

Goal: To improve keyboarding techniques   5 minutes

Key handwritten copy without pauses.

In the United States, coins and paper money make up only about 20 percent of all the money in circulation. The other 80 percent consists of checking accounts, bank deposits, and various kinds of credit, such as credit cards.

LESSON 31

Margins: Default or 1"
Spacing: SS or default   Tab ¶

31A
WARMUP

Key each line twice. DS after each pair of lines.

Identify misstrokes.

Goal: To strengthen keyboarding skills   5 minutes

1 The book was thick, so he did not want to read it.
2 Glendon accepted their offer; Lynette rejected it.
3 Use all the numbers except these: 34, 67, and 89.
4 Benjamin asked, "Why won't Quentin accept defeat?"

| 1 | 2 | 3 | 4 | 5 | 6 | 7 | 8 | 9 | 10 |

40D
ROUGH DRAFT

SM: Default or 1"

Read the copy. Then key the paragraphs making the changes indicated by the proofreader's marks.

Proofread and correct all errors.

Goal: To key rough-draft copy   10 minutes

Key boarding is a psychomotor skill that combines muscular activity with mental processes. Like playing tenis or the piano, key boarding is a skill that can be learned. The lerner must first be shown how to make the proper movements. At first, the movements are slow and deliberate.

Like a beginning tennis player who concentrates on each and every aspect of swinging the racket, only to miss the ball, the key boarder may try to concentrate on all of the aspects of proper technique.

40E
PRODUCTION TIMING

Take a 2-minute timing on these closing lines.

Repeat the timing.

Goal: To build speed keying closing lines   5 minutes

1 Sincerely
↓ QS

Cheryl A. Martin
Systems Analyst DS

xxx DS

Enclosure

2 Sincerely yours
↓ QS

Tony M. Taylor
Project Director DS

xxx DS

Enclosure

40F
APPLICATION: LETTERS

JOB 1

File name: L40F1

Letterhead

Send to:

Mr. Alan Redmond
Office Manager
Anderson and Doyle
4389 Stout Street
Wichita, KS 67201

From:

Jennifer R. Middleton
Account Executive

Goal: To key block-format business letters   20 minutes

Most business travelers know that traveling is not an easy job in itself. As a frequent business traveler, you must plan ahead. You shouldn't put off what you can do now, and you must stay in touch with your office. The last thing you can afford is to waste time. You often find that you need to be in two places at once. Of course that's impossible, or is it?

Our specialy seminars for busy executives can show you how to use time in airports, planes, and hotel rooms to do more work than you'd accomplish sitting at your office desk. Special attention is focused on developing high-level managerial skills, such as delegating responsibilities to your support staff.

We want to get the latest in technology and research working for you, on your team Call me today, and I will show you numbers that prove what we can do for you.

(Continued next page)

31B
NEED TO KNOW

Goal: To learn how to use other keyboard symbols   7 minutes

Refer to the illustration to help you locate each new symbol key on your keyboard.

Determine which finger strikes each key.

Note: Some symbols may not appear on your keyboard.

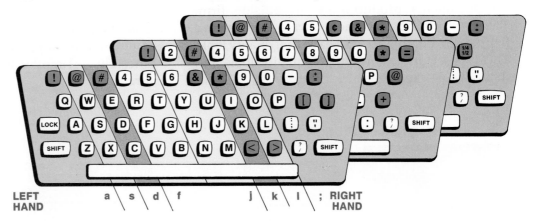

LEFT HAND   a   s   d   f   j   k   l   ;   RIGHT HAND

Symbol	Spacing	Example
General Use:		
! (exclamation)	2 spaces after	Ouch! That hurts.
@ (at)	space before and after	2 @ $1.69
# (number/pound)	no space between figure and symbol	#47 (number) 50# (pounds)
¢ (cent)	no space before	75¢ each
& (ampersand/and)	space before and after	Smidt & Sons
* (asterisk)	no space between symbol and word	*Note Total*
$\frac{1}{2}$/$\frac{1}{4}$ (one-half)/(one-quarter)	no space before	5$\frac{1}{2}$ oz.; 2$\frac{1}{4}$ lbs.
Math Use:		
+ (plus)	space before and after	2 + 2
= (equals)	space before and after	2 + 2 = 4
Programming Use:		
@ (at)	no space after symbol	@4
+ (plus)	no space before or after	A+B
[(left bracket)	no space after	[UC
] (right bracket)	no space before	[UC]
> (greater than)	space before and after	AMT > 10
< (less than)	space before and after	A < B
* (multiply)	no space before or after	5*8
= (equals)	no space before or after	C=C+1

31C
KEYBOARD PRACTICE

Goal: To practice proper keystroking   20 minutes

Key each line twice.

Identify misstrokes.

1 Max cried, "Help!" Sue screamed, "I'm over here!"

2 Sharon bought 6 dozen @ $2 per dozen and paid $12.

3 Randy purchased 500 gallons of #2 grade oil today.

4 This order is for 350# of potatoes @ $1.98 per lb.

5 He bought at 60¢ apiece; she bought at 50¢ apiece.

(Continued next page)

documents that have been photocopied and type-set documents produced by an outside firm. The photocopied documents were inexpensive to produce, but they did not have that quality look. The typeset documents had a quality look, but they were expensive to produce. ¶ SUPER CAP, our computer-aided publishing system, is inexpensive to use and provides a quality look. Fill out and return the enclosed form to receive more information on the SUPER CAP. / Sincerely / Timothy Jordan / Manager / Enclosure

Margins: Default or 1"
Spacing: SS or default   Tab: ¶

40A
WARMUP

Goal: To strengthen keyboarding skills 5 minutes

Key each line twice.

DS after each pair.

"ble" combinations

```
1 stable able table reasonable marble fable remarkable capable
2 The terrible and horrible comedian was not laughable at all.
3 Judith was able and capable of blowing the invisible bubble.
```

| 1 | 2 | 3 | 4 | 5 | 6 | 7 | 8 | 9 | 10 | 11 | 12 |

40B
ACCURACY PRACTICE

Goal: To build keyboarding accuracy 5 minutes

DS after each group of lines.

Take a 2-minute accuracy timing on the lines in 40A. Repeat the timing. Try to improve your accuracy.

Checkpoint: Did you improve your accuracy?

40C
NEED TO KNOW

Goal: To learn proofreader's marks 5 minutes

Proofreader's marks are used to indicate corrections or changes in copy. Refer to the table here to learn what each mark means, how to use it, and what the corrected copy looks like.

Mark	Meaning	Example	Corrected Copy
∧	insert	Improve▵your keyboarding	Improve your keyboarding
℘	delete	using ~~your~~ software	using software
		Keying a documents	Keying documents
#	add a space	you#think	you think
⌢	close up space	in denting	indenting

Key each line twice.
Identify misstrokes.

6 The Martin & Watkins Company was closed yesterday.
7 *Note: Every score should be listed individually.
8 Suzanne very quickly added $30\frac{1}{4}$ to $60\frac{1}{4}$ and got $90\frac{1}{2}$.
9 Please check this problem: 10 + 11 + 12 + 7 = 40.
10 180 PRINT "TYPE @12' "TO PRINT AN INCOME STATEMENT
11 A sample line in a program might read: PRINT A+B.
12 The program command to begin underscoring is [UC].
13 1050 IF AB IS > 18 THEN PRINT "MONTHLY DEDUCTIONS"
14 1060 IF AB IS < 18 THEN PRINT "PAYROLL DEDUCTIONS"
15 In a program 5*8 means 5 is to be multiplied by 8.
16 280 IF A=25 THEN PRINT "THESE PEOPLE MAY NOW VOTE"

31D
GOAL WRITING

DS or default.

Take two 3-minute goal writings.

Key at a pace that is comfortable for you.

If time allows, start again.

Identify misstrokes.

Determine your GWAM.

Goal: To measure timed-writing progress   10 minutes

	1'	3'
A typical day for a social worker involves	9	3
helping people to identify and to solve their	18	6
problems. To be effective, a social worker must	28	9
be sensitive, yet objective at the same time.	37	12
A bachelor's degree is often needed for	45	15
entry-level jobs. Many states give school grants	55	18
to those workers who want to earn a master's	64	21
degree and to advance in their careers.	72	24

1' | 1 | 2 | 3 | 4 | 5 | 6 | 7 | 8 | 9 | 10 | AWL
3' | 1 | 2 | 3 | 5.7

31E
TECHNIQUE TIMING

Take a 3-minute timing on each group of lines.

DS between timings.

Goal: To improve keyboarding techniques   8 minutes

Key the numbers as quickly as you key the words.

1 sign 2856 work 2948 down 3926 then 5636 rich 4836
2 firm 4847 when 2636 form 4947 rush 4726 city 3856
3 wish 2826 owns 9262 both 5956 pals 0192 girl 5849

Quickly release the shift key and return to home-key position.

4 The decisions affected Sam, Rose, Mark, and Wilma.
5 Enterprise; Calendar; Maintenance; Mortgage; Brief
6 Has Fay Jacks passed the CPA or the CAM exams yet?

Key the lines of each address in the correct order.

1 Garfield Trust Company / Detroit, MI 48205 / 306 Grover Lane / Mrs. Kris Eberhart / Loan Officer
2 P. O. Box 28 / Devon, DE 06460 / Dr. Alice Hinton / United Fund Campaign / Chairperson

3 Abe Computer Company / President / Atlanta, GA 30344 / 1286 Marsh Street / Mr. C. J. Inmon
4 Kansas City, MO 64128 / 1844 North Piedmont Drive / Mr. Jon Takata / Compu Data / Manager
5 Mrs. Laura Fernberg / P. O. Box 33 / Omaha, NE 68105 / Fine Arts Council / Administrator

39E
APPLICATION: LETTERS

Goal: To key block-format business letters   21 minutes

JOB 1

File name: L39E1

Letterhead

Send to:

Ms. Jane Craft
1937 Tamarac Court
Portland, OR 97223

Supply a salutation.

From:

Richard Cozza
Safety Manager

CUE: DS after reference initials to key Enclosure.

The state of Massachusetts is pleased that your bicycle touring club will be visiting our state this summer.

Many cyclists who come to this state are unaware of the basic traffic laws. These laws are the same for cyclists and drivers of automobiles. This means obeying all traffic signals, following laws for one-way streets, and giving proper turn signals to fellow cyclists and motorists. As I am sure you are aware, a motorist cannot react as quickly as a cyclist. With the amount of traffic on the roads today, everyone must be aware of the laws and follow them.

I am enclosing a booklet detailing the traffic laws and regulations of our streets and highways.

Sincerely

Checkpoint: Did you use your reference initials?

JOB 2

File name: L39E2   Letterhead

Mrs. Jill Kronhart / Administrative Assistant / TeleComx, Inc. / 92 North Jupiter Drive / Chicago, IL 60624 / (supply salutation) / Whatever happened to the "paperless" office? That concept seems to have gone by the wayside for everyone except hi-tech and science advocates. ¶ Experts estimate that the average office worker must read at least 900 pages of hard copy information per month. This figure is projected to grow yearly. Paper will obviously remain the dominant means of communication for a long time. ¶ In the past, offices have depended on two kinds of hard copy communication: simple typewritten

(Continued next page)

Measuring Mastery

32A
WARMUP

Key each line twice.
DS after each pair of
lines.

Goal: To strengthen keyboarding skills   5 minutes

1 The new cook heated thick soup for the tired boys.
2 I am enclosing the four copies that you requested.
3 "Send him water-marked stationery," said Marjorie.
4 Invoice Nos. 2938, 4720, 3820, and 7564 were paid.

| 1 | 2 | 3 | 4 | 5 | 6 | 7 | 8 | 9 | 10 |

32B
GOAL WRITING

DS or default.

Take two 3-minute
goal writings.

Key at a pace that is
comfortable for you.

If time allows, start
again.

Identify misstrokes.

Determine your
GWAM.

Goal: To measure timed-writing progress   10 minutes

	1'	3'
Australia is the home of an earthworm that	9	3
can grow to an amazing length of many feet. The	19	6
huge worm, like all worms, is blind, deaf, and	28	9
very harmless. It lives on rotting vegetation and	38	13
prefers to remain underground.	44	15
Australians feel that the huge worms are	53	18
quite a sight, but do not use the worms for	62	21
anything other than occasionally scaring the wits	72	24
out of unwary tourists.	76	25

1' | 1 | 2 | 3 | 4 | 5 | 6 | 7 | 8 | 9 | 10 | AWL
3' | 1 | 2 | 3 | 5.7

32C
PUNCTUATION
PRACTICE

Key each line twice,
using correct spacing
around the punctua-
tion marks.

Goal: To review spacing with punctuation   9 minutes

1 Wm. R. Jones Co. -- the state's leader -- can exhibit.
2 Ship the following: 8 red, 12 blue, and 12 green.
3 The correct numbers are 1 5/16, 15/32, and 19 3/32.
4 "She can win it," said Jane. "Jack can win also."
5 Call Mary at 7:30 a.m.; I'll call you at 7:00 a.m.
6 He built 2,450 units; however, we sold only 1,830.
7 The figure is $65.39, but only $56.93 was written.
8 She told us <u>not</u> to go. Let's do what she says to.
9 Isn't Bob's car insurance just as good as Henry's ?

39B

GOAL WRITING

DS or default.

Take two 3-minute goal writings.

If you finish before time is called, start again.

Record your speed and accuracy.

Goal: To measure timed-writing progress   10 minutes

	1'	3'
The study of personality deals with human emotions, | 11 | 4
actions, and thoughts. It is often described as the | 21 | 7
ability to get along well with others socially, but to a | 22 | 11
psychologist, personality is much more complex. | 42 | 14
Many things can make up personality. Sometimes we link | 54 | 18
personality to the mood a person is in most of the time. | 65 | 22
For example, we may say that a person has a sad or a | 76 | 25
cheerful personality. Other times, personality may be | 87 | 29
linked to a trait, such as sincerity. | 94 | 31

1' | 1 | 2 | 3 | 4 | 5 | 6 | 7 | 8 | 9 | 10 | 11 | 12 | AWL
3' | 1 | | 2 | | 3 | | 4 | | 5.7

39C

LANGUAGE ARTS

Read the rules in the box at the right.

For each word in the list below the box, key the word and a colon (:).

Then,

1. Key the word in syllables.
2. Show how the word is divided.
3. Key the number of the rule(s) that apply.

Use a comma to separate items as you key them across the page.

Check your work with the key in Appendix A.

Goal: To review word division rules   8 minutes

> **Rule 4.** Avoid dividing figures, abbreviations, dates, or proper nouns.
> **Rule 5.** Divide a compound word between the elements or after the hyphen.
>
> **Examples:**
>
> | Word | Syllables | Divided Word | Rule Number |
> |---|---|---|---|
> | AFL-CIO | — | (avoid dividing) | 4 |
> | basketball | bas ket ball | basket-ball | 5 |
> | $46,668.17 | — | (avoid dividing) | 4 |
> | Dr. Howard Jones | — | (avoid dividing) | 4 |
> | self-evident | self ev i dent | self-evident | 5 |
> | June 16, 1985 | — | (avoid dividing) | 4 |

Example: understand: un der stand, under-stand, 5

1 Thanksgiving
2 September 5, 1989
3 grandmother

4 Mr. John Roberts
5 $17,845,890.17
6 self-confidence

7 superhuman
8 well-behaved
9 Detroit

39D

READ AND DO

Goal: To format inside addresses   6 minutes

The inside address of a business letter usually contains the following information keyed in the order given: (1) addressee's name, (2) addressee's title (in some letters, this might be omitted), (3) company name, (4) street address, and (5) city, state, and ZIP Code.

(Continued next page)

32D
KEYBOARDING REVIEW

Key the statement number (followed by a period and two spaces) and your answer.

Goal: To review keyboarding procedures   8 minutes

True/False

1. Space once before and after a hyphen.
2. Always leave one space after a quotation mark.
3. Space twice after a semicolon.
4. Space twice after a period that ends a sentence.
5. Space once after a period used as a decimal point.
6. To figure the number of words in a line, divide the number of strokes in the line by 5.

Fill-in-the-Blank

E T 7. The _____ sets a tab stop at any point on a line.
8. The _____ allows you to key beyond the left and right margins.
9. The _____ moves the carrier to the left one space at a time.
10. Use the _____ to key all capital letters.

M 7. Use the _____ to key all capital letters.
8. A command to the printer within text is called an _____ command.
9. Use the _____ keys to move through text.
10. The automatic return feature of a microcomputer is called _____.

32E
TECHNIQUE TIMING

Take two 2-minute timings on each pair of lines.

If time allows, start again.

DS after each timing.

Goal: To demonstrate correct keyboarding techniques   13 minutes

Keep your eyes on the textbook copy when keying and returning/entering.

1 I inquired about proposed subordinated debentures.
2 Invoices 38209, 39576, 40730, and 41829 were paid.

Key without pausing between words or lines.

3 Then--and only then--will I get the majority vote.
4 Nu-Ore has multi-million dollar lease obligations.

Keep hands and arms in correct position.

5 The Governor of Arkansas expressed his opposition.
6 Long-term debts exceed total shareholders' equity.

32F
TECHNIQUE TIMING

Take two 2-minute timings.

Use auto return or the margin signal to determine line endings.

Goal: To demonstrate correct keyboarding techniques   5 minutes

Tab, underline, and key all caps correctly and efficiently.

Dental insurance has become a very important benefit. About one of every three Americans has some kind of dental insurance plan supported by employers and the American Dental Association (ADA).

Conference calling furnishes a "meeting place" for anyone who wants to share knowledge and experience—without the time and expense of travel. A conference call placed from an American Telecomex System allows you to discuss a business matter over the telephone with people in up to 58 other locations.

I would like to demonstrate what conference calling can do for you. I will call you next Wednesday to set up a time that is convenient for you.

Sincerely

Ms. Jeanne Garvey
Sales Manager

xxx

Checkpoint: Did you use your reference initials?

JOB 2

File name: L38F2

Key the letter in 38E. Make these changes:

1. Change the inside address to:

   Mrs. Marilyn Martinez
   Sales Manager
   Edgewater Office Supply
   670 Boylston Place
   Minot, ND 58701

2. Supply an appropriate salutation.
3. Change the complimentary close to: Yours truly
4. Change the originator's name and title to:

   Donna Hudson, Administrative Assistant

5. Use your own reference initials.

LESSON 39

Margins: Default or 1"
Spacing: SS or default   Tab: ¶

39A
WARMUP

Goal: To strengthen keyboarding skills   5 minutes

Key each line twice. DS after each pair of lines.

Speed   1 When he lets us take his machine, the analysis will be done.
Accuracy   2 Miriam, atom, boredom, coliseum, condominium, stream, claim,
Number/Symbol   3 My policy (#L-48356-G) for $50,000 was paid up May 27, 1982.

| 1 | 2 | 3 | 4 | 5 | 6 | 7 | 8 | 9 | 10 | 11 | 12 |

Careers

Movie Industry

Want to work in the movies? You may be surprised to find out what a large part computers play in the movie industry.

As part of the office staff in accounting, marketing, and production, you would use computers all the time for billing, communications, scheduling, and inventory. As a writer or assistant, you would use word processing programs designed especially for movie scripts.

If you worked as a composer for movies, you would use computers to record music, sometimes keyboarding the instrumentation directly into a computer. As a film editor, you would use computers to cut and fit together film.

And if special effects is your interest, consider this: most of the spectacular optical effects in movies today are done not on the movie set but in the studio — by effects specialists working on state-of-the-art computer equipment.

PART 2 Building Formatting Skills

38E
PROJECT PREVIEW

Goal: To key a business letter in block format   8 minutes

File name: L38E

SM: Default or 1"

Key as much of the letter as you can in 5 minutes.

Use the current year in the date.

Ignore misstrokes.

If you finish before time is called, start again.

September 23, 19-- ↓ line 15

Mr. Paul Johnson R/E
Head Librarian R/E
Des Moines Public Library R/E
113 Newport Way R/E
Des Moines, IA 50311 DS

Dear Mr. Johnson

Thank you for your inquiry into our database services for public libraries. We have several software programs that will fit your need for a computerized card catalog. DS

A computerized card catalog will save your library users and your staff hours of valuable time. Users will have access to much more information in much less time. DS

I am enclosing one of our brochures. If you need additional information, you may call me at (402) 691-3110. DS

Sincerely
↓ QS
Eleanor Hererra
Director DS

jac DS

Enclosure

38F
APPLICATION: LETTERS

Goal: To key business letters in block format   15 minutes

JOB 1

File name: L38F1

Letterhead

SM: Default or 1"

CUE: Use your own initials as reference initials.

(Current date)

Mr. Henry Rodriquez
Marketing Manager
Perrine, Inc.
2240 Alamo Heights
Lubbock, TX 78209

Dear Mr. Rodriquez

Have you ever explored the benefits of conference calling?
Do you know how much other marketing managers, in business-es like yours, value conference calling?

(Continued next page)

UNIT 3

Personal/Business Letters

One way of applying your keyboarding skills is through the preparation of business correspondence. In Unit 3, you will learn the parts of the block-format letter, both personal and business, and how to format these parts to prepare attractive letters.

UNIT OBJECTIVES

In this unit, Lessons 33–44, you will:

1. Increase your keyboarding speed and accuracy.
2. Prepare personal and business letters in block format.
3. Use open punctuation for salutations and complimentary closings.
4. Name, store, retrieve, print, and delete documents.
5. Key documents containing proofreader's marks.
6. Key envelope mailing addresses in OCR format.

ELECTRONIC CONCEPTS

default settings (p. 90)	documents (p. 81)	file names (p. 84)	retrieve (p. 87)
delete (p. 87)	file (p. 84)	printing (p. 90)	store (p. 86)

LESSON 33

Margins: Default or 1"
Spacing: SS or default   Tab: ¶

33A
WARMUP

Key each line twice.

DS after each pair of lines.

Goal: To strengthen keyboarding skills   5 minutes

```
1 Teresa truly tried to treasure her trophy for a trapeze act.
2 Verbal brevity is a valuable trait a volleyball devotee has.
3 The dominant horseman rode a palomino through a wheat field.
  |  1  |  2  |  3  |  4  |  5  |  6  |  7  |  8  |  9  | 10  | 11  | 12  |
```

33B
ACCURACY PRACTICE

DS after each group of lines.

Goal: To build keyboarding accuracy   5 minutes

Take a 2-minute accuracy timing on the lines in 33A. Repeat the timing. Try to improve your accuracy.

Checkpoint: Did you improve your accuracy?

38C

LANGUAGE ARTS

Goal: To review word division rules   10 minutes

Read the rules in the box at the right.

For each word in the list below the box, key the word and a colon (:).

Then,

1. Key the word in syllables.
2. Show how the word is divided.
3. Key the number of the rule(s) that apply.

Use a comma to separate items as you key them across the page.

Check your work with the key in Appendix A.

> Divide words only when absolutely necessary to maintain proper line lengths. Refer to a dictionary or word book as needed for syllabication.
>
> **Rule 1.** Never divide a one-syllable word or a word with less than six letters.
> **Rule 2.** Divide only between syllables.
> **Rule 3.** Include two or more letters with the first part of the divided word and three or more with the last part.
>
> **Examples:**
>
> | Word | Syllables | Divided Word | Rule Number |
> |------|-----------|--------------|-------------|
> | sought | sought | (do not divide) | 1 |
> | undue | un due | (do not divide) | 1 |
> | consume | con sume | con-sume | 2 |
> | carefully | care ful ly | care-fully | 3 |
> | abandoned | a ban doned | aban-doned | 3 |

Example: thought: thought, do not divide, 1

1 bought
2 frequently
3 equally
4 obtained
5 compared
6 around
7 deleting
8 length

38D

NEED TO KNOW

Goal: To learn the block format for business letters   7 minutes

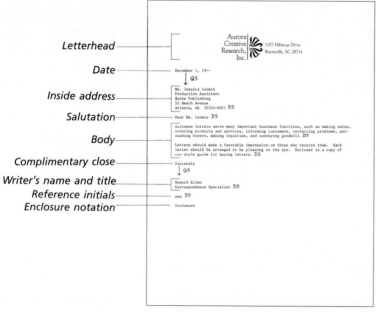

Letterhead
Date
Inside address
Salutation
Body
Complimentary close
Writer's name and title
Reference initials
Enclosure notation

Business letter in block format

1. Business letters are usually prepared on **letterhead** stationery. Letterhead is printed with the name and address of the originator's company.

2. In **block format,** the margins, spacing, and position of the date line are the same as for personal business letters.

3. Business letters may contain parts not found in personal business letters: writer's title, reference initials, and (if needed) an enclosure notation.

4. The **writer's title** is keyed as part of the signature lines immediately below the printed name.

5. The **reference initials** are the initials of the keyboard operator. They are keyed in lower-case letters a DS below the signature lines.

6. When additional items are sent with a letter, the word **enclosure** is keyed a DS below the reference initials.

Goal: To learn the block format for personal business letters   7 minutes

The **block format** may be used for personal business letters. Refer to the illustration as you read about how to prepare a block-format personal business letter.

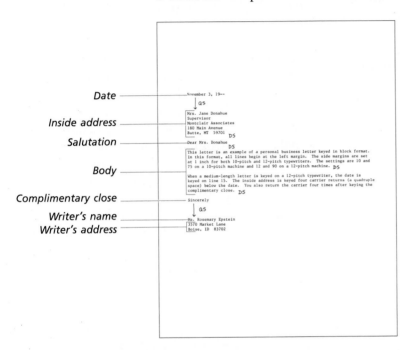

Date
Inside address
Salutation
Body
Complimentary close
Writer's name
Writer's address

November 3, 19--

QS

Mrs. Jane Donahue
Supervisor
Montclair Associates
180 Main Avenue
Butte, MT 59701
DS

Dear Mrs. Donahue
DS

This letter is an example of a personal business letter keyed in block format. In this format, all lines begin at the left margin. The side margins are set at 1 inch for both 10-pitch and 12-pitch typewriters. The settings are 10 and 75 on a 10-pitch machine and 12 and 90 on a 12-pitch machine. DS

When a medium-length letter is keyed on a 12-pitch typewriter, the date is keyed on line 15. The inside address is keyed four carrier returns (a quadruple space) below the date. You also return the carrier four times after keying the complimentary close. DS

Sincerely
QS

Ms. Rosemary Epstein
3570 Market Lane
Boise, ID 83702

Personal business letter in block format

1. Key all lines beginning at the left margin.
2. Use default side margin settings if available. Or set 1-inch side margins.
3. The position of the date line varies according to letter length. For the medium-length letters you will be keying in this unit, key the **date** (month, day, and year) on line 15.

   E M Use the return/enter key to space down to line 15. Most electronic equipment has a default top margin setting. That is, a certain number of lines are set aside for a top margin. The auto page insert on electronic typewriters automatically spaces down the number of lines in the default top margin. Include these lines in your count to line 15. For example, if you have a top margin default of 6 lines, count down 9 more lines (6 + 9 = 15) to key the date on line 15.
4. Key the **inside address** 4 spaces—a quadruple space **(QS)**—below the date. (For QS, press the return/enter key four times.) The inside address contains the name, title, company name, and address of the addressee (the person to whom the letter is written).
5. Leave two spaces between the two-letter state abbreviation and the ZIP Code. (ZIP-Plus has a hyphen and four numbers following the ZIP Code.)
6. Key the **salutation** 2 spaces—a double space **(DS)**—below the inside address. The salutation usually begins with *Dear* followed by a courtesy title and the addressee's last name (for example, Dear Mrs. Hayes). For open punctuation, do not key a colon after the salutation.
7. Single space **(SS)** the **body** of the letter. DS between paragraphs; do not indent paragraphs. Allow auto return or word wrap to determine line endings, or listen for the margin signal to determine when to press return/enter.
8. Key the **complimentary close** (for example, Sincerely) a DS below the body. For open punctuation, do not key a comma after the complimentary close.
9. Key the **writer's name** (the person who wrote the letter) a QS below the complimentary close. This will leave enough space for the writer's handwritten signature.
10. Key the **writer's address** below the writer's name. SS the writer's address.

37F

APPLICATION: LETTERS

Goal: To key personal business letters in block format   17 minutes

JOB 1

File name: L37F1

Dr. Robert Orsi / Director of Admissions / Alston City College / 4389 School Street / Boston, MA 02176 / (supply salutation) / I am interested in pursuing a career in accounting or computer science. I understand that your college has an excellent computer science program. ¶ Please send me a course catalog, a registration form, and a schedule of classes for the fall term. As I am not a state resident, I also would like some information regarding tuition and housing. ¶ I would appreciate receiving any other information that you feel would be helpful to a prospective student. / Sincerely / (supply your name and address)

Checkpoint: Did you supply an appropriate salutation?

JOB 2

File name: L37F2

Ms. Catherine Morello-Simmons / Station Manager / Radio Station KRXB / 1734 Lincoln Avenue / Seattle, WA 98107 / (supply salutation) / Last Sunday evening I listened to your "Evening Serenade" program that was broadcast between 7 and 9 p.m. It was one of the most enjoyable programs I have heard in many years. The selection of music, from classical to soft rock, was outstanding. Your disc jockey, Alvin Calhoun, makes the program even more interesting with his little bits of humor. ¶ I am interested in changing my career. I would like to work in the field of broadcasting. Would it be possible for me to visit your station to see for myself how a program like this is put together? I can be at your station any time after 6 p.m. / Sincerely / (supply your name and address)

LESSON 38

Margins: Default or 1"
Spacing: SS or default   Tab: ¶

38A

WARMUP

Key each line twice. DS after each pair.

confusing words: it's and its

Goal: To strengthen keyboarding skills   5 minutes

1 It's too soon to tell whether Anne passed the algebra class.
2 Northwest High chose its principal from the three finalists.
3 It's certain that Pamela's sense of duty was its own reward.

| 1 | 2 | 3 | 4 | 5 | 6 | 7 | 8 | 9 | 10 | 11 | 12 |

38B

SPEED PRACTICE

Take two 30-second timings on each sentence. Try to increase your speed on the second timing.

GWAM = 1'GWAM × 2

Goal: To build keyboarding speed   5 minutes

	1'
1 The one wish of the city panel is to have downtown activity.	12
2 England is to handle the usual profit for their marine work.	24
3 The downtown chairman of the coal firm is to work for a day.	36
4 This cup is neither fir nor oak, but this cane chair is oak.	48

| 1 | 2 | 3 | 4 | 5 | 6 | 7 | 8 | 9 | 10 | 11 | 12 |

33D

Goal: To key a personal business letter in block format   7 minutes

SM: Default or 1″

Body: Auto return or margin signal.

Key as much of the letter as you can in 5 minutes.

Use the current year in the date.

Ignore misstrokes.

If you finish before time is called, start again.

October 10, 19--   ↓ line 15
   ↓ QS
Mrs. Kerri Mullins R/E
Sales Manager R/E
InfoTech, Inc. R/E
2903 Wadsworth Avenue R/E
Inglewood, CA 90303-1001 DS

Dear Mrs. Mullins DS

Last month, I purchased a SERIES IX PLUS computer system from your company. I'm very satisfied with my system; however, as I discover more uses for my SERIES IX PLUS, I find that I need additional components. DS

Do you stock a 20-megabyte hard disk drive and a screen for color graphics? A hard disk drive would improve my storage capacity, while color graphics would enhance the quality of my work. DS

Please send me a price list of all the components you have available for the SERIES IX PLUS system. DS

Sincerely
   ↓ QS
Mr. Scott Farrell R/E
8260 County Line Road R/E
Whittier, CA 90609 R/E

33E

NEED TO KNOW

Goal: To learn about Production Timings   2 minutes

The Production Timing in 33F allows you to practice keying the opening lines of a letter. The purpose of a Production Timing is to help you learn to move quickly through a frequently used format. Production Timings are the first step in the process of developing your production skills—your ability to prepare quality **documents** within a specified time period.

33F

PRODUCTION TIMING

Goal: To build speed in keying opening lines   6 minutes

Take a 2-minute timing on these opening lines.

Repeat the timing.

Resume keying without pausing after each return/enter.

1 February 12, 19--
   ↓ QS
  Ms. Ellen Babb
  Human Resources Director
  Rapid Print Documents
  780 Murphy Lane
  Duluth, MN 55830-3081 DS

  Dear Ms. Babb

2 June 7, 19--
   ↓ QS
  Mr. Norman Ford
  Office Manager
  M. Bradley, Inc.
  3491 Downing Road
  Portland, OR 97219 DS

  Dear Mr. Ford

5. The first section that I read in a newspaper is ____.
6. My favorite dinner to prepare is ____, and its main ingredients are ____, ____, and ____.
7. The brand name of the keyboard that I am using is ____, and its color is ____.
8. Some careers that might use my keyboarding skills are ____, ____, and ____.
9. The name of this class is ____.
10. I'd like to compose a letter to ____ who lives in ____.

37D

READ AND DO   **Goal:** To learn about salutations in letters   8 minutes

The salutation is a greeting to the person receiving the letter.

1. The correct form to use is the courtesy title (*Mr., Ms.,* etc.) and the person's last name. (If you know the person well, you may address him or her by first name.)
2. The salutation generally used in personal business letters is *Dear,* as in *Dear Dr. Groves.*
3. If the letter is addressed to a company or department, the accepted salutations are *Ladies and Gentlemen* or *Dear Sir or Madam.*
4. You also may use a business title if you do not know the individual's name, as in *Dear Credit Manager* or *Dear Executive Editor.*

5. For open punctuation, do not key a colon after the salutation.

Key the first line of each inside address given below. On the next line, key the appropriate salutation. DS between items.

1. Mr. Richard Koeppe
2. The Norton Corporation
3. Mrs. Charles Picco
4. Merit Life and Casualty Company
5. Dr. Sandra Chamberlain
6. Mr. David Blake
7. Margaret Atwood
8. Mr. Norman Sanford
9. Personnel Specialist
10. R. Minichiello Associates

37E

SELF-CHECK   **Goal:** To review the salutation in business letters   5 minutes

Key the statement number and your answer: True or False.

Check your answers in Appendix B.

1. Leave a triple space between the salutation and the body of a business letter.
2. An accepted salutation in a letter addressed to a company is *Dear Sir.*
3. The correct courtesy title to use when you do not know a woman's marital status is *Mrs.*
4. The person named in the salutation of a business letter is the same one whose name appears in the first line of the inside address.
5. If the first line of the inside address is *Mrs. Maggie Creighton,* the salutation is *Dear Mrs. Creighton.*
6. If a letter is addressed to *Mrs. Maggie Creighton, Marketing Manager,* an appropriate salutation to use is *Dear Marketing Manager.*

Goal: To key personal business letters in block format   18 minutes

SM: Default or 1"

Body: Auto return or margin signal

Use the current year in the date line.

CUE: Remember to include the default top margin in the 15 lines.

November 12, 19-- ↓ line 15
    ↓ QS
Mr. Robert Turner
Director of Admissions
Tri-State University
1164 College Road
Fort Collins, CO   80521 DS

Dear Mr. Turner DS

I want to attend Tri-State University's College of Business.
I graduated in the upper 10 percent of my class at Pueblo
City High School with a grade point average of 3.75. While
attending high school, I studied business subjects, including
accounting, communications, office procedures, and information
processing. DS

I am very interested in entering the field of business.
A bachelor's degree in business administration will help me
reach this goal. DS

Please send me an application for admission to the College
of Business and a course catalog. I would also appreciate any
available information on financial aid. DS

Sincerely
    ↓ QS
Mr. Steven Terry
421 Orman Avenue
Pueblo, CO   81004

Checkpoint: Did you remember to include the default top margin in your line count?

Key the letter in 33D. Make the changes shown to the right.

1. Change the date to:

   today's date

2. Change the inside address to:

   Mrs. Lois Gonzales
   Manager
   Marks Business Systems
   8502 East Santa Fe Trail
   Taos, NM 87571

3. Change the salutation to:

   Dear Mrs. Gonzales

4. Key your name and address as the originator.

JOB 2

File name: L36G2

Mrs. Mae Roe / Recreation Director / Snowmass Recreational Center / P. O. Box 711 / Aspen, CO 81611 / Dear Mrs. Roe / Thank you for taking time to talk with me yesterday about working in your accounting office. The information about working conditions, benefits, and salary makes the position of accounts receivable clerk perfect for me. (¶) The Snowmass Recreational facilities are impressive. The employees I met yesterday seemed to be happy and to enjoy their work. (¶) I look forward to hearing from you next Friday. A position as an accounts receivable clerk at your center sounds exciting. / Sincerely / Ms. Ruby Chow / 1710 Ivy Street / Durango, CO 81301

LESSON 37

Margins: Default or 1"
Spacing: SS or default   Tab: ¶

37A
WARMUP

Goal: To strengthen keyboarding skills   5 minutes

Key each line twice. DS after each pair of lines.

Speed
Accuracy
Number/Symbol

1 In the future, their information should be sent only to her.
2 Cr., bus., amt., bal., and acct. are business abbreviations.
3 Invoices 22-348 and 23-902 (10/8 and 10/19) total $1,104.70.

| 1 | 2 | 3 | 4 | 5 | 6 | 7 | 8 | 9 | 10 | 11 | 12 |

37B
GOAL WRITING

DS or default.

Take two 3-minute goal writings.

If you finish before time is called, start again.

Goal: To measure timed-writing progress   10 minutes

	1'	3'
Running is now one of the most popular sports. Many	11	4
people talk about jogging and running as if the terms	22	7
were the same, but running is usually faster than jogging	33	11
because people who jog do not aim for speed.	42	14
The nice thing about running is that it takes no	52	17
special skill or facilities. The only equipment needed to	64	21
succeed is proper shoes and clothing. As a precaution,	75	25
older people and those not used to vigorous exercise should	87	29
have a physical exam prior to starting a running program.	99	33

| 1' | 1 | 2 | 3 | 4 | 5 | 6 | 7 | 8 | 9 | 10 | 11 | 12 | AWL |
| 3' | | 1 | | 2 | | 3 | | 4 | | 5.7 |

37C
KEYBOARD COMPOSITION

Key these sentences, supplying words or phrases to complete them.

Goal: To compose at the keyboard   5 minutes

1. I have lived in ____ for ____ years.
2. I can key ____ words a minute on a ____ minute goal writing.
3. My favorite sections of a keyboarding lesson are ____ and ____.
4. ____ is the most ____ class that I am taking this year.

(Continued next page)

34A
WARMUP

Goal: To strengthen keyboarding skills   5 minutes

Key each line twice. DS after each pair of lines.

Speed
Accuracy
Number/Symbol

1 If she signs the document   she may not go with the auditors.
2 Will and Zedekiah will work the west zone with Zoe and Whit.
3 Two changes (2109 N. 1450 E. and 1129 W. 650 N.) were noted.

| 1 | 2 | 3 | 4 | 5 | 6 | 7 | 8 | 9 | 10 | 11 | 12 |

34B
GOAL WRITING

Goal: To measure timed-writing progress   10 minutes

DS or default.

Take two 3-minute goal writings.

If you finish before time is called, start again.

Record your speed and accuracy.

	1′	3′
Sheep are important domestic animals because they	10	3
provide us with both food and clothing.	18	6
Sheep inhabit most countries of the world. In some	29	10
countries, sheep are more prevalent than people. Prosperity	41	14
is gauged by the number of sheep that a person owns.	52	17
Sheep are raised in a variety of ways. One important	63	21
way is on the open range where they are herded in groups	74	25
numbering in the thousands. They may also be raised on	85	28
individual farms where one rancher may have just a few.	96	32

1′ | 1 | 2 | 3 | 4 | 5 | 6 | 7 | 8 | 9 | 10 | 11 | 12 |

3′ | 1 | 2 | 3 | 4 |

AWL
5.7

34C
PRODUCTION TIMING

Goal: To build speed in keying closing lines   5 minutes

Resume keying without pausing after each return/enter.

Take two 2-minute timings on these lines.

Try to increase your production speed on the second timing.

1 Sincerely
↓ QS
Mrs. Lillian Smithe
2400 Kalakaua Avenue
Honolulu, HI 96815

2 Sincerely
↓ QS
Mr. Ernest Dowell
649 Empire Circle
Bozeman, MT 59715-3315

34D
KEYBOARD COMPOSITION

Goal: To compose at the keyboard   5 minutes

Complete each sentence.

Do not correct errors.

1. This weekend I might ____
2. I would like to spend a month in ____
3. During the winter months, I like to ____
4. One of the nicest people I know is ____

(Continued next page)

36E E M

Goal: To learn how to print a document   7 minutes

The final step in document preparation is the **printing** process. Before printing a document, proofread it carefully and correct all errors.

E *Electronic Typewriters*

Documents that have been stored may be printed at a later date. To print a document:

1. Insert paper. Use the same pitch printwheel/element you used when you keyed the document. Also set the same margins, tabs, and line spacing.
2. Position the carrier where you want the document to begin printing.
3. Press the print key or command.
4. Key the file name or the storage area.
5. Press the key or command to start printing.

M *Microcomputers*

Using these steps as a guide, follow printing procedures for your software.

1. Store the document.
2. Select the print option from the main menu, or key the print command.
3. Select the appropriate format for the document. If necessary, change the software's **default settings** to match those of the document. That is,
   a. Key the desired format changes as they are requested by the prompt, or
   b. Move the cursor through a list of default settings, and key the desired changes.
4. Check to see that your printer is on and ready to print. Be sure the paper is aligned correctly.
5. Key the command to start printing.

36F

NEED TO KNOW   **Goal:** To learn to key unarranged copy   3 minutes

Some of the letters in this unit require you to make decisions about the arrangement and spacing of the letter parts on the page.

Diagonal lines (/) indicate the end of a line or a letter part. When you see a diagonal line, decide how many times to press the return/enter key. For example, if the copy reads *Dear Mrs. DiAngelo/*, press the return/enter key twice before keying the body of the letter.

Double space and begin a new paragraph when you see the paragraph symbol (¶).

36G

APPLICATION: LETTERS   **Goal:** To key personal business letters in block format   22 minutes

JOB 1

File name: L36G1

Mr. Isaac Rudnick / Director / Reynolds Computer Company / 2674 Central Avenue / New Orleans, LA 70633-4426 / Dear Mr. Rudnick / As a testimonial to the DATA MASTER 2400 computer your company sold me last month, I would like to tell you how satisfied I am. The DATA MASTER has helped me keep accurate banking records. Information for my banking transactions is easy to input. A running balance is always available. My DATA MASTER also enables me to keep an up-to-date appointment calendar. New appointments and cancellations are made quickly and easily. (¶) Each week I find new uses for my DATA MASTER computer. I expect to enjoy using my DATA MASTER for many years to come. / Sincerely / Kay Castro / 2372 Fairview Avenue / Bogalusa, LA 70427

> **Checkpoint:** Did you space correctly between the letter parts?

(Continued next page)

5. A concept I would like to learn more about is ____
6. What I like about spring is ____
7. Listening to music ____
8. One thing that I wish I could do is ____
9. One of the best things about being in a big city is ____
10. I may use my keyboarding skills in ____

34E

READ AND DO

Goal: To learn how to name a file   8 minutes

Some electronic equipment can save documents for future use. When saving or storing a document, the equipment creates a **file,** which you can name. Files are stored either in memory or on a floppy disk.

Because stored documents are usually referred to by their **file names,** choose a name that will help you remember the file's contents. For example, if your document is a report on tourism in Texas, you might name the file—Tourism in Texas.

Before you can name a file, you need to know the requirements of your equipment or software. Some equipment or software require the file name to begin with a letter instead of a number or a symbol. Other equipment accept punctuation or blank spaces within the name. Still others limit the number of characters in the file name.

If the number of characters in a file name is limited, you may need to abbreviate words. For example, assume you are allowed a maximum of eight characters in a file name. For your report on tourism in Texas, you might abbreviate and use a file name such as TourTX.

Create a file name for each of these documents. Key the number of each document (followed by a period and two spaces) and your file name.

1. Report of spring sales figures
2. Letter to Electronic World
3. Agenda for the monthly directors' meeting
4. Minutes of the monthly marketing meeting
5. Letter to Mr. R. C. Jason
6. Memo about product price increases
7. List of expenses for March
8. Report on new marketing tactics

34F

APPLICATION: LETTERS

Goal: To key personal business letters in block format   17 minutes

JOB 1

File name: L34F1

SM: Default or 1"

Note: Beginning in this lesson and continuing through the book, file names are given.

Unless your teacher tells you differently, use the suggested file names for the documents you prepare.

CUE: Use today's date in the date line.

(Current date)

Ms. Elizabeth Rivera
Fashion Editor
Smart Dressing
5690 Lexington Boulevard
Covington, KY 41011

Dear Ms. Rivera

In the August issue of Smart Dressing, you advertised AERIO shoes (page 45) for those who want to "look professional and feel comfortable." The style in the photo appears to be a shoe that is appropriate for most business engagements.

(Continued next page)

36A
WARMUP

Key each line twice.

DS after each pair.

Frequently misspelled words

Goal: To strengthen keyboarding skills   5 minutes

```
1 Cassy has assured the astonished eastern Asian of the asset.
2 Fong was fatigued with the frightening fight for five frogs.
3 Lanky Luke felt lucky to pluck the nickel from a clear lake.

  |   1 |   2 |   3 |   4 |   5 |   6 |   7 |   8 |   9 |  10 |  11 |  12 |
```

36B
ACCURACY PRACTICE

DS after each group of lines.

Goal: To build keyboarding accuracy   5 minutes

Take a 2-minute accuracy timing on the lines in 36A. Repeat the timing. Try to improve your accuracy.

Checkpoint: Did you improve your accuracy?

36C
NEED TO KNOW

Goal: To learn the correct format for inside addresses   3 minutes

1. The first line of an inside address identifies the addressee, the person to whom the letter is written. The correct form consists of a courtesy title, the individual's first name, initial, and last name.
2. Courtesy titles include *Mr., Mrs., Miss, Ms.,* and *Dr.* Use *Ms.* when you do not know the marital status of a woman or when she prefers this title.
3. The second line of the address usually contains the person's business title, if it is known.
4. The next line contains the company's name.
5. The most important address information is in the last two lines. The second line from the bottom contains a number and street name or a post office box to which mail is delivered.

6. The city, two-letter state abbreviation, and ZIP Code are on the last line. Separate the city and state abbreviation with a comma. Leave two spaces between the state and ZIP Code.

```
Addressee's name ──────→ Ms. Carole E. Lanoff
Business title ────────→ Office Manager
Company name ──────────→ System Design, Ltd.
Street address ───────→ 5681 Hillside Road
City, state, and ─────→ Columbia, MO  65201
   ZIP Code
```

36D
SELF-CHECK

Key the statement number and your answer: True or False.

Check your answers in Appendix B.

Goal: To review the inside address in business letters   5 minutes

1. The first line of an inside address identifies the addressee.
2. The addressee is the person who wrote the letter.
3. *Mr.* and *Ms.* are examples of courtesy titles.
4. An addressee's business title is usually keyed on the second line of the inside address.
5. Always separate the state abbreviation from the ZIP Code with a comma.
6. Leave a double space after the inside address.

I wear a size nine shoe and have difficulty finding that size in styles that are fashionable and suit my taste. Would you please send me a listing of stores in the San Francisco Bay area where AERIO shoes are sold?

Sincerely

Ms. Kristine Malmburg
1613 Pacifica Avenue
Walnut Creek, CA 94597

> **Checkpoint:** Did you use a QS after the date and the complimentary close?

JOB 2

File name: L34F2

SM: Default or 1"

Use current date.

Send to:

Mr. Paul Balentine
Accounting Supervisor
Polo Shop
611 Mitchell Avenue
Baton Rouge, LA 70893

Dear Mr. Balentine

Your billing clerk, Ms. Jeanne Henning, asked me to write to you. My monthly statement arrived today with a $700 charge that I am unable to identify. I have checked my receipts, and I cannot find a charge for this amount. Could this be a computer error?

Please help me resolve this matter immediately. I have always enjoyed shopping at the Polo Shop. Your service and merchandise are outstanding.

Sincerely

Mr. Douglas Newmann
3018 Moline Way
Baton Rouge, LA 70846

LESSON 35

Margins: Default or 1"
Spacing: SS or default   Tab: ¶

35A
WARMUP

Key each line twice.
DS after each pair.

"ing" combinations

Goal: To strengthen keyboarding skills   5 minutes

1 skating dancing talking wishing skiing singing eating buying
2 I feel like singing while I am dancing or skating or skiing.
3 Stopping those running around the swimming pool is her duty.

| 1 | 2 | 3 | 4 | 5 | 6 | 7 | 8 | 9 | 10 | 11 | 12 |

35G

**APPLICATION:
LETTERS**

Goal: To key personal business letters in block format   26 minutes

JOB 1

File name: L35G1

CUE: Supply the date.

Mr. John Lange
Director of Admissions
Tampa Business College
6502 Market Street
Tampa, FL 33690

Dear Mr. Lange

Thank you for the information about computers and careers
you shared with the Temple City Business Club. Most of us
were unaware of the careers available for individuals who
have good keyboarding skills and an interest in computers.

Several of us are interested in learning more about the
course offerings at Tampa Business College. Will you please
send me a fall course catalog? Will you also send me the
name of one of your career counselors?

I am glad you were able to speak to the members of our
business club. As you know, the club was organized to
give young people an opportunity to investigate careers that
are available to them in business.

Sincerely

Ms. Beth Panbaker
81 Downing Road
Tampa, FL 33687

JOB 2

File name: L35G2

Key the letter in 34F, Job 2. Make these changes:

1. Change the inside address to:

   Ms. Rebecca Marshall
   Accounts Payable Manager
   Merritt Department Store
   203 Main Street
   Baton Rouge, LA 70842

2. Change the salutation to:

   Dear Ms. Marshall

3. Change the billing clerk's name to:

   Mr. Rodney Barber

JOB 3

File name: L35G3

Key the letter in 35G, Job 1. Make these changes:

1. Change the inside address to:

   Mr. Gordon Carlson
   Admissions Director
   Lubbock Business Institute
   8720 Old Post Road
   Lubbock, TX 79401

2. Change the salutation to:

   Dear Mr. Carlson

3. Change the name of the business college to:

   Lubbock Business Institute

35B

SPEED PRACTICE

Goal: To build keyboarding speed   5 minutes

Take a 20- or 15-second timing on each line. If you complete a line in the time allowed, go on to the next one.

		20"	15"
1	The girl went downtown in the auto.	21	28
2	Eight emblems make the window confusing.	24	32
3	The author of the civic maps works two hours.	27	36
4	The panel paid the conductor and spent the profit.	30	40

| 1 | 2 | 3 | 4 | 5 | 6 | 7 | 8 | 9 | 10 |

35C

SELF-CHECK

Goal: To review the block format   5 minutes

Key the statement number and your answer: True or False.

Check your answers in Appendix B.

1. In block format, all lines begin at the left margin.
2. When keying a block-format letter, set 1-inch side margins.
3. The date of a block-format letter is always keyed on line 14.
4. The inside address is keyed a double space below the date.
5. The salutation is keyed a double space below the inside address.
6. In block format, the first line of a paragraph indents five spaces.
7. The body begins a TS below the inside address.
8. In a block-format letter, DS between paragraphs.
9. The body of a block format letter is DS.
10. The complimentary close begins a QS after the body.

35D E M

NEED TO KNOW

Goal: To learn how to store documents   3 minutes

A feature of most electronic equipment is the capability to **store** documents for later recall or retrieval.

E *Electronic Typewriters*

The procedure for storing text varies; however, the basic process includes these steps:

1. Insert paper. Determine whether your printwheel/element is 10 or 12 pitch. Then set margins, tabs, and line spacing.
2. Press the store key or begin the store command. You may need to specify a storage area or give a file name.
3. Key the document.
4. Press the store key or end the store command to close storage.

M *Microcomputers*

For some software, storing is referred to as saving a file. Select an option or use a command to store or save

a document. Until you give a store command, a document exists only in the microcomputer's memory. If you turn the microcomputer off without storing the document, you will lose the copy you have keyed.

Each software program has its own menu or its own commands for storing documents. However, the procedure is usually to key the document; then select and follow the steps that apply to your software:

1. Select the store or save option, or key the store command for your software.
2. Key the file name of the document, if prompted to do so.
3. Respond to other prompts that may appear on your screen. If you have a dual disk drive, you may need to tell the computer which disk drive contains the file.

35E E M

NEED TO KNOW   **Goal: To learn how to retrieve documents**   3 minutes

A document that has been stored in the memory of an electronic typewriter or on a microcomputer disk, can be recalled or **retrieved** for use at a later time.

E *Electronic Typewriters*

Some electronic typewriters play back or print a stored document. Others send the document through the typewriter's display screen. To retrieve a document:

1. Insert the paper. Set the margins and tabs if your typewriter prints the document. Position the carrier and paper where you want the document to begin printing.
2. Press the retrieve key or begin the retrieve command.
3. Key the file name or the storage area of the document.
4. Press the appropriate key or use the appropriate command to start the process.

The typewriter either plays back or displays the document. Typewriters that display stored text usually have a command or key that allows you to scroll the text forward. Use this feature to review the stored document.

M *Microcomputers*

Before you retrieve a document that has been stored in a file, you may need to clear your microcomputer's memory or screen. (Remember to store or save an existing document before starting a new one.)

The procedure for retrieving stored files may include the following steps. Follow those that apply to your software.

1. Select the retrieve or recall option, or key the command to retrieve a file.
2. Key the file name of the document being retrieved. If you have a dual disk drive, you may need to tell the microcomputer which disk drive contains the file you want.

If you cannot remember the name of a file, key a directory command to display a list of the file names that are stored on a particular disk.

When you retrieve a document, the microcomputer puts a duplicate, working copy, of the document into the microcomputer's memory. The original document stays in storage. You may change or print the working copy. Any changes you make will occur only in the working copy until that copy is stored. Once the working copy is stored, it usually replaces the original document stored in the file.

35F E M

NEED TO KNOW   **Goal: To learn how to delete a stored document**   3 minutes

When no longer needed, a document or file may be **deleted** or removed from the memory of an electronic typewriter or from a microcomputer disk.

E *Electronic Typewriters*

Some electronic typewriters use a delete key. Others use one or more commands to delete a document or file from memory. Depending on your typewriter, you may use the following steps:

1. Press and hold down the delete key, or key the command for your typewriter.
2. Key the file name or the storage area.
3. Key other commands as necessary.

M *Microcomputers*

Adjust the following procedures for deleting a document or file to fit your software.

1. Select the files option from the main menu.
2. Select the delete option from the files menu.
3. Select the file that is to be deleted.
   a. Either move the cursor to the file you want to delete and enter the command that deletes the file, or
   b. At the prompt, key the appropriate file name (be sure to key the file name correctly).

A Key to Language Arts

Activity 20D

(1) The <u>concert</u> was well attended.
(2) The <u>children</u> played <u>games</u> and broke <u>balloons</u>.
(3) Do you plan to attend the <u>seminar</u> with Nancy?
(4) He spoke to the <u>attorney</u> and to Judge Blackburn.
(5) <u>Baseball</u> and <u>dancing</u> are her favorite <u>activities</u>.

Activity 24E

(1) My friend Susan will enter Roosevelt High School.
(2) His favorite teacher, Ms. Mason, speaks Spanish.
(3) The young man attends the U.S. Air Force Academy.
(4) The Baxters will visit Yellowstone National Park.
(5) Did you go to the Sears Tower in Chicago?
(6) The Lorex Corporation is in Bellevue, Washington.
(7) Is your new address 32 Rosecrans Boulevard?
(8) Basketball is popular at Syracuse University.
(9) Plays by William Shakespeare will be featured.

Activity 38C

(1) bought, do not divide, 1
(2) fre quent ly, fre-quently, 3
(3) e qual ly, do not divide, 3
(4) ob tained, ob-tained, 3
(5) com pared, com-pared, 2
(6) a round, do not divide, 3
(7) de let ing, delet-ing, 2
(8) length, do not divide, 1

Activity 39C

(1) Thanks giv ing, do not divide, 4
(2) Sep tem ber 5, 1989; do not divide, 4
(3) grand moth er, grand-mother, 5
(4) Mr. John Roberts, do not divide, 4
(5) $17,845,890.17, do not divide, 4
(6) self con fi dence, self-confidence, 5
(7) su per hu man, super-human, 5
(8) well be haved, well-behaved, 5
(9) De troit, do not divide, 4

Activity 41B

(1) My letter dated March 29 contained some inaccurate information.
(2) We plan to open our new office on Wednesday, May 15.
(3) We are open for business Tuesday through Friday.
(4) We are closed on Monday, May 25, for Memorial Day.
(5) Our big clearance sale takes place on the Monday after New Year's Day.
(6) July 4 is also known as Independence Day.
(7) We will be open on weekends after Labor Day.
(8) I don't like to work on Saturday or Sunday.
(9) When I work on Christmas, I get paid double time.

Activity 43D

(1) Annie has decided to attend Clement College next year.
(2) The Needle in a Haystack is my favorite needlepoint shop.
(3) Tomorrow's concert will feature The Boston City Orchestra.
(4) Elizabeth's attorneys are with Post, Czarnek, and Pillar.
(5) The omelets at the Sunshine Cafe are simply delicious.
(6) Wendy has belonged to the Daytona Club for 15 years.
(7) Our school tennis team practices at Racquets Unlimited.
(8) The cheerleaders of Westland University won the competition.
(9) Golf practice is available year-round at Pro Golf, Inc.
(10) Don't overlook Ye Olde Corner Cafe in your search.

Activity 47D

(1) Ann Green attends Green Valley Community College.
(2) On Monday, April 15, Richard Dannon will speak here.
(3) John works for Educational Computer Systems of America, Inc.
(4) They work on all holidays, even Christmas and Easter.
(5) Their working hours are 9–5:30, Monday through Saturday.
(6) My work at the hospital will be finished in August.
(7) The words <u>many</u>, <u>staff</u>, and <u>along</u> cannot be divided.
(8) You should not divide the names of holidays.
(9) You should not divide the names of people.
(10) You should not divide a number.

Activity 51B

(1) Because of its value, the museum doubled its security.
(2) Do you remember if it's ever been awarded to their accountant?
(3) A bird always makes its home in a relatively safe spot.
(4) Ms. Whitworth replied, "I don't think it's a suitable reason."
(5) If George thinks it's hectic now, he won't believe the tax season.
(6) A weasel must find its way back home through a set of tunnels.
(7) Because of its great popularity, the rally is held every year.
(8) Rodgers asked whether it's ever happened before at work.
(9) It's going to be one year before it's time to buy a new car.
(10) It's too bad that Harry can't locate its original owner.

input information given to an operator in various forms for processing, or data and instructions given to a computer to enable it to do a specific job

insert the process of adding new copy to text that has already been keyed

laser printer a printer that produces letter-quality documents by using laser technology

letter quality printer a printer that produces high quality output that is similar to that of a typewriter

memory the capability of equipment to store information and to retrieve, delete, or change it at a later time

menu a list of functions that a computer performs in relation to the software program that is being used

merging the combining of a list of variables (such as addresses) with a document (such as a letter)

microcomputer a small computer with enough power and storage capacity to meet the needs of many different kinds of users

modem a hardware device that enables computers to communicate with one another by telephone

monitor the display screen of a computer that allows the user to view all data entered through the software or the keyboard

mouse an input device consisting of a small box with one or more buttons; as the user moves the box, the cursor moves around the screen

network a number of computers or communicating devices linked together to electronically transmit data from one location to another

numeric keyboard a group of keys resembling the keys of a calculator that are used to input numbers

OCR optical character reader, scans typewritten or printed text and converts the characters into electronic signals that a computer can read

option one of the functions that can be selected from a software menu

output the final document produced by a word processing system

page layout the vertical and horizontal arrangement of a document on a page.

peripherals input and output devices such as terminals, keyboards, and printers that are connected to a word processing system

print the process of converting screen or disk copy to hard (paper) copy

printout a document printed on paper

program disk a disk upon which a program is stored

prompt a message that appears on the display screen and asks that the user respond

relocate key returns the carrier to the last keying position in a document

retrieve the transfer of stored documents from storage into memory

ruler/format line usually displayed at the top or bottom of a computer screen to show the left and right margin settings and tab settings

scroll the process of moving text up, down, and to the left or the right in order to view additional characters

software a set of programmed instructions stored on disk that tells the computer what to do

status line a line of information displayed on the microcomputer screen. The status line usually indicates the line and column position of the cursor.

store the placement of documents on a disk or in memory so that they may be recalled at a later time

student disk a disk that stores the data keyed by a student

subscript numbers, letters, or symbols that are printed one-half line below the text line

superscript numbers, letters, or symbols that are printed one-half line above the text line

system disk a disk upon which the operating system of the computer is stored

temporary indent a command that creates a temporary left margin thereby indenting successive lines of text

text editor a word processor with the ability to insert, delete, move, revise, and store text

word processing the use of a computer system to process text—documents such as letters, memorandums, reports, and manuscripts

word wrap the automatic movement of a word from one line to the next when the word goes beyond the right margin setting; same as automatic return

Activity 55C

(1) For the past five weeks, I have worked much too long each day.
(2) Jon said that he, too, went to Florida for two weeks in April.
(3) If you are too tired to work, try one or two days of vacation.
(4) In about two or three months, Debbie will travel to Rome.
(5) Pam said she will need at least two chances to pass that test.
(6) Two of the supervisors took much too long getting the results.
(7) The two operators had to learn a lot about the equipment.
(8) If the batter is too thin, the cookies will be flat and dry, too.
(9) Martha, Frank, and Lauren want to go to the play with us.
(10) Jonathan said that he, too, wanted two weeks off in September for his trip to Hawaii.

Activity 57E

(1) They're planning a visit to Houston to inspect their property.
(2) There are four students who have completed their reports.
(3) Randy should arrive at their house about sundown on Wednesday.
(4) If they're going to stop there first, they should leave earlier.
(5) Their group was selected because they're the most qualified.
(6) There are three reasons they're returning their refunds to us.
(7) They're going to take some aluminum cans there for recycling.
(8) He thinks that their idea to start the project is a good one.
(9) Why can't they wait their turn? They're not showing courtesy.

Activity 58C

(1) If you're sure about your decision, then return your report to me.
(2) When you get your jacket back, you will be fortunate indeed.
(3) When you're through with your notes, please give them to Sue.
(4) You hunch is correct; Paula is the person you're seeking.
(5) Your design was outstanding, and your presentation was superb.
(6) You're undoubtedly the best discussion leader in your section.
(7) Your estimates were close, and your projections were accurate.
(8) After completing your reviews, you must return all your files.

(9) You're the best person, and you're certain to get their votes.
(10) Once you're certified, your salary will increase.

Activity 59C

(1) Most of the groups are sure to have an hour in which to relax.
(2) Can you have our final specifications ready for us in an hour?
(3) They were told that our presentation could last for about an hour.
(4) Our task force will require the full hour to provide a report.
(5) Are they going to require more than an hour to check our work?
(6) Our software and our hardware are due to arrive here on May 8.
(7) If you need an hour, our supervisors will see that you get it.
(8) Frankly, our recommendations are kept confidential.
(9) We must tell Rhonda that our decisions are not binding on her.
(10) Are you sure that our complete report can be ready in an hour?

Activity 61C

(1) Maria's favorite song is "Somewhere My Love."
(2) The title of the first chapter is "My Childhood."
(3) Robert Frost's poem "Birches" is one of my favorites.
(4) Her speech about animal rights was titled "Give a Hoot."
(5) One segment of the news program was titled "Dirty Air, Dirty Water."
(6) I read his article, "Success the Easy Way."
(7) He wrote Chapter 1, "In the Beginning," in one morning.
(8) My poem, "A Ray of Hope," is published in that anthology.
(9) "The Clean Machine: Car Maintenance" is the title of her speech.
(10) The chorus sang "There Is Sunshine."

Activity 63C

(1) The textbook we will use is Business and the Law.
(2) He borrowed my copy of the book The Origin of Words.
(3) I subscribe to three of the most popular magazines: Newsreport, Quest, and Sports Afield.
(4) Jane sold three freelance articles to Campers on Vacation.
(5) My favorite movie, Star Vision, is on television tonight.
(6) Their uncle wrote scripts for many television series, including the series The Golden Days.
(7) Our Time is the play our theater group will produce.
(8) Money Talks is a funnier play than Signs of the Times.
(9) The Wall Street Record has informative articles.
(10) Did you get the August issue of Dancer's News?

Activity 66D

(1) Julio asked, "May I have the reports now?"

archive disk a disk on which a file copy of information is transferred from the system

automatic centering a software or machine function that horizontally centers words or lines of copy when a command is given

automatic return a feature that places a word that is too long to fit on a line on the next line

automatic underscore special keys or commands that underline a word or series of words

character a letter, number, symbol, or space in a line of text

character/column display a screen that allows the user to view a portion of a document. It is stated in line length or column size.

code key a key that is used in conjunction with other keys to perform special functions

column a term often used to refer to horizontal spaces across the screen of a microcomputer. An 80-column screen will hold 80 characters

command an instruction the user gives to the computer, usually by means of the keyboard

correction/cancel key deletes incorrect characters

correction memory a feature that allows errors to be corrected in memory before they are printed

CPU central processing unit, the part of the computer that holds computer programs and data; interprets and follows instructions; and sends the results to the user, the computer's memory, or both

CRT cathode ray tube, the display screen

cursor a spot of light on the display screen that indicates where the next character will be

cursor movement keys special keys that allow you to move the cursor up, down, left, or right on the display screen

daisy wheel a rotating print element composed of a set of spokes, with a character at the end of each spoke

data a general term for the information that a computer processes

database a collection or library of information on a particular subject

data processing the use of a computer system to sort, add, rearrange, or otherwise manipulate data (numeric information)

decimal (dec) tab a software or machine function that aligns columns of figures at decimal points

default settings equipment settings that are preset into a software program or into the equipment's memory. These settings may include margins and tab stops.

delete the process of removing or omitting copy from text that has already been keyed

disk a magnetic recording device that allows the user to store information

disk drive the device that reads or writes information on a disk

DOS disk operating system, a program that controls the storage of information on disks and makes it possible for the computer to use programs

document a term often used to refer to letters, tables, reports, and other information prepared on electronic equipment

documentation the printed information accompanying software that explains the software's use

dot-matrix printer an impact printer that uses pins to strike a ribbon and produce characters made of closely spaced dots

editing the process of making changes in text by inserting, deleting, rearranging, or correcting errors

electronic files data stored on magnetic media or in the memory of the equipment

electronic mail communication that is sent and received electronically between terminals or work stations by telephone, cable, or by satellite network

embedded command an instruction that is given to a computer that often does not appear on the display screen. The instruction is usually carried out when the text is printed.

express cursor moves a command or combination of keystrokes that allows the user to move through blocks of text

file a stored document

file name a name given to a document when it is stored

filing the process of storing information on a disk

footers repetitive information, usually a page number, that appears on the bottom of each page of a document

format the physical arrangement of text on a screen or on paper

format commands commands that are used in arranging text on the screen. Format commands include those to change margins, line spacing, and tab settings.

function key any key on the keyboard that does not produce a letter, number, or a symbol

graphics output in the form of pictures, charts, or graphs

hard copy a document that is printed on paper

hard disk a magnetic storage device that has large data storage capacity

hardware the physical equipment of a computer such as the monitor, the keyboard, and the storage device

headers repetitive information that appears on the top of each page of a document

(2) The secretary answered, "The reports are on your desk."

(3) "If you listen carefully," Lou said, "you can hear his accent."

(4) "I'll see you at the staff meeting," he yelled.

(5) "By the way," Lisa complained, "the copy machine is broken again."

(6) John sighed and said, "I guess we'll have to buy a new one."

(7) "David needs more training on the equipment," Maria explained.

(8) "We won the battle," he said, "but lost the war."

(9) Margaret said, "Mr. Jones, word processing increases productivity."

(10) Paul said, "I have just begun to fight for the new legislative bill."

Activity 67C

(1) "Our committee met for an hour," she said.

(2) Pat said, "I want to see your materials for the national accounts."

(3) They're sure that it's the right bus.

(4) The two critics praised her novel, The Hills of Home.

(5) The critics liked its first chapter, "A Country Boy."

(6) The Delta Chronicle reviewed your play, One Hour to Live, in the morning edition.

(7) Literary Parade will praise its plot, too.

(8) My article, "Artificial Intelligence Today," was published in Reader's Review.

(9) "We need to review problems," said the chairwoman, "before we review solutions."

(10) They're sure that the woman is wise.

New-Key Orientation

Goal: To learn the location of ⊙

1. Locate the ⊙ on the keyboard chart.
2. Next, locate the decimal key on your keyboard.
3. Position your fingers over the home keys. Practice the reach to the ⊙ with your thumb. (Depending on the arrangement of keys on your numeric keyboard, you may need to use a finger other than your thumb for the decimal key.)

Keyboard Practice

Key each column twice.

Press the return/enter key twice after each column.

Remember to keep your fingers in home-key position as you enter the numbers.

Goal: To practice proper keystroking techniques

1	2	3	4	5	6
777	978	998	878	788	879
888	987	879	889	787	798
999	878	787	887	897	989
789	987	878	788	977	987
897	789	797	987	797	789

7	8	9	10	11	12
111	132	231	221	331	223
222	213	211	322	232	321
333	123	223	312	133	122
123	213	233	322	312	113
321	231	321	212	123	312

13	14	15	16	17	18
468	48.2	.8	284.0	41.87	154.88
0.489	02537	5827	100	4058.4	888
214.2	852	.024	8.45	08945	.0082
712	.3978	18.73	560	2.25	20008
63944	257.0	85.00	23.00	20.0	632.48
.58	.2684	1045	0.89	36.248	64.1

Speed Practice

Take two 2-minute timings on these columns.

Try to increase your speed on the second timing.

Goal: To build speed on the ten-key numeric keyboard

1	2	3	4	5	6
61.96	446	2.067	78.3	519.2	3372
96	53.94	595.9	3425	60.5	547.4
452.6	9.520	799	53.59	3.678	48.8
2396	101.8	11.5	94.6	4557	2.9
2.8	78.97	543	6.224	431.9	5.973
42.48	11	97.34	40.08	72.6	8.68

Activity 5D
(1) False (2) True (3) True (4) False (5) True
(6) False (7) False (8) True

Activity 8E
(1) True (2) False (3) False (4) False (5) False
(6) False (7) True (8) False

Activity 11E
(1) 8 (2) 32 (3) 13 (4) 28

Activity 22F
(a) False (b) False (c) True (d) False (e) False
(f) True

Activity 35C
(1) True (2) True (3) False (4) False (5) True
(6) False (7) False (8) True (9) False (10) False

Activity 36D
(1) True (2) False (3) True (4) True (5) False
(6) True

Activity 37E
(1) False (2) False (3) False (4) True (5) True
(6) False

Activity 43F
(1) courtesy title (2) open (3) Ladies and Gentlemen
(4) reference initials (5) salutation (6) date
(7) writes (8) single spaced (9) double space
(10) enclosure notation

Activity 46D
(1) True (2) True (3) False (4) False (5) True
(6) True (7) True

Activity 48E
(1) one (2) three (3) no (4) two (5) TS (6) 23

Activity 50E
(1) True (2) False (3) True (4) False (5) True
(6) False

Activity 59D
(1) False (2) True (3) True (4) False (5) False
(6) True (7) False (8) True (9) False (10) False

Activity 60E
(1) False (2) False (3) True (4) True (5) False
(6) True

Activity 62E
(1) True (2) False (3) True (4) True (5) True
(6) True

Activity 64D
(1) False (2) False (3) False (4) False (5) True
(6) False (7) False

Activity 66E
(1) True (2) False (3) False (4) True (5) True
(6) True (7) True (8) False (9) True

Activity 69C
(1) 13 (2) triple (3) double (4) 9 (5) 1-inch (6) 6
(7) margin (8) alphabetical (9) author name (10) year

Activity 71–73F
(1) False (2) True (3) True (4) False

New-Key Orientation

Goal: To learn the location of ② and ⑧

1. Locate ② and ⑧ on the keyboard chart.
2. Next, locate the keys on your keyboard.
3. Position your fingers over the home keys. Practice the reach from the home keys to each new key. Reach down to ② and up to ⑧ with your **5** finger.
4. Input the columns, keeping your fingers in the home-key position.
5. Practice at a comfortable pace until you feel confident about each key's location.

Technique Timing

Take two 2-minute timings on these columns.

If you finish before time is called, start again.

Press the return/enter key twice after each column.

Goal: To key the middle-column keys by touch

Keep your eyes on the textbook copy, not on your fingers, as you input the numbers.

1	2	3	4	5	6
555	228	885	285	582	828
888	852	285	258	558	825
222	522	825	525	582	852
582	252	588	858	825	258
822	528	258	582	525	885
522	855	852	825	582	282

> **Checkpoint:** How often did you look at your fingers: not at all; once; twice; more?

Keyboard Practice

Key each column twice.

Press the return/enter key twice after each column.

Goal: To practice proper keystroking techniques

1	2	3	4	5	6
582	822	522	228	852	522
252	528	855	885	285	825
588	258	258	285	825	525
858	582	825	582	558	582
825	525	582	828	528	852
852	885	282	555	888	222

7	8	9	10	11	12
888	585	222	828	522	228
222	522	555	825	852	822
852	555	888	852	285	825
258	582	258	258	852	828
582	258	852	885	825	258
528	282	528	282	558	522

LETTERS

Formats

Block format

Modified-block format
Indented paragraphs

Simplified format

Special Letter Parts

Mailing notation. This notation indicates a special postal service, such as *Registered Mail,* is required. Key this notation in letters at the left margin, a DS below the date; on envelopes, a DS below the stamp. Use all caps.

Handling notation. A handling notation indicates special handling, such as *Confidential,* is required. Key this notation in letters at the left margin, a DS below the date; on envelopes, a DS below the return address. Use all caps.

Attention line. An attention line directs a letter to a person/department not named in the address. As the first line of the inside and mailing addresses, key *Attention,* space once, and key the name/department. Use all caps.

Subject line. This line gives the topic of a letter. At the left margin, a DS below the salutation, key *Subject* in all caps, followed by a colon, two spaces, and the topic, with the important words keyed in initial caps.

Separate cover notation. This notation shows something is being sent in another envelope or package. A DS below the reference initials key *Separate Cover* in initial caps, a dash, and a short description of the item.

Copy notation. This notation shows a copy of a letter was sent to a person other than the addressee. A DS below the reference initials key a lower-case *c,* followed by one space, and the person's name (courtesy title, first name, and last name).

Postscript. This is a message added to a letter. At the left margin, a DS below the last item in the letter, key *P.S.* in all caps, space once, and key the message. Carryover lines align with the first word of the message.

Two-Page Letters

When a letter is too long for one page, the letter is carried over to a second page of the same quality as the letterhead. A second-page heading is keyed 1 inch from the top edge starting at the left margin. Use either block or horizontal format. Both formats are shown below:

```
Ms. Evelyn Jacobs
Page 2
April 2, 19--
```
Block format

```
Mr. James Olsen      2      November 19, 19--
```
Horizontal format

Letter Placement

Use the letter placement table that follows to center letters horizontally and vertically on the stationery. Position the date line higher when the letter contains a special part, such as a subject line, or a table.

Letter Placement Table		
Length	Words in Body	Date Line
Short	Under 100	20
Medium	100–200	15
Long	Over 200	12

New-Key Orientation

Goal: To learn the location of ③ and ⑨

1. Locate ③ and ⑨ on the keyboard chart.
2. Next, locate the keys on your keyboard.
3. Position your fingers over the home keys. Practice the reach from the home keys to each new key. Reach down to ③ and up to ⑨ with your **6** finger.
4. Input the columns, keeping your fingers in home-key position.
5. Practice at a comfortable pace until you feel confident about each key's location.

Technique Timing

Take two 2-minute timings on these columns.

If you finish before time is called, start again.

Press the return/enter key twice after each column.

Goal: To key the right-column keys by touch

Keep your eyes on the textbook copy, not on your fingers, as you input the numbers.

1	2	3	4	5	6
666	669	339	966	939	699
999	663	363	393	363	936
333	936	336	966	393	939
963	396	936	633	639	336
639	936	636	393	369	696
399	363	996	993	369	939

Checkpoint: How often did you look at your fingers: not at all; once; twice; more?

Keyboard Practice

Key each column twice.

Press the return/enter key twice after each column.

Goal: To practice proper keystroking techniques

1	2	3	4	5	6
963	639	399	669	663	936
396	936	363	339	363	336
936	636	993	966	393	966
633	393	993	939	363	393
639	369	369	699	936	939
336	696	939	666	999	333

7	8	9	10	11	12
369	333	963	639	669	339
396	666	369	963	663	336
393	999	639	936	636	933
696	369	396	966	363	699
693	963	393	939	939	633
639	639	693	333	393	399

Postal Abbreviations

U.S. States, Districts, Possessions, Territories

Alabama	AL	Montana	MT
Alaska	AK	Nebraska	NE
Arizona	AZ	Nevada	NV
Arkansas	AR	New Hampshire	NH
California	CA	New Jersey	NJ
Colorado	CO	New Mexico	NM
Connecticut	CT	New York	NY
Delaware	DE	North Carolina	NC
District of Columbia	DC	North Dakota	ND
Florida	FL	Ohio	OH
Georgia	GA	Oklahoma	OK
Guam	GU	Oregon	OR
Hawaii	HI	Pennsylvania	PA
Idaho	ID	Puerto Rico	PR
Illinois	IL	Rhode Island	RI
Indiana	IN	South Carolina	SC
Iowa	IA	South Dakota	SD
Kansas	KS	Tennessee	TN
Kentucky	KY	Texas	TX
Louisiana	LA	Utah	UT
Maine	ME	Vermont	VT
Maryland	MD	Virgin Islands	VI
Massachusetts	MA	Virginia	VA
Michigan	MI	Washington	WA
Minnesota	MN	West Virginia	WV
Mississippi	MS	Wisconsin	WI
Missouri	MO	Wyoming	WY

Canadian Provinces

Alberta	AB	Nova Scotia	NS
British Columbia	BC	Ontario	ON
Labrador	LB	Prince Edward Island	PE
Manitoba	MB	Quebec	PQ
New Brunswick	NB	Saskatchewan	SK
Newfoundland	NF	Yukon Territory	YT
Northwest Territories	NT		

MEMOS

Memos can be keyed on printed forms or on plain paper. Printed forms vary in size and format, but usually have the guide words *To, From, Date,* and *Subject* printed on them. Set a tab 2 spaces after the guide word Subject for keying the heading information. Use 1-inch side margins.

When keying memos on plain paper, use 1-inch top and side margins. Key the heading lines SS, then TS to key the body. SS the lines of the body, leaving a DS between the paragraphs. Place your reference initials a DS below the last paragraph of the memo.

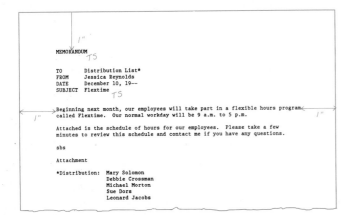

REPORTS

Formats
Unbound Report

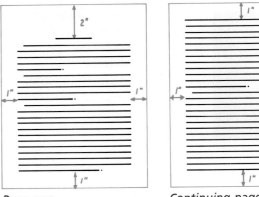

Page one   *Continuing pages*

Leftbound Report

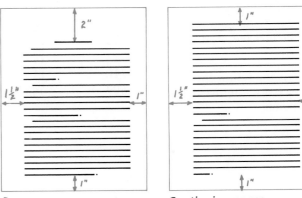

Page one   *Continuing pages*

Topbound Report

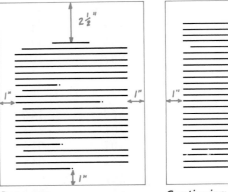

Page one   *Continuing pages*

New-Key Orientation

Goal: To learn the location of ⓵, ⑦, and ⓪

1. Locate the ⓵, ⑦, and ⓪ on the keyboard chart.
2. Next, locate the keys on your keyboard.
3. Position your fingers over the home keys. Practice the reach from the home keys to each new key. Reach down to ⓵ and up to ⑦ with the **4** finger. Strike ⓪ with your thumb.
4. Input the columns, keeping your fingers in home-key position.
5. Practice at a comfortable pace until you feel confident about each key's location.

Technique Timing

Take two 2-minute timings on these columns.

If you finish before time is called, start again.

Press the return/enter key twice after each column.

Goal: To key the left-column and 0 keys by touch

Keep your eyes on the textbook copy, not on your fingers, as you input the numbers.

1	2	3	4	5	6
444	014	140	107	011	141
471	107	701	074	170	117
174	740	701	104	710	417
741	101	704	007	004	047
710	114	471	411	471	104
407	441	117	047	174	114

Checkpoint: How often did you look at your fingers: not at all; once; twice; more?

Keyboard Practice

Key each column twice.

Press the return/enter key twice after each column.

Goal: To practice proper keystroking techniques

1	2	3	4	5	6
741	710	407	014	147	740
101	114	441	140	701	701
704	471	117	107	074	104
007	411	047	011	170	710
004	471	174	141	117	417
047	104	114	444	471	174

7	8	9	10	11	12
170	140	104	111	777	410
701	147	107	147	111	140
107	014	401	174	444	014
741	041	701	741	714	741
147	074	101	710	741	471
410	047	010	410	704	147

Special Report Pages

Title page

Endnotes

Works Cited

The above examples are shown in unbound report format. Key these special pages in the same format in which the report is keyed.

Report References

Parenthetical references. Parenthetical references give credit for information (quotations, facts, or opinions) taken from other sources or used in preparing the report.

When parenthetical references are used, information about the source of the reference is keyed within parentheses in the body of the report. In the author-date format for parenthetical references, key the author's last name and the year of publication, followed by a comma and the page number.

When parenthetical references are used, a reference page is placed at the end of the report.

Footnotes. Footnotes give credit for quoted material. Indicate a footnote at the point of reference by keying a superior figure. The footnote itself is placed at the bottom of the page on which the reference occurs. Footnotes are numbered consecutively throughout the report.

To format a footnote, key a 1½-inch separating line a SS below the last text line. DS, indent 5 spaces, and key the superior figure, author's name, title, publication information, and page reference. SS the lines of a footnote; DS between footnotes. Leave a 1-inch bottom margin.

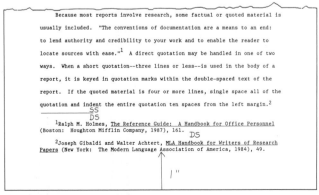

Parenthetical references

Footnotes

New-Key Orientation

Goal: To learn the location of ④, ⑤, ⑥, and return/enter

1. Locate ④, ⑤, ⑥ (the home keys), and return/enter on the keyboard chart.
2. Next, locate the keys on your keyboard.
3. Position your **j, k,** and **l** fingers over ④, ⑤, and ⑥. Reach to return/enter with your **l** finger.
4. Input the columns, keeping your fingers in home-key position.
5. Practice at a comfortable pace until you feel confident about each key's location.

Technique Timing

Take two 2-minute timings on these columns.

If you finish before time is called, start again.

Press the return/enter key twice after each column.

Goal: To key the home-row and return/enter keys by touch

Keep your eyes on the textbook copy, not on your fingers, as you input the numbers.

1	2	3	4	5	6
444	555	666	456	554	664
555	666	454	654	445	446
666	444	545	465	564	566
456	654	446	556	664	645
564	546	646	656	565	465
646	465	546	465	655	654

Checkpoint: How often did you look at your fingers: not at all; once; twice; more?

Keyboard Practice

Key each column twice.

Press the return/enter key twice after each column.

Goal: To practice proper keystroking techniques

1	2	3	4	5	6
456	564	646	555	666	444
654	546	465	666	454	545
446	646	546	456	654	465
556	656	465	554	445	564
664	565	655	664	466	566
645	465	654	444	555	666

7	8	9	10	11	12
654	666	464	666	456	555
546	456	565	655	455	554
456	546	656	654	454	545
465	646	546	555	446	454
444	654	654	556	445	456
555	564	546	554	444	654

PROOFREADING/ERROR CORRECTION

Proofreading

Follow these steps to help ensure the accuracy of all keyed documents:

1. Review any special instructions for preparing the document. Be sure they have been carried out.
2. Decide whether the document is properly formatted on the page or screen.
3. Look over the keyed document for obvious omissions or errors. If you have a keyed or printed copy, mark corrections with proofreader's marks.
4. Read the document for understanding.
5. If the document contains unfamiliar content or technical matter, ask a coworker to help. The keyboarder should read from the original, the coworker should follow the keyed or printed copy or the screen.
6. Check names, figures, addresses, amounts, and dates.
7. Proofread again line by line, checking the keyed or printed copy or the screen against the original.

Proofreader's Marks

Symbol	Meaning
℘	delete, take out
CAPS or ≡	use capital letter
lc or /	use lowercase letter
∧	insert here
↻	insert comma
⌄	insert apostrophe
⊙	use period
⌒	close up
#	insert space
¶	indent for paragraph
∿	change the order
⸢	move to left
⸥	move to right
stet	let stand as is

PREPARING A LETTER FOR MAILING

Assembling

Follow the steps listed below to assemble a letter with its enclosure and its envelope:

1. Place the enclosure behind the letter. Both the letter and enclosure should be facing up.

2. Align the top edge of the enclosure with the top edge of the letter.
3. Place the envelope, with the address facing up, over the top edge of the letter and the enclosure.
4. Fasten the top left corner with a paper clip.

Folding

Follow these steps to fold a letter and insert it into an envelope:

1. Fold the lower one third of the letter up toward the top of the letter and crease.
2. Fold the top one third of the letter down to within ½ inch of the first fold.
3. Put the letter in the envelope, inserting the last crease first.

Window Envelopes

Follow these steps to fold a letter and insert it into a window envelope:

1. Turn the letter face down with the letterhead at the top.
2. Fold the lower one third of the letter up toward the top and crease it.
3. Fold the top one third of the letter down to within ½ inch of the first fold and crease it.
4. Insert the letter into the window envelope so that the address is clearly visible through the window.

D Ten-Key Numeric Keyboard

The ability to key numbers by touch is an important skill. You have already learned to key the top row of numbers on the alpha-numeric keyboard by touch. In the following activities, you will learn to key the ten-key numeric keyboard (keypad) by touch.

Ten-key numeric keyboards are usually found on microcomputers or electronic calculators. When you are keying quantities of numerical data, your ability to input numbers by touch will make the task easier and faster.

The ten-key numeric keyboard is especially useful when large quantities of numbers are to be keyed. The arrangement of the ten-key keyboard into three columns down by four rows across allows for more rapid keying of numbers than is possible with the top row of the alpha-numeric keyboard.

The location of the ten-key numeric keyboard varies on microcomputers. Some microcomputers have the ten-key numeric keyboard located to the right of the alpha-numeric keyboard. Other microcomputers have a separate ten-key keyboard that is attached to the microcomputer when a large quantity of numerical data is to be keyed. Regardless of its location on the microcomputer, the ten-key keyboard has the same basic key positions to be learned by touch.

Key Locations

The locations of the numbers from 0 to 9 are usually the same on all equipment. The locations of the return/enter and decimal keys, and of other function keys, vary from one model of microcomputer to another. Locate the number keys, the return/enter key, and the decimal key on your keyboard. The following illustrations show some typical ten-key numeric keyboard arrangements.

Home Position

On the ten-key numeric keyboard, ④, ⑤, and ⑥ are the **home keys.** When the **j** finger is over ④, the **k** finger is over ⑤, and the **l** finger is over ⑥, the fingers are in home-key position. The **j** finger is also used for ① and ⑦. The **k** finger is used for ② and ⑧, and the **l** finger is used for ③ and ⑨.

Fingers used for the keys return/enter, ⓪, and ⦁ depend on the arrangement of the keyboard. On some numeric keyboards, the thumb is used for ⓪ and the **l** finger is used for return/enter. Study your equipment's keyboard to see which finger should be used for return/enter, ⓪, and ⦁.

Entering Numbers by Touch

Your primary objective while using these materials is to learn to locate the ten-key numeric keys by touch. Your practice materials consist of columns of numbers. After you key a number in a column, strike the return/enter key to force a line break. That is, each time you strike the return/enter key, the cursor will move to the next line. At the end of each column, press the return/enter key twice to leave extra space between the columns.

You are not to total these columns of numbers. You are learning a new key position—not how to add numbers. Also, most microcomputers require a special software program that enables the microcomputer to add columns of numbers.